Talking

with

Young Children

about

Adoption

Talking
with
Young Children
about
Adoption

Mary Watkins and Susan Fisher

Yale University Press

New Haven and London

The opening epigraph of the Afterword is from *The Prophet,* by Kahlil
Gibran, copyright 1923, by Kahlil Gibran and renewed 1951 by
Administrators C.T.A. of Kahlil Gibran Estate and Mary G. Gibran.
Reprinted by permission of Alfred A. Knopf, Inc.

Designed by Sylvia Steiner.
Set in Sabon type by Tseng Information Systems, Inc., Durham, North
Carolina, and printed in the United States of America by Vail-Ballou
Press, Binghamton, New York.

Library of Congress Cataloging-in-Publication Data
Watkins, Mary, 1950–
Talking with young children about adoption / Mary Watkins and
Susan Fisher.
p.   cm.
Includes bibliographical references and index.
ISBN 0-300-05178-6 (cloth)
        0-300-06317-2 (pbk.)
1. Children, Adopted—United States.   2. Parent and child—United
States.   3. Adoption—United States.   I. Fisher, Susan M., 1937–   .
II. Title.
HV875.55.W38   1993
362.7'34—dc20   92-44529 CIP

A catalogue record for this book is available from the British Library.

The paper in this book meets the guidelines for permanence and
durability of the Committee on Production Guidelines for Book
Longevity of the Council on Library Resources.

10 9 8 7 6 5 4

To our children:
Ben and Jane,
Jeff, Rachel, Ani, and Lily

Contents

>   Teddy: I don't want [my birthfather] to find me. He'd take me
>   away. He'd change his mind.
>   Anna: You know, [in adoption] somebody wins and
>   somebody loses.

>   Laura: Mommy, you're not *really, really* my mommy, are you?
>   Maya: Let's call [my birthmom] Forsythia.

>   Jeff: Why didn't my real mom want me? . . . I think she didn't
>   like me.
>   Melissa: I was always wanted. My parents who adopted me
>   wanted me even before I was born.

Acknowledgments

The collaborative effort that made this book possible extends far beyond the two authors. Many people helped us in a variety of ways. We want especially to acknowledge:

—Kay Liebmann, psychotherapist and adoptive mother, whose early conversations with us about young children and adoption inspired the creation of this book.

—the late Arnold and Helen Gurin, of the Heller School at Brandeis University and the Judge Baker Child Guidance Clinic of Children's Hospital, Boston, who were there at the beginning of our families and of our collaboration, for their careful reading of chapters 1 and 2.

—Nancy Clayman, director of adoption services at Concord Family Services, for her group on talking with children about adoption.

—the many who gave us scholarly advice on chapter 2, the research chapter: Viola Bernard; Harold Grotevant from the University of Minnesota; Martha McClintock, Robert Perlman, and Susan Stodolsky from the University of Chicago; and David Reiss from the Center for Family Research, George Washington University School of Medicine. For their help in the very beginning: Sara Kushnir and Marilyn Silin.

—Joyce Pavao, founder of the Pre/Post-Adoption Consulting Team at the Family Center in Somerville, Massachusetts, for reading and commenting on chapter 3.

—all our storytellers, some of whose stories are included in this book: Barbara Bartlett, Ginna Donovan, Ann Esse, Lani and Joe Gerson, Sara Kushnir, Elizabeth Roper Marcus, Leslie Marino, Kristin McLane Kehler, Barbara Moline, Dawn Murtaugh, James Redfield, Marilyn Ruschhaupt, Phyllis Sobelman, Judy Stigger, Leslie Travis, Janett Trubatch, and Judy Varland Zurbrigg.

—Jeff Rosenthal, who taught that love between parent and child is a matter of the heart, not the blood.

—our husbands, Robert Rosenthal and Herman Sinaiko, our first and our final thanks. At every juncture in the creation of this book, they shared their wisdom, humor, love, and support.

From Telling
to Sharing:
Changes in
Adoption Practice

Ideas about children and the best way to parent them change drastically over time. In the 1920s the influential behaviorist John Watson (1928) advised parents never to hug or kiss their children. If they must, a peck on the forehead and a handshake at night should suffice. He urged mothers to leave their children alone for part of the day and suggested that they make a peephole to watch their children if this advice proved too hard to follow. Our parents in the 1940s also struggled to adhere to the advice of experts: to feed us on rigid schedules, to confine us to a playpen, not to pick us up at night if we cried. It must have been hard for them at times, trying to follow all this "good" advice: weathering our cries, timidly questioning the rationale for the advice, feeling guilty if they "gave in" to their inclinations or our demands, fearing that holding us at the wrong time might actually "spoil" us, as the experts claimed.

Adoptive parents of that generation had to cope with additional "expert" advice and practices that were also doomed to change. Adoption workers carefully matched children and their would-be parents for race and religion, often for social class and eye and hair color as well, to minimize the importance and even deny the fact of adoption. The attempt to make the adopted child resemble a biological child reflected and encouraged the belief that biological and adoptive parenting were essentially the same. Curiously, this insistence on the sameness of biological and adoptive

1

family life belied intense cultural stigma regarding illegitimacy as well as fears about the potency of inheritable characteristics. Adoption agencies tried to assure adoptive parents that their practices of psychological testing and history taking would guarantee the health of the babies (Reid 1957; Cole and Donley 1990). The record of the birthfamily's history was sealed away, consigned to the past, and the new parents were reassured that family life would now proceed as though the child had been born to them.

The same history that had seemed so important in the selection and matching of child and parents was rarely communicated fully to the child and was often concealed, as the fiction of the "sameness" of adoptive and birthfamilies was promulgated and lived. In retrospect, family normalcy and health seemed to rest on a shaky foundation of minimization or denial of differences between adoptive and birthfamilies and secrecy about the birthfamily. A corollary of this denial was the advice given to birthmothers: to put the experience behind them and forget it—advice many found impossible to follow.

Many parents carried this philosophy of "sameness" into family life by telling their children once about their adoption and then dropping the topic. Some enacted denial by keeping adoption a secret from their children. Others, to "protect" the children from having to deal with the fact of two sets of parents, told them that their birthparents had been killed, short-circuiting discussions of illegitimacy, as well as the possibility of the children's searching for and meeting the birthparents. Many parents lived in perpetual fear, never knowing if their children would find out their secret. Many children who learned of their adoption from others or from documents never spoke of it directly with their adoptive parents for fear of hurting and upsetting them.

Adoption experts split into two camps: those who urged parents to tell their children about adoption and to do so early, and those who contended that revealing the fact of adoption would harm the child's psychological development and should be done, if at all, as late as possible. Parents were caught in this fiery debate, unable to feel entirely right about following either course.

When their children raised the subject of adoption, many parents—and even many professionals—worried that this was a sign of maladjustment rather than understandable curiosity. To his adoptive parents, the child's questions about his birthparents often felt like disloyalty and rejection rather than a growing child's understandable attempt to put the pieces of his heritage in order.[1] In this atmosphere, it is not surprising that many children said

1. To help parents identify with both their girls and their boys—while making read-

little or nothing about adoption to their parents and that this silence created a distance between parents and child. Ironically, the very steps undertaken to ensure closeness in the adoptive family—minimization and denial of the special nature of adoption—were what disrupted it, leading the adoptee to bear his feelings and unanswered questions silently or to go outside the family for needed emotional support.

As these children, adopted within an ethic of secrecy and minimization, matured, many spoke out about the shock of hearing about their adoption from a stranger or at the deathbed of an adoptive parent (Kornitzer 1968; McWhinnie 1967; Raynor 1980; Triseliotis 1973). Many adult adoptees resented having been denied access to their history, as though they were still children to be protected from a shameful truth. They were denied information not only by a bureaucratic system but often by their adoptive parents as well. In a study of 288 adoptive families, Raynor (1980) found that fewer than 40 percent of the adoptive parents had given the adoptees all the information they had. More than 25 percent admitted having falsified or omitted information, even to their adult children.

Adult adoptees have described the feelings of unreality that came from never being able to fit together the pieces of their life. Many intuitively sensed that there were secrets in their household, but they were left alone with their often frightening fantasies of what those secrets might be. In Raynor's study, only one in four adult adoptees remembered having been told the following basic facts: "why they had been relinquished for adoption; when and where they had been adopted, including the name of the agency and why the adopters took them; and the personal and social characteristics of their biological parents" (1980, p. 95). In another study, 25 percent of the adoptive parents said they had given their children full and truthful information about the birthparents, but only 10 percent of the adult adoptees agreed. Half of the adoptees felt that they had pressed their parents for more information, whereas only 20 percent of the parents gave the same report. Finally, three times as many parents as adult adoptees reported that, as children, the adoptees had never voluntarily raised the subject (Jaffee 1974).

Fortunately, many adults who experienced adoption have described what was helpful and what was harmful in their discussions of adoption with their adoptive parents. In Triseliotis's (1973) study of adoptees who later searched for information about their birthparents, the adoptees were clear in asserting that early, positive disclosure of their adoption gave them the sense of being wanted and led to greater feelings of satisfaction. It was

---

ing as smooth as possible—we will alternate the use of the feminine and masculine pronouns: the child will be "she" in chapter 1, "he" in chapter 2, and so on.

important that when birthparents were mentioned a good image of them was presented. Although the full meaning of adoption evolved through childhood, the adoptees' early self-identity included the awareness of being adopted. Those who had been told about their adoption early and in a positive way had a sense of "well-being," of being "special," and of having something to be "proud" of. Those adoptees who were told late—after age ten—felt that the lateness had a profoundly adverse effect on them, shaking their self-image and leaving them confused, bewildered, and later angry at their adoptive parents, particularly the mother. Upon finally learning about their adoption, they were faced with the task of redefining themselves. Those who were told in a hostile manner—young or old—were left with a conviction that adoption was something "shameful," "terrible."

Notice how the fact of being adopted varies in meaning from being a source of pride to being something shameful, depending on how and when the child is told. The adult adoptees regarded as unjustified their adoptive parents' fears of losing their children's affection if the children knew they were adopted; these parents, the adoptees said, were the ones they knew and had feelings for. Truth and honesty, they argued, would have increased their trust and faith in their parents. Most adoptees dismissed their parents' explanation that they were trying to protect the children by concealing the truth. They viewed this kind of protection as misguided. Many adult adoptees have fought to revise agency practices in order to encourage parents to deal with adoption earlier and more honestly with their children, to grant adoptees access to their files, and to make it possible for them to meet their birthparents if both parties wish to do so.

When we began to parent our adoptive children, we, like our parents before us, followed the prevailing expert advice—now, thankfully, more unified: to use the word *adoption* early (in babyhood) and lovingly, to speak about adoption to our toddlers and preschoolers as the way our children entered our families, to acknowledge with respect our children's birth-families and cultural heritage, to create an atmosphere in which questions, feelings, and concerns about adoption could be spoken about openly. As with our parents, however, the advice paid insufficient attention to how we would feel in following it through and particularly what the process would be like with and for our children. Now the advice is not simply to *tell* the child *once* about his adoption but to *talk with* him across developmental stages throughout childhood.

When our children began to ask if they had been in our tummies, to request that we repeat ad infinitum their adoption stories, to think they saw their birthmothers in the supermarket, to worry about what would have happened to them if we had not adopted them, we turned to the adoption literature for guidance and found none. Books on adoption had several pages on telling the child about adoption, but very little about their evolving understanding of it. Cognitive developmental research was helpful in clarifying that young children are not capable of understanding adoption as adults do, but not as helpful in illuminating what kinds of sense children *do* make of adoption as they pass through early childhood. Guidelines were available for parents of latency-aged and adolescent children, but there was very little for parents of young children, reflecting researchers' relative neglect of how young children construct their understandings, often so differently from adults.

Despite our psychotherapeutic work with young children and our knowledge of child development, as adoptive mothers we were surprised to hear how adoption thoughts were voiced in the play and conversation of our own toddlers and preschoolers. We were aware of the guiding principles sketchily set forth in the adoption literature about what to tell the young child, but nothing we had read remotely prepared us to enter into the kinds of play and conversation that arose spontaneously between our children and us. The book we needed was nowhere to be found.

As friends we turned to each other with our fears and anxieties, replaying for each other in detail our adoption conversations with each of our children. In this sharing between ourselves and then with other adoptive parents, we gradually came to realize that our children's concerns and understandings were normative, and our own difficulties and worries largely reflected the emotional work adoptive parents have to go through to be full partners with their children in living with the realities of adoptive family life together.

We realized how helpful it would have been to us to hear what adoptive conversations with young children sound like, how they evolve, to know in advance how children go about understanding this thing called "adoption." In this book we have done two things: first, in chapter 1, described the psychological work parents must do in order to be able to talk effectively with their young children about adoption; and second, in chapter 3, let what young children have shared with their parents in conversations and play teach us how they experience and understand adoption.

The longest section of this book, chapter 4, consists of accounts by adoptive parents of their conversations and play with their young children concerning adoption and their own working through of adoption issues. We feel that sensitive parents, not researchers, are the best reporters of young children's thoughts about adoption, as these thoughts are often shared only in intimacy in the course of daily living. Interviews by strangers cannot elicit or convey the richness of how young children live their understandings about adoption, preconceptually as well as conceptually, in action and play as well as words. Giving parents a voice in this book reflects our belief that what is most helpful to adoptive parents is not more advice from the "experts." Too often adoptive parents are disempowered as parents through the multiple intrusions of the adoption process, necessary though many of them are. What is most helpful is hearing from individuals who are living the adoption experience and finding ways to share this experience with one another.

These stories reflect not the smooth and effortless interactions that we too often think we should have with our children but the interaction of children and parents in the trenches of family life. We hear parents learning to listen to their young children's messages and concerns, sorting out their own psychic laundry to make room for their children, struggling with how best to answer questions and proceed—often feeling in doubt or believing they have failed, rethinking the situation, and going back to it. We have found this sharing among adoptive families profoundly supportive and empowering to us as parents, and we hope that these stories, as intimate glimpses into adoptive family life, will support our readers as well.

Although a three-year-old may begin to pursue adoption themes with curiosity and interest, his parents may be burdened by anticipation of the child's sense of loss, by a sadness that they did not give birth to this child, by their understanding of and sympathy for the birthparent's difficulties. In chapters 1 and 3 our concern is therefore twofold: we explore the meaning of adoption first from the perspective of the parent and then from that of the child. In chapter 1 we look at the emotional world of the parent who worries over what the child should be told and when, or whether he should be told at all; who carries the sadness of the adoptive situation long before the child does; who, like all parents, does not want something to hurt her child, and yet lives in apprehension and knowledge that adoption inevitably carries some pain.

Despite a climate of seeming acceptance, even praise, adoptive parents have to deal with subtle and not so subtle cultural prejudices against adoption. The research on adoption outcome that filters down from academia to parents is often outdated or disheartening, reflecting not scientific truth but cultural bias and apprehension about adoption. In chapter 2 we review some of this research at some length, not to inform parents of each and every adoption study, but to share ways of thinking about adoption research that may liberate our children and ourselves from the often bleak prognostications we labor under.

In chapter 3 we shift to the perspective of the child and explore the ways in which young adoptive children understand and communicate about adoption, using an analysis of the stories. We give our readers an idea of how adoption conversation evolves between a parent and a young child, what the child understands and does not understand at different developmental stages, what his adoption questions and play may sound like, and how they may reflect his more general developmental concerns.

In our analysis of what young children said and played out regarding adoption themes and how their parents responded, two things became clear to us. The first contradicts the prevailing opinion and research indicating that only in mid-to-late latency is the child able to understand and experience the losses and conflicts of adoption. According to this view, as children's conceptualizations of adoption become more similar to those of adults, they begin to perceive the losses inherent in adoption (the loss of birthparents and extended family, often the loss of birthplace and cultural heritage, the loss of relatives who have a shared genealogical history). It is argued that toddlers and preschoolers have a predominantly rosy picture of what adoption means, since they do not yet have an understanding of relinquishment, of genetic relatedness, or even of conception. Thus, in this way of thinking, adoption is a cause of celebration and joy for the child. Happiness in bringing his parents joy is indeed an important part of the young child's sense of adoption. But, though it is true that different aspects of loss come into focus as cognitive ability and social knowledge increase, we found that preschoolers and early-latency-age children experience some difficulties regarding adoption that are consonant with their developmental stages and the kinds of concerns typical of these phases.

Our focus on the young child fills a gap in the adoption literature that has led parents to believe that talking with their young children about adoption will be easier and more problem-free than talking with them in late latency and adolescence. Although it has been acknowledged that initiating talk with one's young child about adoption is often difficult because of the parents' emotions and attitudes, too little emphasis has been given to the emotional work the young child often begins to do at this juncture. Our intention is to highlight this so that parents will be prepared to hear their children's concerns and establish early on their openness and availability.

The toddlers, preschoolers, and early-latency-age children in these stories experienced their own adoption-related losses and issues: the sadness of not having been in the adoptive mother's "tummy," the yearning many children (particularly those in interracial families) feel to look like their adoptive parents, their difficulty in understanding the multiple caretakers often involved in their history, the desire to have entered their family in the same simple way as their peers with more continuity between past and present, the occasional worry about the imagined dangers in a complex early history, laden with transition.

Although uncovering such issues might lead some researchers to an even gloomier sense about adoption than they already have, our second impression contradicts this conclusion. When adoption is openly and freely discussed in a context of loving family life, the child's concerns can surface, be addressed, and, in time, yield to his growing sense of mastery, emotional and cognitive.

We want to emphasize our strong impression that it is not the adopted child's wonderings, conflicts, and losses that give rise to later difficulty in some adoptive families but the manner in which these are or are not shared and respected. Our data do not reach into adolescence, but it is clear from the stories reported here that early sharing about adoption and the young child's fears, joys, and concerns establishes a strong emotional foundation from which the adolescent's feelings of loss can be dealt with.

Through this early sharing both parent and child become comfortable and familiar with thoughts about adoption. Through mutual listening it becomes clear that adoption means different things for a parent than for a child, that true dialogue can be established only if the parent extends herself or himself into the child's experience, learning from it and respecting it. Crucial to this early phase—as, indeed, to later ones—is the adoptive parents' positive attitude toward adoption. This does not mean a simplistic picture founded on a minimization of differences and a denial of the child's heritage but a hearty sense that despite its conflicts and losses, being adopted is not merely survivable but can be enriching and deepening.

It is our hope that in focusing on these two worlds—the inner world of the parent and that of the child—we can begin to see how they converge in actual dialogue with our young children. In these dialogues—in play and in words—living together with adoption becomes a positive prototype of how families can share truthfully and feelingly, across developmental understandings, all the issues of deep concern in family life.

In the case of many difficult family problems—the illness or death of a parent or sibling, divorce, alcoholism, abuse, economic deprivation—all members may have to cope with them at the same time, often without warning. In contrast, adoption is known by the parents far in advance of the child. Parents have time to think, to worry, to plan together how it will be talked about and dealt with in the family. Although this undoubtedly causes some anxiety for adoptive parents, it also provides the opportunity to anticipate our children's questions and feelings, to make room for them.

An essential feature of adoptive families is their integration of differences (Kirk 1964). Our own collaboration reflects this heterogeneity as well: one of us adopted by choice, the other by necessity; one adopted intraracially and domestically, the other interracially and internationally; one arranged an open adoption, the other followed a traditional route; one of us is a psychoanalyst and child psychiatrist, the other a developmental and clinical psychologist; one a specialist in early child development, the other in adolescence; one Jewish, one Quaker. In the end this book represents such a mutually enriching integration of these differences that we flipped a coin to decide first authorship. Likewise in our selection of stories, we have tried to represent a variety of kinds of families: nuclear, single-parent, lesbian; interracial and intraracial; families who adopted infants and those who adopted three- and four-year-olds; families with only adopted children, families with both biological and adopted children, and families who adopted a child after first foster-parenting him; families who chose closed adoption and families who opted for open adoption; and, finally, families in which the early sharing about adoption was experienced as comfortable and easy, and those in which it was felt to be difficult, at times disturbing.

Usually the first family member to receive the young child's questions about adoption is the mother, partly because of the child's preoccupation with how babies emerge from mothers. Triseliotis's (1973) research on adoptees who chose to find out more about and/or to search for their birthparents revealed that when adoption was disclosed by adoptive parents it was usually the mother who told the child. Further, adoptees in his study, male and female, felt that it is the adoptive mother's responsibility to disclose adoption information, and when such disclosure had not been forthcoming, their anger focused on her.

Twenty years later, despite radical changes in the family and in our understanding of gender, it is significant that in almost every family we asked to contribute a story it was the adoptive mother, not the father, who wrote the story. In these accounts the first member of the family to receive queries and fantasies about adoption was the adoptive mother, who relayed them to the father.

Although this early focus on the mother (as children mature they are more apt to initiate dialogue with the father) is explainable by the fact that the young child is interested in how he emerged from the mother's tummy and in nursing, it is nonetheless true that in most families mothers still bear the heavier burden of child care. It is the mother who is more likely to witness the unfolding of a child's thoughts and concerns in play and conversation. And since adoption is an alternate form of carrying a baby into family life, the mother—the biological carrier—tends to be assigned and to feel responsibility for adoption-related tasks far into the child's life. We suspect that this division of responsibility goes largely unquestioned, as merely a piece of our unconscious cultural assumptions about gender. To have at least one perspective from a father, we have added an interview with a man who shares his experience as both a birthparent and an adoptive parent.

The parents whose stories we report have different styles of speaking with and being with their young children, just as the children vary in their verbal facility, the ways they incorporate adoptive themes into their play, their understandings of adoption, and their degrees of worry and wonder. This diversity is important, because as some research shows (Raynor 1980, p. 97), neither the amount of information disclosed nor the frequency with which adoption is talked about is correlated with successful outcome; rather, it seems to be a matter of positive parental attitudes toward adoption.[2] Most of the children described here were not participants in open adoption, where the children have an opportunity to have an actual relationship with the birthfamily, but all of the families were open about the existence of the children's birthparents.

This is not a "scientific sample" of adoptive children and families. We were interested not in conveying the norm per se but in sharing concrete family life where adoption is discussed early and openly—to convey what this early talking sounds like, in what kinds of contexts it occurs, how it is experienced emotionally by parents and children. We sought out parents who had been attentive to how their children's wondering about adoption had unfolded and who were willing to share this experience.

Although we address this book to our fellow adoptive parents, our hope is that teachers, extended family members, adult adoptees, birthparents, mental health professionals, and adoption workers will also read it to acquaint themselves more fully with the inner worlds of adopted children and their parents and how these are negotiated through dialogue and play.

The chapters in the book do not need to be read in sequence. Chapter 2, which deals with recent research on adoption, relates to both chapter 1 and chapter 3. Some readers may wish to go directly to the stories in chapter 4, for in the end, it is our children who teach us what adoption means to them at various times in their lives. Their thoughts and fantasies around adoption themes far surpass our dry adult definition of adoption. Our hope is that this book will help parents to be good and compassionate listeners to their young children, children who, when given the chance, are eager to tutor us on all the different ways they experience adoption. Our task is not simply to tell them what adoption is but to assimilate into our abstract notions of adoption their experiences and understandings of adoption.

2. In Raynor's sample of adult adoptees (1980, p. 99), one-third reported being content with the information given them, even when very little or none was given; one-third were reasonably content but would have welcomed more information; the remaining third were dissatisfied and wanted to learn more, usually one or two things in particular, such as the reason for their relinquishment or whom they resembled in their birthfamily.

Chapter 1

Adoption and the World of the Parent

A mother is likened unto a mountain spring that nourishes the tree at its root, but one who mothers another's child is likened unto a water that rises into a cloud and goes a long distance to nourish a lone tree in the desert.

—The Talmud

One of the most powerful resistances to talking with one's child about being adopted is the feeling of many parents that they have just walked through that desert all by themselves. They have endured frustrations and disappointments, in many cases while trying to resolve their complex feelings about infertility. By the time they get this wonderful baby, usually quite suddenly, without the "normal" nine months of preparation, they just want to sit back and feel like a "regular" family and not have to deal with their child's questions about whose tummy she came from, why she looks different from her parents, and who her "real" parents are. Adoptive parents don't want to have to figure out what adoption means to them as parents. Nevertheless, they have an implicit conception of adoption that will either enrich and help or confuse and inhibit them when talking to their child. They just want to relax and enjoy the work and pleasure of raising this remarkable baby whose arrival is the happy culmination of so much effort and turmoil.

Yet there are extra tasks for adoptive parents. They have to deal with the birthparents in their own minds and, in an open adoption, in ordinary reality. They often have to struggle with what is unresolved about their infertility. Many must grapple with the various issues involved in becoming a multiracial family. For some, intense family feelings arise because the bloodline has been interrupted and the adoptive family ties will be only of the spirit. Only?! And just when the parents are beginning to unwind and put all the past anxiety, distress, and waiting behind them, the young child starts asking questions that open up new anxieties and old wounds.

When we examined the stories you will read in chapter 4 we discovered that many parents anticipated talking to their children about adoption with anxiety, dread, sadness, and fear. Yet as each story unfolded, the parents moved from these initial feelings to a greater sense of comfort, deeper understanding, even humor, and eventually matter-of-factness. Parents began to see that the conversations were often more difficult for them than for the children. In fact, very often the young children were simply curious and interested in talking. In this chapter we try to illumine why parents start out with such dread, in the hope that understanding will alleviate some of this anxiety for new adoptive parents.

As we deal with what adoption means for each of us, we are assailed by experiences, ideologies, and research findings that can be powerfully troubling and can interfere with talking to our children about being adopted. For parents struggling to come to terms with their feelings of disappointment and loss about their barrenness, these reflections of cultural attitudes, myths, distortions, prejudices, and convictions are especially trying. But for all adoptive parents—those who choose to adopt instead of, or in addition to, having a biological child as well as those who adopt because of infertility—our culture's assumption that adoption is somehow inferior to biological parenting deeply affects us and may make talking with our children about adoption more difficult than it need be.

In some cultures adoption is not seen as an inferior way of coming to parent children. Children are experienced as belonging to the larger group and deserving love and care from all adults, not just those with blood ties. There is no sense that the child without blood ties to her parents is inferior, unsafe. How different this is from our culture, in which some parents beg their grown children not to adopt and the laws of most states differentiate adopted from biological children, excluding them from inheritances unless otherwise specified. Ours is a culture in which some couples will spend years trying to conceive a child and then prefer to remain childless rather than "risk" adoption or attempt to love a child who is experienced as not their own. It is a culture in which infertility is often viewed as a judgment, a "sign" that one is unfit to have children, rather than as simply a biological state.

Our culture, like most cultures, considers "our" genes to be better than those of "others"—whether they are other classes, other races, other religions, other nations, other cultures. Contrary experience does not change this attitude. Yet few of us know our own genetic lineage more than one or two generations back. And those who do are—if they are honest—frequently appalled. The best family trees shelter an assortment of paranoid schizophrenics, depressives, hypochondriacs, alcoholics, or horse-thieves along with saints and successes. Extended family gatherings often present us with more diversity than gatherings of close friends.

Once adoption has taken place—often without the wholehearted support of friends, family, and, sadly, even of one's spouse—one is frequently reminded, subtly or overtly, that this way of becoming and being a family is somehow tenuous, flawed, not quite right. Well-intentioned friends may search for resemblances between parents and child as though this would be a source of reassurance. Strangers innocently comment on differences: "How did you get a baby with such red hair?" To the adoptive parents this may suggest that the child is not quite theirs, as though redheads are never born to brunettes. After staring for a few minutes, someone in the beauty shop announces to your two small daughters, "You couldn't be sisters. You have curly hair and you have straight hair." A passerby asks you, "Where did you get him?" as your baby innocently flashes a beautiful smile to this intrusive stranger. A close friend says, "Aren't you worried how it will all turn out?" as though your baby is more likely to become a juvenile delinquent than her little darling. A friend asks in front of your four-year-old, "Did she have any brothers and sisters?" Since the friend knows all your children, you realize she means "the real ones," born of the same birthparents. Your nine-year-old does very well on a math exam and a good friend exclaims, "How lucky it is that she came to you. Think what might have happened to her in another family!" A friend comments, "Wow, you really knew how to pick 'em!" Though obviously well-intentioned, these remarks convey the sense that your adopted daughter is either infinitely plastic or totally predetermined—and something like a creature carefully selected and purchased at an animal fair.

Although there is a great deal of genuine acceptance of adoption, we have found ourselves in social gatherings being criticized by normally pleasant dinner companions for doing something dangerous, stupid, or threatening, or assaulted by intrusive questions about the state of our reproductive equipment or our marriage—questions that are far more personal, impolite, and offensive than is customary in these situations. Sometimes the questions and comments betray racial and cultural prejudice in particular, but they always reflect a general prejudice against difference.

For many people, breaking the bloodline by adopting symbolizes a loss of control. For people for whom control over their own lives, feelings, and impulses requires everything to be negotiated in a particular "normal," "natural" way, adoption can be very threatening indeed. The biological tie gives people who fear loss of control a fantasy of power and certainty over what will occur in the future. For them adoption means genetic chaos. People who see biological parenting as superior—safer, more controllable—have a strong inclination to demote adopting to an inferior status.

Again and again, strangers, friends, family, friends of your children, convey that what you have done by adopting is different, risky, offensive, second-best. What is worse, you yourself may have shared in these judgments before you knew you were to adopt, and in difficult moments you still may.

When we talk with our children about their adopted status while we are clouded and confused by this cultural baggage about blood ties, it can feel to us that we are telling them that there is something wrong with them and with their lives. Further, we may feel that our connection to them is tenuous, not real, and we may communicate this to them without being aware of it.

Adoptive parents must confront their own conceptions and misconceptions about what makes a family good and come to understand—as it turns out very young children do naturally (Pederson and Gilby 1986)—that it is love that defines family relationships.

That our child has a history that predates us, is a separate person when she comes to us, in no way indicates that there is something wrong with her. Rather, adoptive parents can use this fact to arrive earlier at a perception that birthparents must eventually come to as well—that our children are separate persons from the beginning. Some birthparents have described such a feeling of separateness from their newborn at birth. They will talk about the enormous gulf between their fantasy of the child within them when they were pregnant and the actual baby lying on the mother's belly after delivery. The born baby is so separate! Other birthparents feel a fusion with the baby that lasts into the first year of life and sometimes beyond. That feeling of fusion has often been romanticized and idealized, but the fact remains that feelings of closeness, attachment, and bonding develop over time, are quite separate from fusion, and occur whether the child has been born to you and felt separate from the beginning, whether the separateness developed slowly, or whether, as in an adoption, the child is brought to you quite abruptly and the attachment process begins without benefit of pregnancy.[1] Attachment takes time for some birthparents and some adoptive parents.

---

1. "Attachment" refers to the emotional connection developed over time between parent and child. "Bonding" refers to a now widely challenged theory that there is a

Others—both birthparents and adoptive parents—describe attachment as instantaneous.

All parents have many moments when they worry about their attachment to their children and their children's attachment to them. Healthy attachment requires that parents be able to bear feelings of rage and anger at the child's helplessness, dependency, and needfulness, at the demands of the child, her lack of gratitude, and the changes her presence has made in their lives. Adoptive parents are frequently reluctant to admit experiencing these ordinary mixed feelings about becoming a parent because they fear that in the eyes of others this admission might compromise their "suitability" for parenthood—and it could!

Birthparents can fall back on the biological attachment at such moments, but adoptive parents do not have this abstraction to turn to. In its place they must build a strong understanding and acceptance of these painful feelings of ambivalence and negativity as an inevitable and essential component of parenting—not a threat to basic ties but intrinsic to them. In our conversations with adoptive mothers some describe, with extreme guilt and lack of acceptance, feelings of anger and rejection that are common to all parents of young children. One mother, upon seeing the new baby for whom she had waited with devotion and anticipation, thought, "She looks like a scrawny chicken!" Another described her fear that she would get angry at the baby and throw him off the balcony. *All* mothers experience the temporary wish that the child would go away or the thought that she is disgusting or ugly, though many will deny such feelings. Because adoptive mothers have often spent years trying to get a baby and to prove themselves worthy of a child, it is hard for them to allow themselves to accept these moments when their benevolence fails. A preoccupation with the possibility that the birthmother will reclaim the child at times like these may disguise an all too understandable desire to have a little holiday.

The adoptive parents must leave their images of who they wanted their biological child to be and their preoccupation with blood ties in order to join their actual child in the present moment. In the period before the child arrives, all parents have fantasies about what she will be like—and the fantasies are largely the same by whatever route she comes. For both birth and adoptive parents, the actuality of the real baby initiates a gradual relinquishing of the fantasy baby so that the real child may have space to develop her own identity and separate existence. This process of constructing a fan-

biologically determined time period immediately after birth when mother and infant can form an intense attachment and that if they do not, the child's later behavior can be powerfully affected. The bonding literature and assumptions will be discussed in chapter 2. In this book we refer to the development of "attachment."

tasy child during the waiting period is a necessary prelude to the parent's attachment to the actual baby. One mother put it this way:

> When we were first planning to adopt, . . . I was against it. . . . It was not something I would ever choose to do, but we went ahead and put our name on an adoption list. When it came time to adopt I was ready to adopt, and to fully accept that as a choice. But what I had to do to become ready was to grieve the loss of not having a biological child and what that meant *for me*. I think it means different things for different people. And when I had really come to some resolution about not giving birth to a child, it was clear that the next task was that I had to separate from my image of the child I had imagined having, in order to have an actual child. And I said to . . . my husband, I think that that is the work all parents have to do, whether or not they are biological or adoptive: they have to separate from their image of who and what the child will be, whether it is that she will be skinny or athletic or whatever. . . . I think my work was in separating from the image I had for my child. I realized that whoever the child was—whether he or she came by birth or adoption— I was going to have to separate from that image, because the child was not going to be an extension of me. That was the hard work I had to do. I feel that I have been really free to let Virginia become who she is going to be. And I probably would not have been forced to realize this so early in the parenting process [if adoption had not been involved]. I was really aware of learning that. The child needed to be free to become whoever he or she was going to become.

With an adopted child there is less likelihood of "seeing" one's own talents in the child and misusing that perception, projecting onto the child what isn't there at all or overemphasizing what is there only a little bit. Adoptive parents rarely think, "Johnny will be a genius at math like me," or "Johnny will be a football star like me." Adoptive parents do not have the pleasure of seeing themselves physically mirrored, as sometimes occurs when a birthchild is an uncanny replica of a parent. It is quite striking, however, that over time adoptive parents will say, in the same way birthparents do, "He has my long fingers," or "She has my allergies," or "She giggles like I did when I was her age." The line between physical resemblances, such as the fingers and the allergies, and identifications that emerge with love and attachment, like the giggle, begins to blur and then fade.

All parents have a ringside seat at the fascinating and immensely interesting unfolding of the child as an unknown quantity, a sense that they truly do not know who the child will become—a sense that retains the mystery of individuation. The powers of imitation and identification will produce all sorts of similarities. But adoptive parents are deprived of the experience—and the expectation—of seeing themselves reproduced in a concrete way. Their relations to their child will not have that physical "flesh of my flesh" quality that some parents care about very deeply. When otherness is respected, however, a fine opportunity is created for a unique individual to develop, and this can more than compensate for the absence of blood ties. Respect for the unfolding of the child's qualities is a mark of good parenting, be it adoptive or biological. There can be great joy and pleasure in witnessing ways of looking and being that are different from our own—with both birth and adopted children.

With the adopted child's first question about her beginnings—typically, "Was I in your tummy?"—the parents confront the necessity of coming to terms with their feelings about the birthparents. Although the answer to the child's question is a short one—"No, you were in another lady's tummy," or "No, you were in your birthmother's tummy"—our journey as parents to that answer is a long and complex one. We must ask ourselves who the birthparents, usually complete strangers to us, have become for us symbolically and imaginally. Often they become stand-ins for parental or authority figures in the adoptive parents' lives. Sometimes they become objects onto which adoptive parents project all sorts of inner feelings with which they have trouble.

Every woman worries at times that she will not be a good enough mother. Sometimes she compares herself to her own mother or to a friend. At stressful moments, an adoptive mother may use the birthmother in this way: "*She* would have done a better job." Sometimes an adoptive mother has feelings of jealousy because she didn't "do it all" and a fantasy that everything would have been fine if only she had given birth to the child. Normal feelings of rivalry may be focused on the largely unknown birthmother. The adoptive mother may think of herself as inadequate and may have a feeling of foreboding or inevitable failure; meanwhile she has an internal representation, or mental picture, of the "other mother" as perfect. Meeting the birthparents, even becoming acquainted with them, sometimes eases adoptive parents' worries; but the task of coming to terms with their feelings about the birthparents remains.

Sometimes the adoptive mother has images of how sad the birthmother must be to have relinquished the child—an empathic projection of how she would feel about giving up this much-loved baby. Sometimes the adoptive parents feel guilty, as though their desire to adopt caused the separation between the child and the birthmother, giving pain to both. Sometimes the adoptive parents remain preoccupied with the birthparents in an unhealthy way, reflecting their low self-esteem and lack of confidence as parents. In contrast, a birthparent can sometimes be a source of courage and inspiration, as in this example:

> Teresa interrupted and addressed her mother directly: "No, it is not my baby any more. It is their baby now." Then she turned directly to me. "It is your baby now." . . .
>
> Keeping one's baby if you are a domestic maid in northeastern Brazil means traveling the long road back to the village you were born in. . . . More than that, it means watching your own child be locked into the same privations and lack of possibilities that you had as a child. It means the very real possibility of your child dying as an infant, the near certitude of her being undereducated, of her working in the fields until she could no longer.
>
> Teresa was clear that she was not going to do that kind of watching. . . . She wrote in a letter to Laura, "I do not want you to have the same sadnesses I had as a child." . . .
>
> I still carry about the guilt that I have the good fortune to mother this wonderful little girl, and that someone I know has had the bad fortune to part with her. I feel as though I have to do it right, not just for Laura, but for Teresa. I have to prove that she was right to be confident about me, to have chosen me for her child's mother.

Some of the feelings of jealousy of the birthparents are more complicated and difficult to face. Concern about the impact of the child's biological heritage may mask jealousy of the "other" mother for her role in the child's life and frightening fantasies about her coming to take the baby back—if not literally, then through the unfolding of the child's genetic heritage. There is always genuine and powerful gratitude to the birthmother for giving this baby to the adoptive family, directly or indirectly. But along with gratitude there may be fears and other negative feelings that may be projected onto seemingly unrelated concerns, such as the child's I.Q. and excessive, ungrounded preoccupations with unreported disease in the birthfamily's history.

A part of some adoptive mothers' jealousy and inner relationship with the birthmother may have to do with sexuality. If the child was born out of wedlock, the adoptive mother may have the fantasy that the birthmother was a beautiful, sensual young woman—with resulting feelings of jealousy. An infertile woman may, after all, erroneously link fertility and sexuality.

These fantasies can lead to projections onto the adopted child as she matures—the "bad seed" notion that the child will inevitably come to resemble
in character what the adoptive parents fantasize about the circumstances
surrounding her birth. Absurd as it sounds, this is a common fear of adoptive parents, who tend to confuse the social circumstances of the baby's
birth with her biological endowment.

For all these reasons, adoptive parents often dread the child's first mention of her birthmother. It is hard to remember that what the birthparents
have come to represent for us lives only in *our* imaginations. The child
adopted in earliest infancy has neither an accurate image of her birthparents
nor prolonged experience with them. To us a birthmother may be a brave,
courageous woman from an impoverished situation who has sacrificed her
tie to her child for the sake of the child's welfare, even survival. She may
embody a flamboyant, expressive sexuality that mocks our infertility. She
may stand for the youth and energy we feel are flagging in us as we embark
on child rearing as somewhat older parents. Sometimes our fear that she
will reclaim the child expresses our habitual anxiety that good things in our
lives will be taken from us—and sometimes it reflects our own ambivalence
about the child. After all, birthparents who clean up spilled paint for the
twelfth time in one day cannot take refuge in the fantasy that some "other
mother" will come and get the child.

An essential component of successful parenting is the deep conviction
that "this is my kid, for better or worse." Fantasies that the birthmother
still wants her child, that she would be a better mother, that she might reclaim her child, that because of the blood tie the child would be closer to
her if given the chance—these can diminish the necessary sense of healthy
entitlement to having that child. Developing such a sense does not mean
denying the existence of the birthparents or the significance they may come
to have for the child. It means that the adoptive parents have accomplished
the paradoxical task of being unwavering in their conviction that this is
their child forever and still having room in their heads and hearts for the
parents who brought her into the world.

Sometimes adoptive parents evade some of the difficulties of parenting
by sustaining a lack of entitlement to the child—never connecting deeply
enough with her, never developing fantasies and expectations about her.
Such parents, when the child has problems, often will make her adoptive
status the sole reason for them and thereby avoid a sense of responsibility
and hope for change. Parents may fear that talking with adopted children
about the birthparents will attenuate their own feelings of claiming the
child—but it needn't. There are two realities: *we are the parents; the baby
has a history.* They are not contradictory. It is the parents' unfounded sense

that these two facts are incompatible that can be passed on to the child and may give the relationship between parents and child a sense of tentativeness. Come the ordinary problems of development, this tentativeness can lead parents to attribute problems to the fact of adoption itself, thus surrendering their sense of responsibility and connectedness to the child, unwittingly extruding her into an unsupported and lonely space.

Parental ambivalence about entitlement and parenting (obviously present in birthparents too) can therefore use the birthmother's existence as a rationalization; and sometimes the leap from the real situation is quite fantastical. Some birthmothers do long for and wonder about their adopted-away children and might be happy to meet them at some point; but many are contented with the adoption, want to put it behind them, and describe their fears of a stranger coming to their door one day. Such birthmothers have truly surrendered their children and moved on, and adoptive mothers need to appreciate this. This is often very difficult for them to believe, since they wanted their children so desperately and feel they would never have given up a child.[2] Adoptive parents need to become aware of their fantasies about the birthparents so that they do not inadvertently ask that the child join them in whatever their internal dialogue with the birthparents may be. In this way a space is made for the child to create her own fantasies of her birthparents that will reflect her changing concerns as she develops, fantasies to which the adoptive parents need to be attentive.

An enormous amount of attention has been paid to the idea of loss for the adopted child: the loss by abandonment of the birthparents at birth or later; the loss of her extended biological family; the loss of her birthplace and particular cultural heritage; the loss of the ability to see herself in relation to blood relatives. This is a very complicated issue to which we shall return again and again. For a child given up at birth by parents who genuinely want something better for her, the birthparents' sacrifice, renunciation, and altruism can be too easily overlooked. Talking about this to the

---

2. For example, one adoptive mother in our stories was surprised to find that the shame of out-of-wedlock birth is so great in India that often birthmothers do not even visit their babies when living in the same facility. Utter anonymity is preserved by Indian orphanages to protect the birthmother from further shame and to help her move on in her life. Different cultures have different attitudes. In the United States today there is considerable pressure on young mothers for open adoption. The problem with such uniform solutions to complex problems is that they are not responsive to individual situations: some young mothers might want to surrender their children with no further contact; others may prefer open adoption in one form or another. Similarly, adoptive parents need to feel free to choose the form of adoption that suits them, be it open, modified open, or traditional (Demick and Wapner 1988; McRoy and Grotevant 1988).

child at the appropriate time may help transform a feeling of rejection into one of thoughtful care. In addition, it is important to emphasize that the "rejection" is not of the child herself but of the role of parenting at that particular time in the birthparents' lives. After all, you have to know a person in order to reject her meaningfully, so that, most emphatically, the rejection is not of the person the child is or was—and the child can gradually come to understand this, with her parents' help.

All this having been said, however, there is no question that there is some loss for the adopted child, though the dimensions and character of that loss are often overdramatized by parents and the helping professions. The child will make it dramatic enough as it is! As the distinguished psychiatrist and psychoanalyst Viola Bernard says, "Adoption is a repair of trauma, not a trauma in itself (except for unsuitable placements); it is not a losing or a taking away of what never was, but a mutual giving and gaining of affirmative family relationship" (1974, p. 531).

It is very easy and common for adults to project onto the feelings of the adopted child their own experiences of abandonment by people they have known. Adoptive parents tend also to project their own unresolved feelings about their inability to conceive or bear a child—that poignant loss of their own—onto the child. There is, after all, a difference between a child's loss in reality and the fantasies the child creates about that loss. It is very important to keep the two separate and to remember that the content and impact of the fantasied loss depend to a great extent on the spirit and atmosphere in which the adoption is experienced by the parents and discussed with the child.

The experience of losing one's birthparents is obviously different for a child adopted at birth than for a child adopted at five years of age. To help parents hear these differences, we include two stories of children adopted after infancy: one at age five and the other at seven. Children adopted in infancy can have no memory of what has been left behind, and therefore their actual experience of loss does not include all the losses usually anticipated by the adoptive parents. Rather, such children feel a yearning to have been in the adoptive mother's tummy. It is the loss of being inside her body that the child most often speaks of first and that the adoptive mother must help her with. On the other hand, young children who are adopted after infancy will experience a concrete sense of loss for places and people they remember.

When all is said and done, however, there *is* loss, and all the dimensions of that loss have to be dealt with within the family over time—what it meant then, what it means now, and what it might mean in the future. These losses unfold with the child's understanding and capacity to deal with them. They need not permeate her mood and create her character. Questions appear at odd times, and if they are dealt with on the spot they may not reappear for months or even years—or they may recur frequently.

While the young child's sense of loss is largely focused on not having been in her adoptive mother's tummy, the parents must grieve their loss of their biological baby—that symbol of innocence and absolute purity, that perfect and romantic embodiment of the family they should and would have had if they had been able to bring a child into the world directly. They need to grieve the loss of that perfect family, that anchor against despair and uncertainty where ancestry and origins are certain, that magical, enchanted, protected harbor, the source of strength for life's later hardships. We do not think such families really exist; rather, it is the quality of the actual relationships within the family, among family members, that provides the trust and strength to deal with life's trials. In this context, dealing with adoption at the right time and in ways suited to the temperament and cognitive development of the child becomes just another opportunity to share and to tolerate many kinds of feelings about life's disappointments and rewards.

What makes it so difficult to surrender our romantic fantasies about family is that there is no stronger symbol of purity, innocence, wholeness, and perfection than a newborn baby, experienced by the parents as having come into being almost miraculously. The parents try to protect their child's innocence and purity as long as possible. For adults already torn by experiences of disappointment, struggle, fear, loss, or even death, the baby is a welcome epiphany of all that is not yet sullied and damaged. The baby stands for new possibilities. Worldly reality first imposes itself on the child through the figures of the parents. And so parents wisely strive to protect the child from unduly harsh reality as long as possible—by not showing impatience, by not allowing the child to cry for long periods uncomforted, by scrupulously attending to the child's needs. But we adults do not protect the child only for the child's sake. *We* need this sense of the baby's pristineness, of her being set apart from the world she must eventually enter. *We* feel revived playing with the baby, laughing and cooing, down on the floor again.

But the world and its problems have left their imprint on our adopted children's histories before they come to us, and this is one of the most difficult aspects of beginning to talk with our children about adoption. The baby need not have arrived emaciated from the third world for this to be so. Whether the child's story involves an unwed teenager, a destitute mother, illness or death of the mother, a rape, a conception not from love, a mother who used drugs during pregnancy, the harshness of life has already been demonstrated. In many cases of international adoption these intensely personal issues are compounded by such wider factors as economic and social inequities for women and girl children, U.S. intervention in a country's internal affairs, the country's impoverishment and inability to support mothers and children in severe need.

To deny the adopted child's history in our own minds is in part an attempt to restore the child as a symbol of purity for us as adults. Parents who have difficulty separating from their children are often fearful of the impact of the world on them. In the end, however, every child grows up, and as an adult she must have a dialogue with the world beyond her family. The adopted child has a history of origin that involves her with the world apart from her parents right from the beginning, whether or not she knows it. H. David Kirk, in his remarkable classic *Shared Fate* (1984), cogently describes how adoptive parents need to renounce an "enchanted" view of family in order to honor their child's origin:

> In an enchanted plot, the actors play parts of a plan which presupposes wholeness and which enshrines flawlessness. . . . The world view, the plot, and the role are indicative of the meaning of enchantment—an undivided whole, a seamless robe, reflecting the "original" and the "natural" view of things. . . .
>
> In our society parenthood is still widely held enchanted—that is, whole and indivisible—from the beginning of the love of mates, through conception, pregnancy, birth, and child rearing. . . .
>
> The dilemma for adoptive parents consists essentially in what picture of themselves and their role they select. . . . They can either say, "I am just like any other parent," and reject the objective and subjective differences. . . . If they choose this way of defining themselves and their place in the drama they will be rewarded by conforming to the regulation model of parenthood and thus feeling fewer pangs about the differences visible to the audience beyond the stage. But such adoptive parents will more likely pay a price in the process of seeking and keeping sound relations with their principal fellow-actors, namely their children, around the meaning of adoption. If, on the other hand, they choose to acknowledge their differences by retaining a memory of their original deprivations and a recognition of their current substitute position on the stage, then their problem will more likely be with the audience rather than with their fellow-actors. (pp. 43–44)

Every parent has the wish not to give the child pain. Lancing an abscess is the pediatrician's problem. In that situation the parent merely holds the child—and that is difficult enough. But we ourselves, we alone, must inflict whatever pain or distress the knowledge of being adopted will entail. When we first talk about it, we are presenting information that will eventually introduce difference and disappointment into our child's life—an extra burden that other parents do not have to deal with in this particular form. And knowing that how we deal with it will affect how the child will deal with it does not make the burden lighter.

There is an extraordinary remark by a child quoted in *Shared Fate:* "The child who is born into his family is like a board that's nailed down from the start. But the adopted child, him the parents have to nail down, otherwise he is like a loose board in mid-air" (Kirk 1984, p. 160). On the basis of our own experience as adoptive parents, our research in the extensive literature about adoption, and, finally, the stories we have collected for this book, we think that listening to the child, talking with her, and helping to create her story with her are all part of "nailing" her down, of making her certain of her home and our love for her.

Chapter 2

Adoption
Research

Research and theory do not exist in an objective realm but inevitably reflect the culture in which the study takes place. This is clearly the case with the research and theoretical reflection that have structured psychological thinking about adoption. Adoptive parents need to understand the scope, limitations, and character of this research.

As adoptive parents all of us have been influenced by the cultural prejudice and myth pervading this research. This atmosphere contributes to the sense that telling our children they are adopted is bringing them bad news. Most of us, however, are not familiar with these research traditions and do not understand that much about them was ill-founded in the first place and is now thoroughly outdated.

The more recent research, whose results are more comforting to adoptive parents, has not yet filtered through the network of adoption agencies and adoption literature down to adoptive parents themselves. And some of the older literature that ran counter to the "bad news" tradition never received the attention it deserved, probably because it went so strongly against the grain of the prevailing cultural myths and prejudices about adoption.

Lacking familiarity with the literature, the adoptive parent is ill-prepared to dispel and dispute this powerful sense that discussing adoption with one's child is bringing bad tidings. We think it is important to discuss this literature in some detail so that parents will be able to find their own more informed place to stand rather than being overwhelmed by misinformation. Otherwise, it may appear as though "the experts" have confirmed what everybody else has been intimating or telling us outright—that our families are defective, our children doomed to psychological pathology, and that genes will "win out" over nurture. Some examples of theory and research can show how to take a more critical stance toward what is presented to us as fact and help us to discriminate what is scientifically unsound and culturally biased from well-conceived and executed research.

The Psychiatric-Psychoanalytic Tradition

"Does the mere fact that he is adopted mean that our child can't develop a good sense of self?"

There is a long-standing conviction in the psychoanalytic literature,[1] which has flowed into the counseling and social work professions, that the adopted child has a more fragile identity, experiences more difficulty integrating a solid sense of self, and will be at greater risk for emotional problems than a child reared by his birthparents. Adopted children of course have their work cut out for them, as do their parents! But to describe difficulty and limitation as inevitable is both unfounded and very troubling. We must remember that we are listening to theory and that theory is not truth but merely a way of organizing experience and asking questions—albeit a powerful way. To generalize from a clinical sample—a small group of troubled children— to the general population, to treat theoretical speculation as natural law, is dubious science at best. Adoptive parents need to be protected from the dogmatic tone of this psychoanalytic research, which has influenced a whole generation of adoption workers—and knowledge is the best defense.

Many influential psychoanalysts are convinced that adopted children inevitably face grave difficulties in development because of their supposedly unique response to the "family romance" and the loss of their birthparents (see Brinich 1980; H. P. Blum 1983; Nickman 1985; Panel 1967; Peller 1961; Schechter 1960; Wieder 1977a, 1977b, 1978).[2]

According to Freudian theory, every child passes through the Oedipus complex—a phase from age two and a half or three to about six—in which the child desires to be the central love of the opposite-sex parent and conse-

1. In this section we examine the large body of psychoanalytic theorizing about adoption. Because our views on this literature are by and large quite negative, with the notable exception of the work of Viola Bernard (1963, 1970, 1974), we want to be clear at the outset that our complaints are not with psychoanalysis in general either clinically or theoretically but with this particular body of speculation. Both of us in fact work within one or another branch of psychoanalysis, and our critique is offered from the perspective of friends, not enemies.

2. This conclusion is strikingly similar to the literature on children born to Holocaust victims in assuming that the children will be psychologically scarred. Clinical experience shows that damage is not inevitable.

quently feels rivalrous toward the same-sex parent. As part of the Oedipus complex and its resolution, the child imagines that he has been adopted and actually is the offspring of some fairy tale "other" couple from whom he has been separated. He does this in order to cool the intensity of his passion to be more intimately connected with his mother, to distance himself from her, and to protect himself from the disapproval and retribution he fantasizes are forthcoming from his father. The child, in this phase, experiences his own parents as bad and depriving, unlike the fantasized "other" parents, who would not so frustrate him. This fantasy, called the "family romance" (Freud 1909), is the final phase of the Oedipus complex, which results in the consolidation of personal and gender identity. Now the child identifies with the same-sex parent and is able to delay the gratification of his passion and wait for a substitute for his mother to appear later in his life. As part of this ability to delay gratification and to identify with the same-sex parent, the child gives up his imagined other family and reluctantly locates himself with his real family. Eventually, by renouncing the split between the "good" and "bad" families and accepting his own parents as containing both good and bad elements, he will be able to integrate and accept good and bad as part of himself and thereby will develop a strong and healthy superego (that part of the mind that is conscience, social critic, and source of ideals and values). He will have a clear sense of values, an ability to criticize his own behavior and distinguish right from wrong, and a set of goals and ideals that reflect the best of himself and society.

It is important to note, however, that most contemporary psychoanalytic theorists emphasize the preeminence of interpersonal attachments that are continuous from early life until well past the oedipal period. These relationships, their character and quality, play a critical role in shaping the expression of conflict at every phase of development, and for many theorists they overshadow in importance such concepts as the family romance, on which the psychoanalytic notions of adoption are based.

On the basis of this early conception of the family romance, some psychoanalytic writers have argued that the oedipal phase will prove a stumbling block for the crucial personality integration of the adopted child. Because in his case these other parents in fact exist or have existed, the adopted child will not have to give them up; consequently, he will fail to identify solidly with the same-sex parent and thus will fail to reach the realistic and tolerant sense of himself and others that results from such an identification. He will therefore unrealistically idealize some people and diminish others, having internalized a polarized and less mature superego—with harsher self-criticism and inappropriate ego ideals. According to this view, adoptive parents should delay telling their child anything at all about being adopted until he is seven or eight, when logical thinking has superseded immersion in fantasy and he is past the oedipal phase, with its family romance. (For a story reflecting this point of view, see appendix A.)

Enriching and illuminating as the oedipal view of child development may be, it has several problems that limit its general applicability. To begin with, as many researchers within the psychoanalytic tradition have themselves pointed out, the theory in its classic formulation is inadequate to the developmental experience of girls. It does not account for a wide range of data acquired through clinical research, child observation, and intensive clinical work and has serious theoretical deficiencies as well (Fast 1978; Person 1980; Schafer 1974; Silverman 1981). More concretely, it does not speak to other factors that might cause a child to be preoccupied with secretly belonging to fantasy families; he might, for example, genuinely and appropriately experience the family he is in as not meeting his realistic needs for care and nurturance. When the family romance is an instance of wish fulfillment, engaged in as a way of dealing with the genuinely harsh realities of a child's present family life, one can argue that rather than being a device to deal with the frustrations of the oedipal phase it represents an adaptive fantasy that helps the child live through the difficult present.

Several additional points need to be made with respect to the application of the family romance to the development of adopted children. Over time, the adopted child will come to see each set of parents—birth and adoptive—in a more complex and more integrated fashion. In instances where the child splits the two sets of parents into a "good" set and a "bad" set, this splitting often reflects not a failure of personality development but a lack of understanding of the adoption process. In fact, there is evidence from both clinical work and child observation that most normal children use splitting as a way to relieve and gradually deal with the painful ambivalent feelings toward parents that inevitably arise.

Two of the stories in chapter 4 clearly articulate this inevitable splitting, which theory warns us is disastrous. One four-year-old imagined her adoptive mother as a bad, witchlike woman who had stolen her from her benevolent birthmother. When she was questioned about this, it emerged that the child, understandably ignorant of how adoption plans are made, had been unable to fathom any other reason for her displacement from her birthfamily. As she came to understand the complexities of the adoption process—the birthparents' motivations for relinquishing her and the adoptive parents' struggle with infertility—her image of each of her four parents became more realistic, integrating what was previously separated into good and bad. Speaking of her birthmother, this same child at age nine said, "She didn't give me away. She had a baby. She gave birth to me. But she didn't give *me* up. . . . She was my mother while I was growing in her uterus, and you are my mother since I was born." Could one truly say of such a child, a child who by age nine had developed some realistic empathy for the important figures in her life, that adoption has made it impossible for her thinking to move from its "mythical," "immature," "unrealistic" beginnings into logical, realistic understanding? Yet this is what the view under consideration would suggest.

The psychoanalytically inspired position implies that a child in normal development integrates good and bad aspects of the parents with whom he will identify because he comes to accept that the "other family" of his family romance is a fantasy. By default, he retreats from dreams and accepts the reality that he has only one family. According to the theory, the adopted child can avoid this acceptance, with alarming results. Yet we see many children today who seem to have little difficulty integrating aspects of diverse caretakers—mother, grandmothers, babysitters, day-care workers, older siblings, stepparents—any number of whom could theoretically provide an escape from the integration of good and bad. And yet such children make solid identifications with their parents and develop solid identities in the face of this array of parenting figures.

Krugman (1964) did developmental appraisals of more than fifty adopted children between the ages of three and seven who had learned about their adoption before she saw them. These were nonproblematic children, being seen for administrative reasons, not because of personal or family problems. Their I.Q.s were higher than would have been anticipated by normal sampling. Psychological testing and play contact showed no patterns distinguishing them from other children of similar backgrounds. Most important for this discussion, however, is Krugman's remark about the test record of a girl aged three years eight months: "On review, this record showed no diffusion of 'good and bad' parental images, but rather strongly indicates that both are fused on the significant persons of the functioning mother and father. . . . *This was characteristic of all but a few of the test records of the adopted children within this age range who were not referred because of problems*" (p. 355; emphasis added).[3] No splitting, no failure of integration, no fragile identities, no damaged superegos!

Schwartz (1970) compared adopted and nonadopted boys on their perception of their status in their families and of their parents as role models. The adopted boys had no problems of superego formation and showed "adequate expression of impulse controls and acceptance of the basic values

3. We would argue from the stories presented in chapter 4 that the adoptive situation does indeed often influence the *content* of fantasy life, but that it does not distort or impair the *form* of thought or fantasy.

and prohibitions of their parents." They did not create fantasied alternative parents, their interest in their birthparents was limited, and there was no evidence of difficulty in identifying with their adoptive parents, no sign of identity confusion or faulty superego formation. Farber (1977) confirmed these findings, and a Danish study by Eldred and his colleagues (1976) on a sample of 216 adopted adults reached similar conclusions. We could cite many more studies to the same effect, but the point should be clear.

The alleged importance of postponing talk about adoption until the oedipal phase is over is not supported by empirical evidence from nonclinical studies or by follow-up assessments of adoption outcome. The impact of talking about adoption depends largely on the quality of parent-child relationships and overall family functioning. "None of the other ostensibly important aspects of the telling—the timing of the initial revelation, the nature and amount of material revealed, or the frequency of subsequent allusions to adoption—were appreciably correlated with outcome" (Jaffee and Fanshel 1970, p. 313). Raynor (1980) reached similar conclusions when she studied British adult adoptees and their families. The adoptees' sense of satisfaction was related to their contentment with the information they had and the ease they felt in reaching out to their adoptive parents.[4]

Many psychoanalysts claim that a child who appears to have no problem about adoption may have unconscious reactions that are being overlooked. Schechter, for example, speaks of "deeper, non-observable feelings and reactions to the event" (Schechter et al. 1964, p. 114). This is an example of "heads I win, tails you lose" reasoning. If the child has problems around adoption, the theory is confirmed; but if he has no problems, the theory is still valid because the problems are unconscious. The only response to this sort of statement is that if the postulated damage never appears it is not worth worrying about and may well be merely a figment of the writer's imagination, without foundation in reality.

There are a few other psychoanalytic theories that adoptive parents should be prepared for. Frisk (1964) suggested that, having been separated from their birthparents, adopted children lack a healthy "genetic ego" and instead develop a "hereditary ghost." Sants (1964) talks about "gene-

---

4. As we will make clear in chapter 3, we are *not* proposing that parents deliver an information-packed speech to a young child, filled with concepts and contexts beyond his possible understanding. A three-year-old child should not be told that he has four parents, two of them strangers to him; that he is the product of illegitimacy, rape, or incest; or that he is lucky not to be abandoned or poor any longer. Rather, he deserves a comfortable and comforting answer to whatever question he is asking at the moment, an answer framed in the parents' own language and responsive to who the child is and in language he can understand.

alogical bewilderment" and a "genealogically deprived" child.[5] There are certainly issues to be dealt with by adopted children in relation to their background and their feeling informed, connected, and comfortable with whatever information is available about their biological heritage. The importance placed on biological continuity by these theories, however, and the emotional disruption they assume is caused by lack of complete knowledge of one's biological roots do not appear to be confirmed by empirical studies of adopted children. They also reflect a conviction that biological ties represent greater reality than social connections.

Krugman (1964, p. 353) notes that Schechter uses the word *real* seventeen times and *own* twice when talking about the birthparents of adopted children but never when speaking of their adoptive parents. She describes the terminology in some adoption literature as appearing "to grow out of a primary acceptance of a biologically oriented definition of the reality of parenthood," a terminology that also implies "the converse, that the adoptive parents must then be not real, or less real." Terms like *genetic ego* and *genealogical deprivation* are pure constructs treated as if they were concrete social and psychological realities. Once reified, they have been attributed to adoptees as though they are inevitably going to be experienced. This is not to deny that late adolescent and adult adoptees sometimes do wonder about their genealogical histories and seek information in order to answer their questions. To want to know about one's genetic history, however, need not imply inevitable or pathological deprivation. Stein and Hoopes (1985) emphasize quite vigorously that reifying concepts such as "genetic ego" and "genealogical deprivation" are derived from theory in an attempt to account for the responses of disturbed patients and are then projected onto a nonclinical population. These theoretical reifications would be comic were they less destructive.

There is an underlying assumption in these theories that the ideal world for a normal child consists of a special version of the nuclear family in which a single monumentally influential parent, the mother (the father is barely in evidence), has an impact more profound than current research indicates. Recent work reveals, for example, that the impact of siblings on personality development is much stronger than had previously been thought (Daniels 1985). Quite independent of parenting, and regardless of whether the siblings are biologically or adoptively related, sibling relationships have

---

5. Genealogical bewilderment, if experienced by an adoptee, becomes possible only in adolescence, when understanding of genetic lineage is conceptually possible. Then this confusion about who the real parents are is part of a larger age-appropriate confusion and quest for adult identity.

a dynamic of their own. They are asymmetrical in character (one child dominant, another passive; one outgoing, another timid), powerful, and often controlling of personality outcome (personal communication, D. Reiss 1992). In most other cultures and times children had multiple caretakers (Margolis 1985). The idealized family of psychoanalytic theory in which the mother spends hours alone with her young children is an anomalous arrangement historically and is of questionable benefit to the mental health of young children and their mothers. Nevertheless, these writers idealize the nuclear family and deem a child's awareness of other early caretakers destructive to his mental health.[6] One three-year-old in her play imagined her two mothers—her tummy mother and her adoptive mother—as a supportive network, each being a source of care and protection. (See the story of Laura.)

As we will show in chapter 3, the way in which the child's understanding about his birthparents unfolds reflects his psychological development in general. Although adoptive parents may use the word *adopt* with a child as young as age two, it evokes no images of birthparents for such a child. When at age three or four the child's questions about whose tummy he came from evoke the response "another lady," his curiosity about this other woman is extremely limited; interest in and ability to understand her reasons for relinquishing him are virtually absent at this age. The wise parent follows the child's lead, not arbitrarily initiating a discussion but allowing the child's questioning to indicate what he is prepared to understand and integrate. It is only when the child begins to comprehend that other people have thoughts and motivations separate from his own that wonderings about relinquishment will surface; only then will conversations about when and why he was given up for adoption make sense to him. Premature or unasked-for information can indeed confuse a child, though often it will pass right by him. On the other hand, information that a child is capable of understanding can enrich and consolidate his experience.

Late-latency and adolescent adoptees we have met strike us as having integrated good and bad characteristics not just of themselves and their adoptive parents but of their birthparents as well, whatever their level of information and experience of them. Often they have a feel for situations of social complexity, poverty, and early motherhood that their nonadopted peers do not. Rather than polarize good and bad, ricocheting between two sets of parents, these children have established a rich sense of themselves and the world.

----

6. The Woodlawn epidemiological study, the largest of its kind ever done, found that only mother-alone families produced significant problems for the first-graders evaluated. Children in mother-grandmother, mother–significant other families did quite well (Kellam et al. 1977).

The psychoanalytic writers we have been discussing all based their specu-
lations on a very small sample of patients in clinical treatment. Studies of
adopted children in nontreatment settings come to very different and far
more positive conclusions both about the mental health of their subjects
and about when to tell them about adoption.

Current infant and child development research supports our sense that
the family romance may be a significant marker in development for some
children but is barely evident in others; even when it is deeply experienced,
it is but one part of the child's real and imaginal experiences with other
people. Few contemporary child therapists and analysts report organized
evidence of family romance fantasies in their patients and in their child observations. As described by Freud and others, the family romance was probably a sociocultural phenomenon of a particular historical period rather
than a necessary component of the oedipal phase (personal communication,
J. Fineman 1992). Development is an ongoing dynamic process, not a mechanical and inevitable unfolding of the oedipal phase, which forever limits
further growth. (See the work of infant researchers Emde 1988a, 1988b;
Sander 1983, 1985; Stern 1985.) This is an important theoretical revision.
Many of the psychoanalytic notions that led to the bleak view of adoption
were based on views of development that did not give sufficient emphasis to
the shaping power and flexibility of human attachments. In sum, the simple
truth is that one cannot predict from either statistics or theory the individual outcome of any particular experience. Thus, being adopted, however
tortuous some of its pathways, has no predetermined or inevitable character
outcome.[7]

Some psychoanalysts have based their grim views of adoptive development on the adopted child's loss of his birthparents. This loss is deemed
detrimental both in and of itself and because of the child's mistaken assumption that he was rejected by his birthparents because he was flawed
or inadequate. Some writers even speak of the "image" or "ghost" of the
parents that lives on in the child.

Just who is it that the child adopted in infancy has lost? We must not
confuse our adult knowledge about the birthmother with the young child's
image of her. In fact the child has no remembered images and may have
had no postnatal experience of her. Therefore his feelings of loss in relation to her will develop only in step with his ability to develop imaginal
images of her. These imaginal images, though vivid and powerful, will still
not represent an actual "other" whom he has known and experienced and

---

7. Dr. J. Reiss wittily suggests that psychoanalysts have a gloomy view of adoption because so much of psychoanalytic developmental theory revolves around the
myth of Oedipus—who was adopted and got into trouble when he started asking
questions!

lost. They are essentially the same as the images that every child, biological or adopted, creates in his mind—of monsters, of Uncle George whom he has never seen, or of dead grandparents. They are created and develop in response to the people he is living with, the vicissitudes of his development, and the fertility of his imagination. The striking fact is that these images tell us more about the current experience of the imaginer than about his past. Parents must always try to understand what is going on at the present time in their child's life that contributes to or elicits a particular image and emotion. For instance, a four-year-old girl speaks of missing "my people" and "my beautiful place," the people and place of her birthcountry. She does this when she is on an extended vacation away from the New England home where she lives with her adoptive parents. On another occasion, the same four-year-old longs for her birthmother to visit her at a time when she needs to identify with a mother who could have a baby in her tummy. In contrast, for the child who has had remembered contact with his birthparents or with foster parents before his adoption there are realistic images of real people to be dealt with. That is quite a different story and involves a different order of grieving.

It is imperative that adoptive parents understand that all children, biological and adopted, have in their minds idealized, fantasied parents. These are universal fantasies, experienced by everyone. But because adoptive parents often think that such fantasies of idealized parents are unique to their adopted children, they feel threatened by them, and their existence can become problematic. Their important function is to help the child—every child—deal with the inevitable disappointments and frustrations with parents who set limits, thus arousing anger and guilt in the child—as in the family romance. Having recourse to these idealized images is one of the many normal mechanisms that children use to cope with the vicissitudes of everyday life. It is no different from an adult's holding in mind the image of a flawless spouse who would meet our every need and fulfill our life in a perfect, idealized way. Such an image asserts itself at times of neediness, disappointment, or anger and then usually fades until another time of turmoil.

The hypothesis that the early loss of the birthparents impairs the child's imaginal development is also dubious. On the contrary, the experience of loss may enhance imaginative life. At times of stress many people use traditional myths and stories drawn from their culture to help heal the pain of disappointment and loss. We have only rarely seen a loss of imaginative capacity in children, and only where there has been massive trauma of an assaultive nature or demands from very early in the child's life for excessive self-control and management of himself and others—for example, three-year-olds obliged to manage for themselves, negotiating meals alone, traversing heavy traffic, caring for younger siblings. But these instances of "premature ego development" are very different from the supposed trauma of the loss of someone the child does not remember.

Because the young child first understands what others do in terms of himself, and because he has no knowledge of the social factors that lead to adoption, it is not surprising that he will think he was rejected by his birthparents for being flawed or unworthy. This is not a reason not to tell young children about their adoption. Rather, it is a reason for parents to be alert to this very natural interpretation so that they can help their child understand. One child at age four and a half blurted out, "Why didn't she want me?" His mother replied, "Not want you? She didn't even *know* you. She was too young and too poor to be a mommy. To reject someone you have to know them." This seemed to make sense to the child and allayed his feelings of rejection. Let us emphasize here that such a child can also counter his imagined rejection with the multiple daily experiences of being accepted, valued, respected, tolerated, and loved in his actual family. In time, the fantasy of rejection is replaced by a more mature understanding. By the time latency arrives, the child who has grown up knowing he was adopted is now able to appreciate that who he was had nothing to do with the motivations for his relinquishment. If, however, daily experience in the adoptive family is actually rejecting, the child may be unable to credit any other reason for his having been relinquished, despite his intellectual understanding to the contrary. His fantasy about his adoption will reflect his experience—his adoptive experience.

An incidental finding of Stein and Hoopes's 1985 study of identity formation in fifty adopted adolescents is of considerable relevance to our discussion. They found that 92 percent of the youngsters in their study had been told about their adoption by the age of six, most of them between three and five, and that almost all of them were satisfied that this was the right time. Most of their subjects gave realistic reasons for their relinquishment by their birthparents, citing financial difficulties, emotional immaturity, out-of-wedlock pregnancies and the illegality of abortions, altruistic reasons, and the desire of the birthparents not to have children. Only four of the fifty adoptees referred to the possibility of their own inferiority. The authors note how startlingly different these findings are from those based on psychoanalytic theories.

The disparity in findings between clinical and nonclinical populations is even more striking in studies of adoptees' fantasies about their birthparents. Wieder, a psychoanalytic theorist, states that his patients' fantasies "were not fantasies of idealized or exalted images unsullied by misdeeds

[but] images of debased and feared people for whom they had an unrelieved hatred" (1977a, p. 189). Later he notes that birthparents were represented as "corrupt, immoral, sadistic, lower class and uneducated" (p. 197). He quotes a seventeen-year-old patient who remarked, "I only see my father as a killer and my mother as a whore" (p. 191). Only very late in the clinical description of this patient, and only casually, almost as an afterthought in a sentence about wish fulfillment, does Wieder mention that this adolescent's adoptive family was marked by "violent interactions between the parents who demonstrated little affection toward each other."

In our view, the image of the birthparents often reflects life in the adoptive home. In sharp contrast to Wieder's conclusions, Stein and Hoopes found that of the thirty-five adoptees in their study who were able to fantasize about their birthparents, none made disparaging remarks. Most of these adolescents projected a quality of sameness onto the birthparents— "tall like me" or "work a lot like me." Even an unhappy boy, who disliked his adoptive home, said, "They'd be outgoing like me . . . reasonable and fair . . . pretty athletic . . . on the go." The authors note that there are more constraints in a research interview than in a psychoanalytic session, but they too were impressed by the great discrepancy between the two sets of fantasies.

Infant Research and the Issue of Bonding

> "Will the fact that I wasn't there at the absolute beginning mean that my child won't be attached to me?"

There is a vast literature on bonding and attachment: on the early experience of the infant, his connection with his mother, his responses to the world, his development of affect, empathy, and cognition, his capacity to grow, adapt, survive, and thrive, and his responses to deprivation, frustration, and neglect.

Often, however, there has been confusion between the development of emotional attachment over time and "bonding," an event purported to happen shortly after birth, predominantly between mother and child. Eyer (1992), in a careful and penetrating study of the persistent popularity of bonding theory, despite its discredited status among scientific researchers, concludes that the concept of bonding was a magical one, invoked to distract childbirth reformers, necessitate medical interventions, and single out mothers for blame regarding the emotional problems of their children rather than place appropriate focus on the socioeconomic and cultural issues that militate against proper care and nurture of children.

The myth of bonding as a magical rite that confers emotional protection on a child has haunted adopted mothers, as well as the mothers of premature infants and others who were unable to bond at the appropriate time because they or the infants were ill; for such mothers, bonding is a maternal event that they have already failed to perform in the prescribed hours after birth. Without an understanding of the mythical nature of the bonding notion and its confusion with healthy attachment (which adoptive children do achieve in loving, caring settings), adoptive families, educators, and therapists can blame any later difficulties of adoptees on either the failure of bonding or the separation of even a several-day-old infant from the birthmother he has already "bonded to."

Infant research is notorious for the way in which bits and pieces of it have been used to bolster one side or the other in ideological debates. Findings on the resiliency of the infant, for example, have been used to argue for the positive side of adoption; work on the effects of the disruption of bonds has been cited to support negative prognostications about adoption. That the infant early on recognizes mother's smell, for example, is used to support the contention that the adoptee is wounded by the adoption process because the infant has switched from one smell to another as he leaves his birthmother. A fact about olfactory perception is given a psychological significance one would be hard-pressed to prove.

On the one hand, a romanticization of the mother-infant relation permeates modern psychology, and with it goes an image of the baby as easily harmed by separation (Rutter 1981). On the other hand, the studies on resiliency offer a quite different, hardier image of the infant. From our current cultural viewpoint we have taken it for granted that the mother-child relationship in infancy and early childhood is all-important. Now studies question these commonplace assumptions, focusing on other highly significant variables, such as sibling relations, that correlate with adult outcome. These studies suggest that early experience may not matter as much as we thought it did, that children can make up for lost time—at least cognitively (Clarke and Clarke 1976; Kagan 1980; Anthony 1987; Cohler 1987, 1992). Moreover, as we have noted, in most cultures infants and children have multiple caretakers, and concern focuses on the quality of care rather than on the presence or loss of a particular caretaker.

It is important to think carefully about the implications we draw from simple pieces of infant research. Just as the fact that a very young baby can imitate a smile without its carrying a meaning of happiness, so the fact that a baby can recognize its mother's smell does not tell us what the meaning of being separated from that smell is.

Psychoanalytic theorists and clinicians have constructed explanatory accounts of early childhood that obviously entail some projection of adult experience. That is to say, they attempt to extrapolate from the present situation of a person in trouble to a past that is no longer directly accessible. They are trying to create, retrospectively, a developmental story/myth that leads up to and accounts for the present impasse. As babies are not yet verbal and nobody remembers much about infancy and early toddlerhood, these phases are fertile ground for extrapolations and fantasies. The danger is that the researcher may go beyond what is known and accessible to draw conclusions from what cannot be known but only conjectured.

Adoptive families with a child who is experiencing difficulty can easily distance themselves from present-day problems by invoking concern about the long-ago disrupted mother-infant bond. We are not saying that there is no actual loss but rather that one must be cautious about how that loss is invoked and used and avoid talking with certitude when existing knowledge cannot corroborate it.

Clinical versus Nonclinical Populations: Outcome Research

"Is my child more likely to be unhappy or emotionally disturbed because he's adopted?"

Research indicates a greater use of mental health facilities by adopted children and families and greater representation of adopted children among patients in mental hospitals. This finding has led to the feeling that all adopted children will inevitably be troubled because of their adopted status alone.

Many of the studies revealing these statistics do not differentiate between groups of children adopted at birth and groups of children adopted later in life after multiple placements. That is a serious contaminant, for there is a substantially greater likelihood of emotional trauma in children adopted relatively late and in those who have experienced multiple separations than in adopted children placed in stable situations early in life. Many of the existing studies do not control for such significant factors as socioeconomic status, age, or distinctions between intrafamilial and extrafamilial adoption.

It remains a given of psychological research, however, that adopted children are overrepresented in clinical populations. In 1963, Goodman, Silberstein, and Mandell assessed the percentage of adopted children seen at the Staten Island Mental Health Clinic between 1956 and 1962 using estimates of the number of adopted children in the local community rather than in the national population. They concluded: "The overrepresentation of extrafamilially adopted children in our clinic caseload (2.4%) as compared with their rate in the community (1.7%) is of a magnitude which, though statistically significant, is not believed sufficient to warrant social consequence." They went on to say that "extrafamilially adopted children who had been adopted in the community of the study, and who had remained there, were seen less frequently than were non-adopted children. Sampling and choice of base rates for assessing emotional morbidity of adopted children were thought to explain the higher rates found in other studies."

This 1963 study has been cited both to support and to challenge the contention that there is a major difference between adoptive and biological populations in their use of psychiatric facilities. Smith (1984) cites the Goodman study as finding little or no difference. Yet McRoy, Grotevant, and Zurcher (1988) refer to the same study as one of three showing a higher incidence of mental health usage by adopted children. This difference in interpretation is an example of the unconscious bias that creeps into adoption research. It also is indicative of a more general bias in which the search for statistical significance replaces a concern for social or personal meaning.

The fact remains that it is repeatedly asserted that adopted children in diverse countries and cultures are referred for psychological care more frequently than their nonadopted peers (Grotevant, McRoy, and Jenkins 1988). Yet this claim remains controversial. Carole Smith, in her excellent book *Adoption and Fostering,* discusses the distortions that can occur from inadequately assessing the proportion of adopted children in the general population and whether such a figure, even if it could be accurately determined, can ever be a proper baseline for comparison. It may make better sense to calculate the proportion of adopted children in a local population so as to take into account the social-class factors operating within that community. Smith concludes her long discussion by saying, "Any association between adoption and the prevalence of psychiatric referral rates remains problematic and open to argument" (1984, p. 33).

Smith also points out that there are as many studies claiming that adopted children, as patients, have unique symptomatology as there are studies showing that their symptoms are much the same as any assortment of troubled nonadopted children. If the difficulties of adopted children are in some way related essentially to the fact of their being adopted, one would expect to find specific symptoms. Menlove (1965) found more hyperactivity, hostility, and negativism in adopted children. Sweeney, Gasbarro, and Gluck (1963) and Raleigh (1954) did not find significant differences between adopted and nonadopted adolescents in symptoms or diagnoses, nor did the recent work on hospitalized patients, adopted and nonadopted, by McRoy, Grotevant, and Zurcher (1988). So again we have research studies with contradictory findings.

Adoptive families frequently are familiar with mental health professionals who helped them locate their child and process the adoption; therefore they may be more likely than birthparents to turn to such personnel in times of turmoil and to use them earlier in the evolution of an emotional problem. Furthermore, adoptive parents tend to be from middle or upper socioeconomic groups, are likely to be quite alert to signs and signals of conflict and behavior problems, and are more willing to use mental health facilities. An unpublished study of adoptive parents whose children were patients at McLean Hospital, a psychiatric facility outside of Boston, found that the parents had used therapy productively in all areas of their lives well before adopting (personal communication, J. Fineman 1988). So it is not surprising that they would do the same for their children.

The statistics about the heavier use of mental health facilities by adopted children may also reflect a self-fulfilling prophecy. When our toddlers and older children exhibit disturbing behavior and feelings—as *all* children do occasionally—we adoptive parents are apt to worry, "Is it because of the adoption?" Our own fears about the effects of the adoption may cause us to dwell on, reinforce, and overemphasize our child's difficulties. This can lead us to invoke a psychological community that is all too willing to corroborate our fears.

In a study comparing adopted and biological children in inpatient treatment settings (McRoy, Grotevant, and Zurcher 1988) a common pattern was discerned in the adoptive group but in only one nonadoptive family. A significant number of adoptive families noted discrepancies between their children's personalities and what was felt to be acceptable within their own family. Following this perception, "a self-protective, attributional process typically began: 'It's not our fault. It must be because he is adopted.' Abdication of ownership of the problem by the parents often signalled an early stage in the emotional distancing of the adoptive parents from their child. Over time, this distancing served to reinforce the child's feelings of rejection not only by birthparents, but now by adoptive parents as well" (p. 160). Forty percent of the parents in both inpatient groups, adoptive and birthfamilies, were alcoholic, abusive, and quite pathological. Parents in both groups were considered deficient in parenting skills.

It also may be that children in the adoptive pool are at higher risk for certain kinds of behavior patterns that become particularly problematic in adolescence, the time of greatest hospitalization of adopted children. Children whose birthmothers were abusers of alcohol or drugs may be more vulnerable to attention deficit disorders, learning disabilities, and conditions associated with hyperactivity and impulsivity as symptoms. These conditions lead to the kind of social conflict and maladjustment that were seen in this hospitalized group. Birthmothers who are substance abusers may have more difficulty caring for an infant and therefore may be more likely to give them up for adoption—hence the greater weighting in the adoptive pool.

We turn now to studies based on adoptive families in the population at large rather than clinical populations. Researchers have conducted studies based on high school and college populations of adopted children located through agency placements rather than mental health sources and matched with nonadoptive control groups. Strikingly, these studies reveal equivalent, and occasionally greater, mental health among adopted teenagers.

Bohman did a two-stage longitudinal study of 624 children who were candidates for adoption as infants. Some of these children were adopted, some were placed in foster homes, and some remained with their birthmothers, who had changed their minds about giving them up for adoption. The three groups of children, always compared to a control group of classmates, were studied at ages eleven and fifteen (Bohman 1970, 1971; Bohman and Sigvardsson 1980). At age eleven all 624 of these children ran a greater risk than the control group of developing nervous disturbances and symptoms of maladjustment, regardless of whether they were living in adoptive homes, foster homes, or with their birthmothers. Further, "there were significantly more 'problem children' among adopted children than among their controls. In personal interviews, moreover, the adoptive parents often expressed anxiety about the puberty of the children, which might act as a 'self-fulfilling prophecy.'" At age fifteen, however, there was little difference in adjustment between the group of adopted children and their classmates, although the children growing up with their birthmothers and those living in foster homes displayed more social maladjustment and/or underachievement at school.

The authors analyzed their data in an attempt to account for the better performance of the adopted children than the foster children and those who remained with their birthmothers. They studied birth complications, registered criminality and alcohol abuse among birthfathers and mothers, and the length of time the child was in institutional care before placement. They found no relationship between these factors and the superior performance of the adopted group. They did, however, find that the adopted children had somewhat lower mean grades than the controls at age eleven, although they claim that there is no way to tell whether this was related to a hypothesized genetic link between their intellectual capacity and that of their birthparents or to the stresses and complications that so often mark the adoptive situation, which may have impeded the full development of the adopted children's capacities. They speculate that such negative social stresses could account for the adopted children's falling behind the controls at age eleven, a handicap that was largely compensated by age fifteen. The authors did another follow-up study of only the males in the adopted sample (Bohman and Sigvardsson 1978) at age eighteen and found no significant differences in I.Q. scores between the adopted boys and the controls.

Marquis and Detweiler (1985) compared 46 adopted and 121 nonadopted persons between ages thirteen and twenty-one. The nonadopted subjects were volunteers; the adopted subjects responded to a letter sent by the adoption agency to a random sample of adoptive parents.[8] The two groups were comparable in education and social status. The researchers found differences between adopted and nonadopted teenagers, but not in the direction they expected from previous research based on psychiatric populations. Their findings showed that adopted persons saw themselves as being more in control of their lives and having more internal direction and that they demonstrated significantly more confidence in their own judgment than the nonadopted group. In their assessment of others, adopted persons made more favorable attributions than the nonadopted:

> They rated people who were insiders, who had control of their behavior, and who caused good things to happen as more responsible, independent, brave, calm, friendly, popular, secure and normal. . . . In essence, they have come to expect that a person who is in control and effects a good outcome is considered especially good. Adopted subjects see their parenting as significantly more nurturant, comforting, predictable, protectively concerned, and helpful. (p. 1062)[9]

The authors conclude:

> We have shown that adoptive parenting is different from nonadoptive parenting, and that parenting differences may be important antecedent correlates of attributional judgments. . . . There is not a shred of evidence in this study that indicates any of the previously reported negative characteristics of dependency, fearfulness, tenseness, hostility, loneliness, insecurity, abnormality, inferiority, poor self-image, or lack of confidence. If, as

8. They were given a Locus of Control Scale, a Perceived Parenting Questionnaire, a personal history form, and a set of eight stories, with questions on each.

9. The Delaware Adoption Project (Hoopes 1982) showed that self-confident adopted youngsters had adoptive parents with high self-esteem and confidence about their parenting skills.

the earlier literature implies, there really is an excessive number of adopted persons who have psychological problems, one would expect to find some indication of this in the community population when compared with a similar community population of nonadopted persons. However, we found the attributions weighted on the positive side: not just equal to but significantly more than in the control group of nonadopted persons. Certainly, this suggested that, at the very least the old stereotypic view that the adopted are "at risk" is unfounded. (p. 1064)

Stein and Hoopes (1985) set out to test empirically the major theoretical assumptions about the identity challenges posed by being adopted. They compared fifty adolescent adoptees aged fifteen to eighteen with forty-one nonadoptees, both groups drawn from a nonclinical population.[10] They wanted to explore the following questions:

How does being adopted impinge on the process of identity formation during adolescence? Does being adopted adversely affect an adolescent's consolidation of ego identity, as some of the literature suggests? If significant differences in identity formation and adjustment exist between the two groups of adolescents, are the problems related to the fact of adoption or to other variables that might be compounding the process of identity formation in some adolescents? Finally, what differentiates those adopted adolescents who express an avid wish to search for their biological parents from those who show no such wish?

The authors hypothesized that adopted teenagers would obtain lower scores on measures of identity formation and adjustment. Contrary to their expectations, there were no significant differences between the two groups. Adopted subjects showed no deficits in functioning on any measure of overall identity when compared to the nonadopted, and on one measure of identity—the Tan Ego Identity Scale—they obtained significantly higher scores. They also found no signs of deficits in self-esteem, impulse control, or sociability in the adopted group. They did find that the nonadopted subjects scored more positively on the Offer social-self dimension, which, when analyzed further, was related to the fact that the adoptees did somewhat more poorly in the area of vocational and educational goals. This finding, which is consistent with other studies we have mentioned (Bohman 1972; Hoopes 1982), suggests that adopted children sometimes do less well in

---

10. They used the Tan Ego Identity Scale, the Offer Self-Image Questionnaire for Adolescents, the Social Atom Task, and a semistructured interview.

school. As we have noted, this may reflect a weighting of the adoptive pool toward the average or less than average, or it may reflect a relatively poor quality of prenatal care.

The authors hypothesized that adopted subjects who perceived an open communication style about adoption in their families would obtain higher scores on measures of ego identity. This was indeed the case. Open styles of communication about being adopted produced higher scores on school and self-esteem factors. The authors further thought that adoptees with good relationships with their adoptive parents would obtain higher scores on identity measures than those who experienced their parental relationships as less satisfactory. Again that was the case.

Their prediction that the presence of nonadopted siblings in the adoptive family would impede the adjustment of the adolescent adoptee, as has been suggested in the literature (Hoopes 1982; McWhinnie 1967), did not turn out to be so. In fact, the mixed group got slightly higher scores. The sample size was small, however.

With regard to adopted adolescents who were searching for their birth-parents, the authors hypothesized that this group would comprise both very high-scoring adolescents, with very solid identities and intense curiosity, and very low-scoring adolescents, with identity diffusion and dissatisfaction with their families. They did not find this polarization among the searchers but only low-scoring adolescents with less satisfactory family relationships —findings similar to those of McWhinnie (1969) and Triseliotis (1973). Sixty-eight percent of their total sample revealed no desire to search, though most adoptees were interested in their genealogies. Searching behavior was not connected to styles of communication about adoption issues or family composition. Substantially more searchers (43.8 percent) than nonsearchers (17.6 percent) perceived themselves as physically dissimilar to their adoptive parents, suggesting that mismatch concerns may contribute to the need to search in adolescence, a time of preoccupation with physical appearance. The authors note, however, that their sample size was small and that most of those interviewed were below eighteen, the age when birth records are made accessible, and younger than the young-adult age at which many people become interested in searching (Sorosky, Baran, and Pannor 1975). Therefore, this was not a study of searching per se but of adoptees who search in midadolescence.

The authors concluded the presentation of their research findings with a touching quotation from researcher L. H. Blum (1976) about how adolescents feel about being adopted: "Adopted children feel *curious*, that's how they feel; they may also feel happy, sad, buoyant, anxious, competent, depressed, not because they are adopted, but because they are individual children, growing up in particular families. That's the point that the courts, the experts, and the authors seem to miss: once you accept the curiosity as a given . . . there just isn't that much difference in the rest of it."

Thus we have two distinct sets of studies: those derived from mental health sources, which show a preponderance of adopted children among their populations, and studies of "normal" groups, which show adopted children to be doing very well indeed. Adoptive parents are more familiar with the former, more worrisome studies than with those of nonclinical populations. We have no reason to doubt that there is a greater weighting toward adopted children in mental health facilities. As we have suggested, it might be that adoptive families make greater use of these facilities; there might be a greater constitutional vulnerability among some adopted children; or, for some families, the stresses of adoption may handicap effective parenting. But it does seem clear that there is no reason to think that there is anything intrinsic to being adopted that leads to severe emotional problems. As noted above, in the McRoy, Grotevant, and Zurcher (1988) study, there were no significant differences in symptoms between adopted and nonadopted inpatient adolescents. Issues involving being adopted played a major role in two-thirds of the institutionalized adolescents; in the other third adoption played a moderate role or was not significant in any way. The authors ask a very interesting question: how is it that so many of the healthy adopted children they studied, who faced problems similar to those of the adopted residential treatment families, had such different outcomes?

Adoptive families are entitled to the same amount of human troubles as birthfamilies, and they certainly will have them. Adoptive parents who have not come to terms with their own infertility and who feel, as a result, insecure, inferior, and defective may be rejecting, overprotective, overindulgent, or less deeply attached to their adopted child and thus may contribute to his emotional problems. But this is no different from what happens in birthfamilies in which parents have emotional problems around self-esteem, issues of separation, and the recognition of differences. Carole R. Smith notes:

> The most significant factors in adoption outcome seem to relate to qualitative, and not easily measured, attributes of individuals and the way in which these interact to enable confident, flexible, concerned and warm parenting. In such families adopted children are able to feel secure, unconditionally loved and wanted, comfortable with the knowledge of their adoptive status and free to explore the past in a way which does not threaten relationships with their parents or the integral place which they hold in their adoptive families. There is no indication that adoption is

automatically problematic for parents or children because of its essentially social nature. (1984, p. 24)

David Fanshel, another distinguished adoption researcher, says, "I emerge from the research experience very much aware that the task of predicting the outcome of a human experience such as adoption involves many elusive and unmeasurable elements at this stage of our research competence" (1972, p. 327).

Open Adoption

"Does having contact in childhood with the birthparents improve my child's adjustment to adoption?"

There are no research data to answer this question, despite intense conviction and controversy about this new form of adoption (Demick and Wapner 1988). What is needed is a long-term follow-up study of adopted children and their families in which the families are grouped by style of adoption and followed from the time of adoption into the adoptee's young adulthood, with assessments at various ages.

Such a study is in process. Harold Grotevant and Ruth McRoy are following some two hundred families, interviewing adoptive parents, birthparents, and children from the time of adoption into the adolescent years. They have divided the adoptions into fully open (with a range of contact between the adopted child and the birthfamily), modified open (contact between birth and adoptive parents through letters and pictures, sometimes through an intermediary), and closed. They are interested in learning how the family dynamics work in each kind of adoption. It is already clear that "there is not one best way for everyone" (personal communication, H. Grotevant 1991), and preliminary study suggests that parents select the form of adoption that best suits them (McRoy and Grotevant 1988).

Genetic Research

"Will life in our family make an impact on our child, or is his fate already determined by his birthparents' genes?"

A recently burgeoning field of research in child development, as part of broader research goals, compares children adopted at birth with their birthparents. Many of these studies claim to have found a high correlation in intelligence as measured by I.Q. and in personality traits as measured by personality questionnaires between the adopted child and the birthparents the child has never known. Many adoptive parents interpret this research as meaning that they can have no impact on the child they are raising, that all is decided in advance, that everything is inherited. Is this conclusion warranted?

We must emphasize at the outset that this research was not designed to explore adoption as such and that its relevance for the specific understanding of adoption must therefore be treated with great caution. The purpose of the research was to discover the general relationship of genetic and environmental factors in human development, using three groupings: (1) identical twins separated at birth; (2) adopted-away children compared with their adoptive and birthparents; and (3) people biologically related to one another in families—such as identical twins, siblings, parents and offspring, or cousins. In the first group, the genetic material is the same, so all variance can be accounted for by differences in the environment. The second group also provides an opportunity to examine the relative weight of environment and genetics.

The early long-term adoption studies were begun at a time when many healthy white newborns were being placed for adoption. These children were routinely put into families highly similar to their birthfamilies in race, religion, and social class—reflecting the prevalent adoption theory at that time. This is a continuously confounding factor in many outcome studies of adoption because it makes it difficult to distinguish the effects of the birthfamily from those of the adoptive family. If both birthparents and adoptive parents have high I.Q.s, for example, there is no way to tell if the child's high I.Q. is due to heredity (being born to parents with high I.Q.s) or environment (being raised by parents with high I.Q.s). In contrast, a Minnesota study (Scarr and Weinberg 1978a) examining the inheritance of I.Q. demonstrated that when a group of children whose birthparents' I.Q. would predict a mean I.Q. of 101 in the children were adopted into families of high socioeconomic status and high educational motivation, the children had I.Q. scores six to nine points higher than anticipated. Scarr and Weinberg (1986) also did a study demonstrating that low-socioeconomic-status (SES) black children adopted into higher-social-class white families achieved I.Q. scores comparable to those of other children in the higher SES adoptive families.

Researchers in this field assess heritability by determining what proportion of the variability of a trait in a given population is associated with heredity and what proportion is derived from experience. It is important to remember that this concept treats heritability as a property of a group; it cannot be applied to individuals. Furthermore, the heritability of a trait can differ dramatically on the basis of the population in which it is measured. For example, among Japanese in the post–World War II generation the heritability of height was high, but when their parents were included in the sample, the heritability was found to be quite low. Obviously the biology had not changed; in the combined sample the difference in nutrition between the two generations dramatically reduced the relative contribution of genetics to height. This example highlights the conceptual difficulty of separating heredity and environment that marks all this research; heritability is not a simple fact of nature but a mathematical construct determined by the design of the research project.

Many studies of I.Q. have estimated its heritability as ranging from 12 to 80 percent (Block and Dworkin 1976). What do these numbers mean? First, given what we know about heritability, the numbers refer to the influence of heredity on the variance in a group of people and say nothing about any individual performance. Second, the convention is always to speak in terms of the *genetic* variation, even when most of the variance is due to environmental factors—.25 heritability means that 75 percent of the variance of I.Q. in a population reflects the effects of the environment plus random variation.

Furthermore, measuring the heritability of I.Q. in a population tells us nothing about the cognitive strategies used to achieve the I.Q. scores, the degree of similarity and difference on various subtests, and most important, the degree of improvement possible with a little help. Even if we find that I.Q. has a high degree of heritability, knowing the I.Q.s of a particular child's parents does not allow us to predict that child's performance on an I.Q. test. Even if we find correlations between parents' and children's I.Q.s, this tells us nothing about cause but merely shows a relationship between the two measurements.

Robert Perlman, professor of pediatrics and of pharmacological and physiological sciences at the University of Chicago, comments:

> Recent advances in molecular genetics, as reported in the popular press, may lead one to overestimate the role of genetics in human affairs. Because the arguments of behavioral genetics are couched in technical terms, it is easy for non-experts to feel intimidated and unable to evaluate these arguments for themselves. Genes determine the structure of proteins. Intelligence and personality are not controlled by single genes but are affected by many genes as well as by environmental factors, and don't behave like simple Mendelian traits. If one compares individuals in similar environments, as many research studies do, the variations among them will appear to be due largely to heredity. Given the richness and diversity of our environments, as of our genetic

heritage, it is difficult to extrapolate the results of these studies to the population at large. (Personal communication 1992)

Almost no one today would argue that fundamental personal qualities such as intelligence, interests, abilities, and character are either strictly biological or strictly environmental. There is a broad consensus that nature and nurture are interactive, that the presenting characteristics of the child and the environment in which he lives affect each other. Within a given family the characteristics of the biological siblings—whether I.Q. or personality—will show some correlation but not necessarily a very strong one even though these children come from the same biological pool. A nurturing environment will usually produce well-put-together kids, though there will always be some children with problems.

It should also be kept in mind that the notion of I.Q. has become so reified that people talk as if an I.Q. number indicates a precise amount of intelligence in the same way that the number of pounds a weightlifter lifts precisely indicates his strength. Yet even the number of pounds lifted indicates the strength only of particular muscle groups in that particular operation. We never define athletic ability by a single parameter—there is no such thing as an athletic quotient, or A.Q. Athletic ability reflects some combination of strength, speed, stamina, and coordination of countless different muscle groups in combination with training, practice, coaching, and drive as realized in one or another of many very different athletic activities. Similarly, the I.Q. test does not measure all aspects of the intelligence of the test taker but rather measures how he performs on certain mental exercises that correlate to some degree with school performance. The evolutionary biologist Steven Jay Gould writes:

> I began my career in biology by using factor analysis to study the evolution of a group of fossil reptiles. I was taught the technique as if it had developed from first principles using pure logic. In fact, virtually all its procedures arose as justification for particular theories of intelligence. Factor analysis, despite its status as pure deductive mathematics, was invented in a social context, and for definite reasons. And, though its mathematical basis is unassailable, its persistent use as a device for learning about the physical structure of intellect has been mired in deep conceptual errors from the start. The principal error, in fact, has involved a major theme of this book: reification—in this case, the notion that such a nebulous, socially defined concept as intelligence might be identified as a "thing" with a locus in the brain and a definite degree of heritability—and that it might be measured as

a single number, thus permitting a unilinear ranking of people according to the amount of it they possess. (1981, pp. 238–239)

Thus, to equate I.Q. with the multifaceted richness of human intelligence is erroneous. To see I.Q. as describing one component of a person's subsequent ability to do the mental operations required for good school performance in Western middle-class culture is appropriate. Yet admissions officers at the University of Chicago have learned through the years that the best predictor of performance in college is not I.Q. or SAT scores but actual grade performance in high school. This is probably because previous academic achievement reflects such factors as motivation, study habits, interests, and personality integration as well as raw intelligence.

One study is of particular interest to us because it does not fall prey to some of the confusions commonly afflicting the research described above. In 1978, Schiff, Duyme, and their colleagues studied thirty-two French children born to working-class parents and adopted at birth by upper-middle-class families (Group A). The researchers located the birthmothers and some of the birthfathers of twenty-eight of these children and discovered that twenty of the mothers had a total of thirty-nine other children of school age who had not been given up for adoption (Group B). So we have two groups of children of the same birthmothers—Group A, thirty-two adopted-away children, and Group B, their thirty-nine siblings and half-siblings who remained with the birthmothers. Each child was rated for I.Q. Mild failure was defined as a score below 95, and serious failure as a score below 85. In addition, school records were examined and a distinction was made between relatively mild failures—repetition of grades in primary school—and serious failures—placement in a remedial class.

The adopted-away siblings were also compared to a very large representative sample of French schoolchildren in the general population who had been studied by others. The results showed that Group A children, those adopted into upper-middle-class families, scored like other children of professional and business parents—relatively high in I.Q. and with few serious school failures. Group B children, who stayed with their working-class birthparents, scored like other children of clerks, skilled workers, and unskilled workers—with relatively low I.Q. scores and more serious failures in school. The *consistent* differences between these two groups of genetic siblings are likely to be the result of their different environments. This is because the normally observed differences among genetic siblings are random and therefore cannot explain the consistent direction of the differences.

The authors conclude:

> The contrast in intellectual status between the A and B children is close to that prevailing in the population at large between

children of upper-middle-class parents and children of unskilled workers. Moreover, the failure rates observed for the A children are almost embarrassingly close to those expected solely on the basis of the social class of their adoptive parents. We think that the most economical interpretation of these observations is that there are no important genetic differences between social groups for factors relevant to school failures. An alternative interpretation would be that a certain genetic disadvantage of the A children was exactly compensated for by a special environmental advantage related to their adoptive status. In this case, however, one begins to wonder whether there exists any experimental design by which the hypothesis of a genetic origin for the "educational lag of disadvantaged children" (Jensen 1969) could be submitted to scientific test. (Schiff et al. 1978, p. 1504)

Capron and Duyme (1989) masterfully expanded this French study by comparing four groups of adopted children: (1) those born to high socioeconomic status (SES) parents and raised by high-SES adoptive parents; (2) high-SES babies adopted into low-SES families; (3) low-SES babies adopted into high-SES families; and (4) low-SES babies adopted into low-SES families. Like the first French study discussed above, they found that children adopted by high-SES parents scored higher than children adopted by low-SES parents by twelve points on I.Q. tests. They also found, however, that children born to high-SES parents scored fifteen points higher than children born to low-SES parents regardless of the SES of the adoptive parents. The children with the highest I.Q.s were those of high-SES birthparents adopted into high-SES families; the lowest scores were achieved by children from low-SES birthfamilies adopted into low-SES families.

The authors conclude:

> Although these findings clearly indicate that the biological parents' background contributes to observed differences in I.Q. between extreme groups, as does that of the adoptive parents, more detailed interpretation is difficult. The adoption method provides a means of dissociating the pooled effects of genetic and prenatal factors from factors related to the postnatal environment. But it is not equipped to differentiate prenatal from genetic factors. This precludes interpreting the effects of the biological parents' background solely in genetic terms, or concluding that observed effects could be prenatal or prenatal acting either in additive or interactive manner with genotype. On the contrary, the effect attributed to the adoptive parents is clearly environmental. (p. 553)

In sum, the postnatal—that is, adoptive—environmental effect on a child's I.Q. performance is independent of the SES of the birthparents. An enriched high-SES adoptive environment produces higher I.Q. scores than a disadvantaged low-SES environment. However, the later I.Q. scores of a child born to high-SES parents will be higher than the scores of a child born to low-SES parents independent of the adoptive environment. The authors are careful to emphasize that the causes of the higher I.Q.s of high-SES babies cannot be determined. They might be due to genetic factors, the quality of prenatal care, the quality of the immediate preadoption postnatal care, or any or all of these, all of which may reflect socioeconomic status.

Let's take a look at some personality studies using adopted children. Commenting on a ten-year follow-up of the Texas Adoption Project, Loehlin, Willerman, and Horn (1987) point out that the genetic effect on personality is around .25, indicating rather low heritability. Yet they say, "Adoptive children do not resemble their adoptive family members in personality, despite having lived with them from birth but they do show a modest degree of resemblance to their genetic mothers, whom they have never known" (p. 968). They also say, "Whatever the sources of environmental variation may be, they tend to be idiosyncratic to individual family members, rather than shared" by all the siblings in a family—"except for social attitudes." This sharing of "social attitudes" within a family was a finding described in many large-scale studies of identical and fraternal twins (Loehlin and Nichols 1976; Martin and Jardine 1986). The phrase "social attitudes," whatever the authors mean by it, suggests a rather large component of personality. In addition, the authors point out that, in contrast to their findings, the effect of family environment is quite marked when the adopted child changes his social class, as in the Bohman and Sigvardsson study discussed in the section on outcomes.

Scarr and Weinberg (1983) state: "There is evidence for genetic differences in interests and personality. There is little evidence that environmental differences among families account for variability in these psychological domains. However, most of the variance in personality and interest is not accounted for by either genetic or environmental differences among families. Most of the variance lies among individuals within families" (1983, p. 266). Rose and Kaprio (1987), however, point out that Minnesota Multiphasic Personality Inventory (MMPI) attitude scales assessing femininity, religiosity, and an "extraversion factor" provide evidence for the influence of shared experience by age- and gender-matched siblings. There is further disagreement on this point, which we will discuss later.

We must be very careful to define what we mean by a personality trait. Such characteristics as liking the color yellow, preferring salmon to tuna, and wearing a square emerald on the fourth finger of the right hand are very striking, even uncanny, synchronies with an unknown birthparent, and they are indeed part of personality. But they are not character, taste, values, politics, or capacity for concern and attachment—aspects of personality that some researchers seem to lump together indiscriminately as "social attitudes." Some dimensions of temperament are probably constitutional, so that if a child with a synthesizing, integrating personality is adopted into a family of dissecting, anatomizing scientists, some of that child's qualities would be unchanged and some would be shaped by the family environment. But this is also true in birthfamilies, which sometimes cannot identify the source of the musical talent or the ability to do astrophysics—even the red hair—of their progeny.

To put the whole question of heritability into perspective, we can say that even when we know something of the biological history of a family, we cannot know what any particular child born into it will look like or what his individual personality and character will be. For identical twins separated at birth and then studied we can be reasonably confident that there will be a good deal of similarity between them—but identical twins have exactly the same genetic material and are frequently adopted into similar environments. Ordinary siblings share only 50 percent of their genetic material. And one must remember that all these studies are based only on tests of I.Q. and questionnaires of personality, which are limited with respect to the many vicissitudes of life and cannot precisely predict how a child will adapt to them all.

Contemporary behavioral genetics attempts to compare adopted and biological offspring (Plomin, DeFries, and Fulker 1988; Plomin 1990) in settings where there was random placement of adopted children, in an attempt to sort out the genetic factors as they interact with the environment. The fundamental hypothesis here is that genes do not operate independently of the environment, that the environment shapes the expression of the biology, and that, to a very large extent, the environment does most of the shaping of the child regardless of the biological heritage (Reiss, Plomin, and Hetherington 1991; Plomin and Daniels 1987). The findings emerging from this large body of research support the hypothesis that whatever the genetics may be, the environment potentiates them—any child becomes more musical if he has music lessons, but a musically gifted child raised in a musically indifferent family may never develop his musical talent.

These researchers are trying to account for individual differences and conclude that, for some factors, the genetic effect reveals itself increasingly with age. Researchers from the Texas Adoption Project, for example, assert that, with age, "shared family environment has a decreasing effect on

IQ" (Loehlin, Horn, and Willerman 1989, p. 1000) but that "genes seem to continue actively contributing to intellectual variation at least into early adulthood" (p. 1001). Other geneticists strongly disagree, as we will point out shortly.

Kamin emphasizes the importance of studying families with both adopted and biological children. In both the Texas Adoption Project (Horn, Loehlin, and Willerman 1979) and the Minnesota Transracial Adoption Study (Scarr and Weinberg 1978b), the I.Q. of the adoptive mother was found to be statistically as similar to the I.Q. of her adopted child as to that of her birthchild. Kamin also notes that "the data in the Minnesota study show that while there is a correlation between the I.Q. of the birthmother and [that of] the child she placed for adoption, there is a similar correlation between the I.Q. of the same birthmother and a child born to the adopted child's adoptive parents and raised by them" (Melina 1989a).

Behavioral geneticists disagree about the nature of the shared environment between siblings. We would suggest that, in many respects, every child has a unique environment because of the individual way he experiences his parents, his siblings, and his world, and how all these react to and interact with him. What appears shared to an observer may be utterly irrelevant to the family members.

Yet there are dimensions of family life that are powerfully shared. Boomsa (1987) suggests that research methods may underestimate the importance of shared environmental factors. Since adopters tend to be quite similar in social class and I.Q., adoption studies may be biased against detecting the influence of shared family environment per se. "If there is very little variation in a measurement, such as goodness of environment, then you can't see a correlation between goodness of environment and [the] intelligence of a child because all the children have the same environment" (Kamin 1989).

Alternatively, Boomsa suggests, the American population as a whole may experience an environment so uniform that shared environmental effects do not show up in research studies. Willerman (1979) also suggests that the standard deviation of environments sampled in American adoption studies may be too narrow to provide a test of social-class effects. Rose and Kaprio (1987) dispute the claims of many adoption researchers that shared environment does not affect I.Q. and that its impact on I.Q. is negligible by the end of adolescence (see Loehlin, Horn, and Willerman 1989). So once again, we see disagreement among the researchers studying adoption.

Our adopted children bring with them a biological makeup that must have some impact on their development. But whatever that impact may be, adoptive parents have no less influence than birthparents the child no longer lives with. It is only that the one part the adoptive parent cannot influence *came from someone else*. That is the crucial point. It is not our biology but someone else's. So we are back to jealousy of the birthparents and the fear of the unknown! We must remember that even if they were our own genes and he was our own biological child, we would still not know which genes went into that child, the good ones or the bad ones. Our birth-children are not "us"—they tap a complicated gene pool that goes back for generations, and some of those genes we would not wish on our worst enemy! Adoptive parents frequently overestimate the contribution of the birthparents, a fantasy that is strengthened by some of the misconceptions we have been discussing. All parents—both biological and adoptive—are faced with the uncertainties of parenting and their lack of control over many aspects of their children's lives and personalities. A birthparent, when his or her children misbehave, can attribute the cause to the other parent's lineage. Adoptive parents may fasten on "those genes" to give expression to the sense of uncertainty that all parents feel.

In the Finnish Adoptive Family Study (Tienari et al. 1987a, 1987b), a nationwide sample of schizophrenic mothers' offspring given up for adoption was compared blindly—that is, without the comparers knowing who was who—with adopted-away offspring of nonschizophrenic birthparents. Of the ten psychotic adopted children, eight were the offspring of schizophrenics raised by nonschizophrenic adoptive parents. These results were initially cited as evidence of the overwhelming contribution of genetics to the development of schizophrenia. But further analysis revealed that nearly all the adoptees who had been diagnosed as schizophrenic or paranoid had been reared in *seriously disturbed* adoptive families, the lowest in the researchers' rating scales; the one manic-depressive child in the study had been reared in a neurotic family.

In striking contrast, in the forty-nine healthy or only mildly disturbed adoptive families there were no psychotic or borderline children and only three (6 percent) with severe personality disorders. Not one of the forty-nine offspring of schizophrenic mothers who were raised in a healthy or only mildly disturbed adoptive family environment became schizophrenic or borderline. In other words, a genetic vulnerability to schizophrenia in these cases required interaction with a pernicious environment in order to develop the clinical picture of illness. And the healthy families in this study usually had healthy children. One cautionary note: because the adoptive families were not assessed before the placement of the genetically vulnerable children, it remains theoretically possible that the genetic vulnerability of the adopted child was disturbing to the adoptive family and in some way contributed to its pathological rating.

Our final thought is that none of this research is predictive. It is only statistical, retrospective, inferential, and descriptive. The mystery of how the baby will turn out exists for all families. Some birthfamilies are able to ignore it for many years; adoptive families look it squarely in the eye from the very beginning.

We hope it is now clear that you and your child arrive at the moment of talking about adoption from very different places. He has never heard the word and can have no negative associations to it. It does not brand you as an inadequate, biologically defective parent or doom him to have a flawed existence. You are struggling to let your experience of yourself as a real parent counter the cultural subtleties that have undermined your confidence. We need to allow the *child* to teach *us* about his unfolding sense of adoption. In the end, this is all that matters—not theoretical speculation, statistical correlations, ill-founded prejudices. We would do well to begin anew in understanding adoption alongside of him, leaving behind some of our fears, embarking on this adventure together.

Chapter 3

Adoption and the World of the Young Child

As parents we have many zany, surprising, confusing, and moving talks with our young child. An enormous amount is on her mind as she witnesses and engages with the world. She talks with us about the sun and the stars, about her dreams, about death, about meanness and kindness. Perhaps she begins with an action, a question, a segment of play, and we respond in words or play. In talking with her about her interests and answering her questions we craft a version of reality for our young child that we hope she can understand. Then we sit back and listen to the curious ways in which our story is transformed and incorporated into her sense of the world. We may make a revision, add some details, or start all over. Each of us in turn takes the story further. As parents we not only talk; we listen. This listening allows us to form an intuitive understanding of what our child understands at this point in her life. It provides us with a working concept of what we will want to talk about when next given the chance, and in what emotional tone. Listening also allows us to learn to see the world from our child's perspective.

Talking about adoption is no different from talking about the other important issues parents and children live through together. Adoption is a reality our families live and about which we share feelings and thoughts. As in talking about sexuality, for example, we do not expect adult comprehension from a little one. We do want to provide a comfortable, accepting atmosphere in which the child can express whatever she is wondering about, and we want to give answers to her questions that are meaningful to her at her point in development. To do this we must try to hear what she is really asking and help her articulate her questions. At the same time, we must refrain from projecting our adult ways of understanding onto her or from overwhelming her with an agenda of our own regarding what should be discussed with her and what she should understand. (Remember the story of the child who asked his daddy where he came from? The father gave an encyclopedic discourse on the birds and bees. When he finished, the child said, "Gee, Dad, I just wanted to know if it was New York or Philadelphia.") Adoptive parents, anxious to complete their assignment of "telling" their child she is adopted, often present her with a wholly adult version of adoption that is of little interest to her, beyond her ability to comprehend, and often unsettling in its inappropriateness.

When we talk about adoption in ways suited to the child's capacities and age level, in ways she can handle, giving her the lead, the fact of adoption becomes an integral part of her understanding of herself. The frequently debated issue of *when* to tell a child simply disappears because we live with her in the reality of her adoption from the beginning: she hears the various versions we construct for her, appropriate for her level of cognitive development and social understanding, and we, for our part, listen to her play, her remarks, and her questions, which teach us how she experiences her adoptedness at various points and what her wonderings are about.

Most young children are remarkably adept at abandoning a conversation when they have gotten what they need or can handle. Their attention simply turns elsewhere. Many of the children in our stories showed this agility in opening up adoption topics that needed to be discussed and, once satisfied, giving unambiguous signals that the discussion was over. One mother said of her four-year-old, "He told me with absolute clarity that he didn't want to talk about adoption any more, and he'd let me know when he wanted to talk about it again." Parents of all but the most reticent children can respect this coming and going of concern, so typical of young children regardless of the issue.

We may at times be shocked or disturbed by how the child thinks about adoption. We may even take what she says or the frequency of her concern as indicative of pathology. In the absence of realistic descriptions of how young children understand adoption and work through their feelings about it, parents and clinicians alike tend to make diagnoses instead of learning how to support children in their understandable and healthy wonderings about their origins, their dual families, and their identity in the light of adoption. Our task as adoptive parents is not simply to inform our child that she is adopted, nor is it solely to mete out information as she matures. We must learn to listen to the child so we can understand how *she* experiences adoption and what it means to her at different junctures. Talking about adoption with your child involves a sharing between two people who not only are different developmentally but are differently related to adoption.

In this chapter we will use current research and an analysis of the stories presented in chapter 4 to talk about how youngsters understand and misunderstand adoption at various points in early childhood. We will use the children's words when possible, to give you a concrete sense of how young children talk about adoption.

Stages of Understanding Adoption

The important research of Brodzinsky and his colleagues at the Rutgers Adoption Project (Brodzinsky, Singer, and Braff 1984; Brodzinsky, Schechter, and Brodzinsky 1986) can help adoptive parents understand that when young children talk about adoption, they are not talking about what adults understand adoption to be: a legally permanent parent-child relationship, created through the intention and desire of the birthparents to terminate their parental rights and responsibilities and the intention and desire of the adoptive parents to assume them. Notice that this definition of reality, while mentioning the intentions and desires of adoptive and birthparents, neglects altogether the experiences of the adoptee. To understand our adult concept of adoption the child must first develop some knowledge "about birth and reproduction, family roles and relationships, values, interpersonal motives, and the functioning of societal institutions" (Brodzinsky, Singer, and Braff 1984, p. 877). And because a full comprehension of adoption rests on this broader knowledge, adopted youngsters are no more sophisticated or precocious in their understanding of this adult view of adoption than are nonadopted children of the same age.

It may be that adopted children develop an adoption vocabulary before nonadopted children do, but adoption and birth are still fused and confused in the young child's mind. Brodzinsky's research shows that adoptive mothers in particular are likely to overestimate their children's knowledge about and comprehension of adoption. He warns parents not to terminate the process of talking about adoption prematurely on the misconception that the child who can "talk adoption" can necessarily understand it.

On the basis of their analysis of open-ended interviews with adopted and nonadopted children aged four to thirteen, Brodzinsky, Singer, and Braff (1984) delineate six levels of understanding about adoption. There is, of course, no one-to-one correspondence between a child's age and her level of understanding, nor is the sequence they describe necessarily valid for each child. Nevertheless, familiarity with these descriptions can alert parents to what the child may be understanding or misunderstanding at various stages.

Level 0. "Children exhibit no understanding of adoption." This refers predominantly to children up to age five but includes some six- and seven-year-olds as well.

Level 1. "Children fail to differentiate between adoption and birth. Instead, they tend to fuse the two concepts together." This describes children aged four to seven years. For instance, a six-year-old boy asked his parents cheerfully, "Did Daddy plant the seed before or after you adopted me?"

Level 2. "Children clearly differentiate between adoption and birth as alternative paths to parenthood, and they accept that the adoptive family relationship is permanent, but they do not understand why. At best, they rely on a sense of faith ('my mother told me') or notions of possession ('the child belongs to the other parents now') to justify the permanent nature of the parent-child relationship." This level of understanding was expressed by children ranging from four to thirteen years old. The predominant ages were six and seven.

Level 3. "Children differentiate between adoption and birth but are unsure about the permanence of the adoptive parent-child relationship. Biological parents are seen as having the potential for reclaiming guardianship over the child at some future but unspecified time." Again, some children from all the age groups—four to thirteen—expressed this understanding, with the predominant weight among six- to nine-year-olds.

Level 4. "Children's descriptions of the adoptive family relationship are characterized by a quasi-legal sense of permanence. Specifically, they refer to 'signing papers,' or invoke some authority such as a judge, lawyer, doctor, or social worker who in some vague way 'makes' the parent-child relationship permanent." This level of understanding was represented among the six- to thirteen-year-olds but was more prevalent among older children.

Level 5. "The adoption relationship is now characterized as permanent, involving the legal transfer of rights and/or responsibilities for the child from the biological parents to the adoptive parents." This level was represented among eight- to thirteen-year-olds but was far more prevalent among the twelve- and thirteen-year-olds.

We have included the range of ages for each level to emphasize that one cannot assume from a child's age that she can understand only so much about adoption, or that she already understands some aspect of it. There are always exceptions in both directions. Also, this research did not include two- or three-year-olds. Just as the study's four- and five-year-olds were represented among four different levels of understanding, it is likely that two- and three-year-olds also exhibit a range in their understanding.

Brodzinsky and his colleagues also studied how children understand their adoptive parents' motivation in adopting them and their birthparents' reasons for relinquishing them. Most of the young children in their study who exhibited some understanding of why parents would adopt focused on the desire to care for and love a child. "Older children focused as much or more on infertility, family planning, and the needs and welfare of children as a basis for adopting" (Brodzinsky, Singer, and Braff 1984, p. 876).

In general, children in the sample had less knowledge about the reasons for relinquishment than about any other aspect of the adoption experience. Children aged four to seven focused primarily on negative characteristics of the children as the reason the birthparents sought placement for them. These young children also mentioned the parents' lack of money or time to care for them as reasons for placement. Older children mentioned financial problems more often and added illegitimacy, parental immaturity, family disharmony, and parental death as reasons for relinquishment.

Like their ideas of adoption, children's understanding of the third parties involved in adoption—agencies, lawyers, social workers, foster parents—was initially absent, then global and diffuse, and finally more differentiated. When children first envision the third parties, they see them as passive "collection" or "holding" centers having no function of their own. (The mean age of children with this rudimentary understanding was eight years two months.) Somewhat later, children see the third parties as actively trying to meet the needs of the adoptive parents. Only at a mean age of eleven years eleven months did children understand the agency as an evaluative intermediary that protects the rights and welfare of both children and adults (Brodzinsky, Schechter, and Brodzinsky 1986, pp. 215–216).

The Early Evolution of Understanding Adoption

Both research and the testimony of adults adopted as children bespeak the need for adoptive parents to talk with their children about adoption throughout childhood and adolescence. As the child matures she will be able to understand the various dimensions of adoption in increasing complexity. (This, of course, is also true of such concepts as love, democracy, death, and responsibility.) The parent must listen for how the child's understanding is evolving to know at what point she is eager and able to understand something that a few months before would have held little interest for her. The parent must listen not only for the ways in which the child's understanding is coming to approximate an adult's but also for the ways in which it is divergent. These divergences are not simply errors to be corrected but expressions of how adoption is experienced by the individual. They need first to be received, understood, and empathized with.

We have turned this listening ear to the stories shared in this book. Accepting the finding of Brodzinsky and his colleagues that young children do not understand adoption as adults do, we have tried to discern from these stories the various ways in which some young children experience adoption and work toward more complex understandings through their relationships—first with adoptive parents and then with siblings and peers. How do understandings of adoption emerge and evolve within adoptive families? What are children's understandings and concerns en route to an adult conceptualization of adoption?

Young children's utterances and play sequences are like adult conversations in that they reveal only a small part of their thoughts at any moment, and what is revealed is subject to multiple interpretations. Moreover, the young child's thought, laden with emotions and images, is often denigrated by adults in general and researchers in particular. Piaget, the foremost theorist of children's cognitive development, used the scientist, not the poet, to typify the desired apex of cognitive development (Watkins 1986). It is too often the logical thinking of the scientist that we wait for our children to exhibit, often disregarding as irrelevant or merely "cute" utterances that sound illogical to us. Brodzinsky's research also demonstrates Piaget's concern for studying how children's thought begins to approximate the thought of adults. We have tried in our discussion of the stories to focus less on the confusions in the young child's thought than on the particular kinds of sense and meaning she constructs in words and images that express adoption as a lived experience, not an abstract concept.

In appendix B we list everything the parents reported their young children to have said or played that seemed to them to relate to adoptive themes. These are listed according to chronological age, freed from thematic interpretations or orderings, so that our readers can form their own impressions directly from what the children said. In this chapter we present a thematic analysis of this material, attempting to tease out young children's concerns about and understandings of adoption.[1]

From these stories it is clear that the fact of adoption becomes the lens

----

1. After reading through each story, we divided it into meaning units, marking each time there was an introduction of a new meaning with respect to our research questions. Then we posed these questions to each unit and attempted to delineate the psychological relevancy of the unit to the research questions: (1) what does this unit tell us about the meaning or experience of adoption for the child? (2) what does it tell us about the experience of being an adoptive parent? (3) what does it tell us about

through which the child, at certain critical times, sees and deals with many of the normal developmental issues that arise in the course of growing up in a family. For adopted children at each stage of development, the struggles and conflicts, the charms and joys of life, are commonly couched in terms of questions and feelings about being adopted. Adoptive parents often lose sight of the fact that their children's nonadopted peers are fighting the same battles and feeling the same pains but are scrapping on fields other than the adoption front, using other metaphors. For this reason we will locate talk about adoption within the context of the usual concerns of early childhood and latency, recognizing that talk about adoption often occurs intertwined with these other normative concerns.

Allowing In-Between Spaces for Wonderings about Adoption

One of the most consistent "findings" across the stories we report is that conversations about adoption most often occur informally, at times and in places between other activities: in the car, at bedtime, on walks. In these in-between spaces thoughts tend to arise more spontaneously for the child, eye contact does not fix the child's attention, and parents are less distracted by other concerns (or so the child thinks). Other in-between spaces where the child feels free to raise her adoptive wonderings are during imaginative play, vacations, walks, bath or toilet times, or time set aside for a parent and a child just to be together, away from work, other family members, and other commitments. In several instances a parent remarked to us, "no sooner" did the walk or the car ride begin than the child spoke up, as though entering this in-between space was an invitation for her to air whatever concerns she might have. As parents we can in nonverbal ways create or allow for in-between spaces that encourage our children to share their feelings and thoughts about all the important things in life, including adoption.

In terms of process, we found a striking difference between parents and their young children in the ways they experience and process conversations about adoption. Children express their concerns precipitously, erupting like volcanoes. A question seems to appear from nowhere. They are agitated, perhaps highly upset. They are curious, perhaps exhilarated. You talk. They talk. It is over. They are sunny. Parents reflect on and worry about an important exchange far in advance. Concerned, they may refer to it long after it is over, but the child may not even remember it. It has been processed and has receded to a subterranean part of her mind. The parent, who may be a wreck for a week, cannot imagine how the child can deal with so much emotion and curiosity so quickly and completely. She can—until the next time.

---

the ways in which adoptive understandings unfold between people? This is the first part of a qualitative method proposed by Amedeo Giorgi (1975).

The World as Families: Toddlers and Their Play of Caretaking

Before the intense dialogues of endless "whys" between you and your preschooler begin, the toddler shows you in her play what her thoughts and concerns are. Beginning around the age of two, the child makes the whole world into families. A pile of leaves, a group of lambs, the fingers of her hand, all become ready symbols for a mommy, a daddy, and their children, or whatever the family constellation of the particular child is. As you try to read a book to your toddler, you are struck by how she turns all groupings into the primary grouping of her experience: the family. It is into the vortex of this near obsession with the family that the experience of being adopted is first assimilated. Young children who may appear to be preoccupied by adoptive themes are simply showing the intense focus on family that is normal for their age. Since their family story includes adoption, they may deal with it repeatedly, just like all children's "Where did I come from?" questions.

Much toddler play revolves around the theme of caring for small animals and babies. Early in toddlerhood, the child imagines herself the recipient of nurturant care. Gradually, she adds to this enjoyable experience of being cared for the role of the nurturer: cooking for a baby, taking care of a baby rabbit, taking her doll for a ride in the stroller. The toddler establishes in play that she can give back the care she has received (Lowe 1975). Although little boys are often observed building and toppling towers, routing truck convoys, and creating car crashes, even the most macho preschooler tells stories with his he-man and monster figures that embody themes of attachment and separation, aggression and control, care, love, and nurturance—the same themes that girls' play portrays.

This play of caring, which precedes questions about where babies come from, lays the groundwork for adoptive meanings. The child may begin to pretend she is a little bunny found in the woods by loving passersby and taken to their home to live. Does she intend an adoptive scenario in any conscious sense? As an onlooking parent, it is hard to tell. What we do know is that how we respond to this imaginative play, how fully we enter into it, how warmly we welcome this stray bunny, will help our toddler as she begins to grapple with her own adoption experience. Turning away from our tasks at that moment, going down on the floor to stroke the bunny's fur, tending to its feelings of abandonment or sadness, sharing in its joy at being discovered, opening ourselves to be with the bunny in the ways she wants us to be—all this helps establish the world of the child as a place that responds to the needs of little ones, delights in them, and can reestablish care in joy and warmth when it has failed or been lost.

Inviting Play to Express Concerns about Adoption

Our children's play is not only a language to be deciphered by us but a language to be entered into and shared. We allow the child to initiate her own meanings, and we can communicate our meanings and our love through the medium of play as well.

We can be attuned to how she handles the many adoptive themes in the stories she sees or hears—Dumbo's separation from his mother and befriendment by Timothy the mouse; Charlotte's befriending of Wilbur the pig and his subsequent caretaking of her spider children after her death; Cinderella's difficult life in her stepmother's house; or the mutual "adoption" of Snow White and the seven dwarfs. Elements from such stories that interest, worry, or delight the child enter her play and express her concerns. These themes are reworked to express her adoptive experience, dilemmas, and wonderings, helping her develop understandings and resolve conflicts for the time being.

The parent need not intervene to make play realistic or interpret the story line the child is following. Play is like night dreams, in which elements of the day are rearranged and things that never happened are included—all in the service of expressing current emotional experience symbolically. Though play and dreams may depart from literal reality, they express emotional reality. The child who wants to play repeatedly at being inside her mother's tummy needn't be told each time that she was never there. She may be trying to express her experience of or need for intimacy with you. Once she is allowed this imaginal experience, the play moves on. Her tummy play does not necessarily mean that she has not integrated your saying that she was not in your tummy, just as the absence of such play does not mean that she understands her adopted status.

In several of the stories shared here we find parents who were at first hesitant to participate in the story line proposed by their child's play—whether it was pretending that the child was in mommy's tummy, that the mother had picked up the wrong baby at the orphanage, or that a birthparent had died when that was not the case. It was as though the parents were fearful that joining the play would somehow give it the stamp of permanent truth. But once the child was allowed to detour from the literal truth and give full rein to the images and scenes that suggested themselves, the parents could hear the child's concerns, and she literally had a theater for working them through in the close company of loved ones.

Let's see how this looks and sounds in a particular play episode. The day the play took place Laura (3:4)[2] had seen a mother pig suckling new-

2. Three years four months. Ages in parentheses will be given in this fashion throughout.

born piglets at a farm. At first Laura played that she was a small animal in the woods who was discovered by a passerby. She assigned the role of passerby alternately to her adoptive mother and to her sister's godmother, Francine. Upon discovery, the baby animal would ask to go to live at the passerby's house. This was played over and over again. Then Laura directed her younger sister (2:4) to be a piglet, too, and to pretend to suckle from Francine, a mother pig. Laura's mother describes what happened next:

> Laura then directed me in the role she imagined for me. She urged me to take her away from her mother, to take her to live at my house. It seemed to me that she was initiating play around the theme of having two caretakers: one mother you nurse from and one you live with. Since I had not brought up anything about her birthmother, I was frankly surprised at her imaginative leap.
>
> I approached the mother pig and said that her baby would like to come to my house to live. I added, without Laura's direction, that I would take very good care of her. Francine added, "Do you promise?" I did.

Up to this point the mother and her friend have followed the story as Laura presented it. Now mother and Francine have introduced a meaning of their own—that when you take someone else's baby to live with you, you make a promise to the first mother to take good care of her child.

> Laura had us go off happily to a pretend house and seemed in an exuberant mood. She had us play this several times, including suckling from Francine.
>
> I decided to put words to these two caretakers and said that "Francine pig" was her "tummy-mommy" and that I would be the mother she would live with forever. She seemed delighted by and interested in this. Then, after playing it again, she asked me to "squish" her—to hold onto her too tightly. I protested at first, saying, "I will never squish you. I am your new mommy and I love you very much. Also I promised your tummy-mommy that I would take good care of you." But again she insisted on this scenario, so I complied.

Notice how the child assimilates some of the meaning mother has introduced and rejects other aspects because these distract from what she is trying to get at.

> I held her tight and said "Squish." She pretended to cry and ran back to her tummy-mommy, who jumped into the scene to protect her.

Then she asked her tummy-mommy if she could come with me again to live at my house. Her tummy-mommy asked me again to promise not to hurt or squish her. I promised. Laura again went off with me happily, seemingly without regret. Then she announced that I had to squish her again. I once again pretended to, not knowing where this was going. Again the tummy-mommy pig intervened. I apologized and promised not to squish her again. She came with me again happily, seemingly protected by this coalition of mothers, the earlier one keeping a check on the later one. Feeling protected, she went off to play something else.

Mother and godmother have followed Laura on an odyssey about going back and forth between a nursing mother to another person she wants to live with. The nursing mother remains in contact to make sure that the baby piglet is well cared for. The piglet is free to go back and forth as she desires. The adoptive mother introduces some of her own concepts into the play while allowing Laura to disregard some of them. Adults joining the child in play patiently say the lines the child directs them to say and repeat scenes until she is satisfied and finds herself released from the scene. While the child is sharing her image of going between two caretakers, not always without some harm befalling her, her mother shares her own sense of having made a promise of care, her regret when she fails in this promise, and her eagerness to try again. Whether we believe that the child is presenting a view of adoption or is operating at a preconceptual level of understanding, we can definitely describe her as working out the fate of a small creature in a situation where there are multiple caretakers, a working out that is certainly an essential basis for a positive emotional sense about adoption.

The parent who is able to follow the child's lead in pretend-play will become a beloved companion with whom the child delights in sharing her world. Following the child's lead means envisioning the child as playwright, director, and producer of a work that neither we nor she has ever seen before. She hands us our roles. We ask her what the doll should say. We enact with spirit but are ready to be corrected by the director on our nuance or emotional tone. We learn our role from the script she gives us or we ask for direction ("What should the mother say?") and are ready to repeat again and again our scenes as our young companion works out a drama that conveys what needs to be expressed and communicated and resolves what needs to be resolved.

The mother of a five-year-old girl noticed that her daughter seemed dissatisfied with everything her mother did. One evening the child could not get to sleep and the mother offered to play with her, hoping that what was troubling her would find expression in the play. The mother explains what happened over several hours of imaginative play:

> She gave me a doll and told me it was a wicked, mean lady, and she had these two other dolls: a lady and there was a little girl. . . . This kind, wonderful lady was a mother to the little girl. They were happy, playing, doing lots of nice things. A mean, wicked lady, who did not have a child, . . . came over and snatched the little girl away and said the child would be hers now. The little girl [doll] was screaming, "If it hadn't been for you, I would be with my real mother."
>
> When I heard this I said, "No wonder you have been so angry at me lately." I suggested that maybe she had been so angry at me, . . . fighting with me over so many things, because she had been thinking that if it hadn't been for me she would still be with her birthmother and wouldn't have to be wondering about her and why she was given up. And she said, "Yeah, if it hadn't been for you, I would still be with her. You came and took me away."

The play and conversation made manifest what the child had been struggling with alone. The adoptive mother was now able to explain that the birthmother had decided even before the child was born that she could not be a mother, that if she herself had not become the child's mother, some other adoptive mother would have.

In appreciating, witnessing, and entering into the pretend-play of our children we gain a sense of how their understandings evolve, their wishes unfold, and their feelings become transformed. The process may be gradual, is usually playful, and is often surprising.

The Preschooler's Curiosity about Her Adoption Story

The preschooler's mind, play, and conversation reveal her fascination with who she is and where she came from. Her play imagines her both backward in time—playing out being in a tummy, being born, being a baby—and forward in time—whom she will marry, what she will be like as a grown-up. It is as though becoming three years old, with all the new communicative power of that age, allows the child to take a leap toward self-consciousness. Being adopted is usually greeted with the same curiosity as are the other facts a child learns about herself during this period. As one parent put it, "Michael started asking questions about adoption at three and a half years old, but that is also the time he began to talk and ask questions about everything."

The adopted child is interested in what her story is: where she came from, when her parents came to her, how they got there, how she looked when they first saw her, and later, what they felt on first seeing her. The adoption story that is first told can convey all the closeness, warmth, excitement, and joy that are present in any story of birth because for the adoptive parents this union on adoption day is usually the answer to their prayers. The child asks the parents to act out the adoption story or talk about it again and again, not merely so that she can fix its important details in her mind, but so that she can experience over and over again the joy and love of her beginning in her present family. Nevertheless, the adoption story cannot and should not be used as a substitute for the birth story, which the child will also need a little later, as she becomes interested in tummies with babies and the fact of birth that allows each of us miraculously to enter the world.

The adoption story does not need to be romanticized by invoking the motif of the "chosen child." The reality is that most adopters no longer choose their child from a group of orphans. Even if they did, this story line about specialness could become a burden for a child. What is chosen can be unchosen. If one was so special as to be chosen, what will happen if one is "bad" or even "average"? The parents can convey the sense that they and the child were destined for each other without implying any demands about how she should act and what she should be like.

Openness and warmth during adoption talk tell the child that we are interested in her story, that we welcome her questions and concerns—indeed, that we value her curiosity about herself. Through the adoption-day story it becomes clear to the child that "adoption"—whatever that word means to her—was a very happy thing for her parents. Looking through the family photograph album with her, enacting meeting her for the first time, telling the story again in a "once upon a time" fashion—these are intimate exchanges between adoptive parents and their children, just as stories of being pregnant, getting to the hospital, and seeing the newborn for the first time are to birthfamilies.

Many parents mention how their young children loved the simple adoption story first presented to them. Characteristically this is a happy, joyous story of the child as the answer to her parents' deepest wishes, of her joining a family that loves her.[3] As this story is told and retold, acted and reenacted,

3. Some people argue that this is an untruthful narrative because it often does not extend backward in time to the child's birth, her birthparents, and their relinquishment of the child; that the parents are distorting reality to make it seem that the child's history began on her adoption day. This criticism is grounded in the fact that many parents never do go on to the birth story as the child matures, thereby failing to help the child integrate her past history with her present life. Although this concern is valid, one can argue that as long as they are committed to talking with the child eventually about both parts of her history, the adoption-day story is a better place to begin. This story roots the child in her present family and deals with what the

the parents begin to introduce more complex details into the narrative. This also seems true of the child. Children of the ages we studied (two to ten years) asked for the initial adoption story and introduced their own concerns into it. Older children sometimes used the adoption-day story as a way to pose difficult questions about their birth and birthparents.

For instance, the following themes were presented or pursued by the children in the context of being told or enacting the basic adoption story initially crafted by the parents and refashioned by the child:

• Child surprises and delights her parents by her entry into their lives as a baby bunny (2:0).

• Animal child is cared for after the death of her mother (2:6 on; 2:9).

• Someone tries to take a baby away from its mother (2:9; 2:11).

• Child asks if her adoptive mother was sad when she came to India to get the child (3:2).

• Child adopted at eight months asks if she was a little afraid of her adoptive mother at first (3:2).

• Child plays out the possibility of the adoptive mother's having picked up the wrong baby at the orphanage (3:4).

• In play child asks her nursing mother if she can live with another mother. If she is in any jeopardy, the nursing mother will intervene on her behalf and return her to the other mother (3:4).

• Child asks why his first mother did not want him and how old she was. He says he loves her and wants to see her (5:0).

• Child asks for story to be retold, for the first time in the presence of his father. Then he adds, "If anyone had tried to take you [adoptive mother] away from me, you [adoptive father] would have killed them." Child also asks what he looked like when his adoptive parents first saw him, how they felt, how big his eyes were, how happy they were (7:11).

"Was I in Your Tummy?": Melding the Birth Story and the Adoption Story

All three- and four-year-olds are fascinated by how things are made and, most of all, by how *they* were made (Fraiberg 1959, p. 180). That babies are

---

two- or three-year-old is most interested in: how the people she loves and depends on were and are thrilled that she is primary in their lives. Before children become interested in where babies come from and then how they themselves are made, they assume that babies, and themselves, simply always exist. Thus until about four years of age they have no need for a cause (Bernstein and Cowan 1975, p. 86). When this concern does enter the picture, the birth story becomes all-important.

born from the mothers' tummies is a numinous insight to preschoolers. The ubiquitous question "Was I in your tummy?" and the child's announcement that she *was* in her mommy's tummy were among the earliest occasions when these adoptive children and their mothers began to process the fact of adoption together. Some children simply accept as fact that "I was in another lady's tummy until I was born, and then my parents got me and took me home" as part of interesting information about themselves, along with "I was born in a hospital"; "I have two brothers"; "My dog's name is Andy." But for some children, being in the belly of another, unknown lady is frightening and undesirable.

In some three- to five-year-olds a first feeling of loss connected to adoption may arise. Unless one believes that the prenatal and early postnatal experience of the birthmother persists in some nonverbal way, it is not the loss of the birthparents that the child experiences at this early age.[4] If the child was adopted as an infant or a young toddler, she does not remember the birthparents or experience them as known. When we listen to the children, the loss they mourn at this early point is the loss of a symbol of absolute closeness and unity with the person a child is usually closest to at this age: the adoptive mother. The child yearns to have been in the belly of the one she knows best and loves intensely. This was true in open adoption as well as closed. This loss is shared by the adoptive mother, who, even if she is able to give birth to her own children, also desires this ultimate closeness with her child. Many of the mothers in our stories were able to join in the emotion of this intimate moment with their children and acknowledge that they too wished the children had been inside them. This mutual longing, though it was not pregnancy, certainly seemed extremely close and loving. And even on the rare occasions a child expressed acute sadness, it did not persist and was usually never mentioned again.

Here are some of the ways children "talk tummy":

• "Just where does a baby grow? . . . Well, then, I grew in your uterus" (2:5).

• "Did your belly get big and fat when I was inside?" (Parent explains.) "But I want to be in *your* belly" (2:6).

• "The factory does not make baskets . . . because it makes babies. That was where I was made." (Mother explains how babies are made.) "So,

---

4. Most researchers studying infant attachment no longer distinguish between infants raised by their birthmothers and those adopted before the age of six months. Benet (1976, p. 181), in reviewing this research, says it is "now thought to be the third quarter of the first year that produces individualized attachment, with consequent mourning if the mother-figure is changed thereafter."

Mom, I grew in your uterus." (Mother explains.) Later that day, child sobs, "I so sad, Mommy. I so sad I didn't grow in your uterus" (3:2).

• "You know what I want when I grow up? I want to get so tiny I can get into your tummy" (3:5).

• "Did I drink from your breasts like Jeremy does?" (3:6).

• "I don't want you to have gone to Brazil to get me. God says I'm coming from your tummy very soon." (Child then enacts birth from adoptive mother.) (3:9).

• Child exhibits pain in her absolute wish to have come out of her adoptive mother's tummy and insists that her adoptive mother breast-fed her (4:?).

• "You didn't need to go to childbirth class for me because I was in someone else's belly!" (4:11).

An older child (8:1) asked, "Mom, is it better to have adopted me or given birth to me?" When his mother replied that it is just different, that she could not imagine being any closer to him if she had given birth to him, he said, "Me neither. Me neither. I want you for my mother."

We see in some of these comments the child's wish to integrate past and present, her birthparents with her present family. Although the adoption story is often a happy exchange between parent and child, the child begins to need pieces of her birth story as well. In particular, as her interest in being born from a tummy and drinking from breasts evolves, she needs to know that she *was* born from a tummy and drank from breasts or bottles like everyone else, that her moment of birth—not just her moment of adoption—was a happy, wondrous epiphany. She needs to identify with the mother who gives birth just as she identifies with her present mother who gives ongoing care and love. A four-year-old let her adoptive mother (who was not infertile) know this when she stated sadly one day, "Mommy, since I didn't come out of your tummy, I can't have any babies come out of mine." Once this worry was addressed, the child was cheerfully able to fantasize being a mother with a baby inside her.

"I don't want to have been in someone else's tummy!": The Young Child's Desire for Sameness

Just as the age-appropriate wondering about where babies come from is often a starting point for talk and sharing feelings about adoption, so too, from the third year on, does the age-appropriate beginning awareness of differences—whether physical, racial, or how one entered one's family—give rise to adoption talk. Most preschoolers do not register protest around adoption: rather, they ask questions relevant to their age, level of social understanding, and cognitive development. But when a preschooler shouts, "I don't want to be adobeded!" the parent must remember that she is not attacking the institution of adoption or criticizing her parents but is telling us one of the central facts of her preschool world: that she does not want to be different from her peers in any way (unless, of course, the difference enhances the way she is seen by her peers—for example, if she is the only child with a pony!). She may not even be able to understand or pronounce "adopted"; yet she has picked up something ominous about it, something that signals that it means a difference. She learns this from strangers who whisper the question, "Is she adopted?" (and all its thoughtless variations) into her mother's ear at bus stops and supermarkets.

When a child of this age announces her wish not to have been adopted, this is no different from the announcement that she wants to live in a blue house like Amy's, not a brown house; that she wants straight hair like her sister's, not curly hair. At the heart of wanting to be the same is the desire to belong, to be loved, to be safe, accepted, and not separated off. But to adoptive parents a child's declaration that she does not want to be adopted sounds infinitely more serious because adoption cannot be changed or made better, because of the parents' lingering feeling that for the child adoption is less desirable than being reared by birthparents, and because the parents anticipate her fuller understanding of adoption later on.

The young child gradually becomes aware that adoption and birth are two different ways of entering a family and that most people live with the family they were born to. Some young children make this difference a source of pride, announcing gloatingly even to strangers that they are adopted. Many adopted children, however, wish their history could be the simple, straightforward one of their peers. They may try to solve this problem by wishing they had been born to their adoptive family, wishing they could dissolve the difference by looking like their adoptive parents, or, somewhat later, protesting their being taken from their original family and home.

• "I want to get so tiny that I can get in your tummy" (3:5).

• Child says adamantly: "I don't want brown eyes. I want blue ones" (like the rest of the family) (3:?).

• "If it hadn't been for you," child says to her adoptive mother, "I would be with my real mother. . . . You came and took me away" (5:0).

These comments do not necessarily bespeak a dislike for either family—birth or adoptive—but reflect our common desires for continuity and for sameness. They can be likened to the child of divorce adamantly hoping for her parents' reunion—so that the future is like the past, her family like "the ideal" one. If the adoptive parents can hear and empathize with this longing for sameness and simplicity, they can easily comfort the child, rather than become distanced out of a misguided feeling of rejection.

Young children have violent as well as loving fantasies, and these can be quite normal for them albeit sometimes unduly frightening for their parents. Thinking about adoption, children may say harsh and shocking things, but children say harsh and shocking things about a lot of experiences. Their understanding of how their words affect others is still developing. "I want to throw this mother in the garbage can and have my other mother" (4:10). This kind of statement can be made within a loving family as the child struggles with issues of differences and belonging. Don't be misled by the intensity with which the young child announces her sentiments about adoption. Notice the context of her proclamations and their function in the present moment. Doesn't she sometimes express her preference for a flavor of ice cream just as intensely, reaching a hysterical pitch: "I don't want 'nilla, I want 'taschio!"?

The parents' labor around this issue of similarities and differences—be the child biological or adoptive—begins in early childhood, as the child tries to reject anything that is different and clings to all that is familiar, whether foods, possessions, songs, books, ways of dressing, ways of being cuddled and soothed. The task is twofold: to respect the child's need for sameness and consistency while promoting and modeling an active appreciation for diversity on all levels. One wants the child to emerge into latency (seven to eleven years) with a sense that differences can be interesting, curious, cherished, and respected. Such respect for and interest in all kinds of differences will bode well for a later, more sophisticated understanding of adoption as one of many ways to create a family. It will allow some self-love and self-respect around how adoption does entail differentness in our culture.[5]

The Intersection of Racial Differences
with the Differentness of Adoption

Our children grow up in a world that assumes resemblances among family members. They are taught in myriad ways that this is one of the most important things that make a family a family—as the teacher places all the yellow ducks together or an aunt says that Jane "got her red hair from her mother."

---

5. The bulletin published by the Council on Interracial Books for Children (1841 Broadway, New York, NY 10023) is an excellent resource for books and materials that help children appreciate diversity, as is the *Theme-Centered Bibliography of Children's Literature: Books with Themes of Personal, Cultural and Social Empowerment* produced by the Intercultural Training Resource Center and Savannah Books (72 Chestnut Street, Cambridge, MA 02139).

Three-year-olds seem to crave sameness, particularly with those they care about. When they note differences and sameness is sensed as desirable, sadness, longing, and wondering about adoption sometimes come to the fore. At other times, the same child observes such differences impartially or with a curiosity untinged by sadness.

Since a "family" is frequently represented as a group composed of members who look somewhat alike, it is reasonable for little ones to feel apprehensive that they do not look like others in their family. For some children, the early noticing of physical differences intersects with their budding awareness that adoption means having two mothers. One tan child at age three asked her parents to take her skin and hands off and substitute her mother's. A few months later, in the context of a stranger's pointing out that she looked different, she announced that her (adoptive) mother was not her "real" mother. Later the same year, the child expressed the hope that some day her mother could have the same color skin as hers. She then asked about the color of her "waitress or nurse or lady." Her adoptive mother felt that she was trying to talk about whether her skin color matched her birthmother's. Her attempts at dissolving the differences between her appearance and her adoptive mother's (by having one become like the other) were giving way to a beginning awareness of having two mothers, one whom she resembled and one whom she didn't. Another child (3:9) tried to dissolve the difference by seeking a mother of her color: "I don't want you to be my mother. I want a brown mother." At another point this child suggested that her adoptive mother paint her skin the child's color, adding that if it rained, God could keep the paint on. Later that day, she said, "You can be my mommy forever and ever anyway," implying that not matching need not stand in the way of their being mother and child together.

It is normal for three-year-olds, who have emerged into a period of development where differences are fascinating, to notice different skin colors. This early noticing, however, is not yet linked to the five- and six-year-olds' interest in classifying everything that comes before them, including themselves and other people. The more complex understanding that everyone belongs to a racial group and that these groups differ in social status unfolds as the older child grasps more about heredity and social structure.

The early concern with differences in appearance may alarm adoptive parents, who out of love and fear are quick to worry that it may become a problem. Studies of transracial adoptees, however, do not support this worry but show that these children's long-term adjustment is similar to that of white children adopted by white families (Feigelman and Silverman 1984) and result in children with healthy self-concepts and self-esteem (Kim 1976; Gill and Jackson 1983; McRoy, Zurcher, Lauderdale, and Anderson

1982). Indeed, in one study it was found that Korean adolescent adoptees in interracial families actually surpassed adoptees in same-race families in terms of adjustment, though they still harbored their earlier concerns about looking different (Feigelman and Silverman 1984).

We must be careful not to project adult ways of seeing onto children. We often fear that the young child will have identity problems because she has two sets of parents or because her racial-ethnic heritage differs from her adoptive family's. Many of those who speak of "identity confusion" unquestioningly take as normative intraracial families. The fact that transracial adoptees have a task of integration different from that of children in intraracial families does not mean that they are destined to fail that task. The young children we studied were busily knitting together an identity that incorporated the conjunction *and*. A three-year-old anticipated that she would have both her birthmother *and* her adoptive mother at her birthday party. A five-year-old had the fantasy that she and her adoptive family would spend each summer with her birthfamily. A four-year-old drew a picture of her Salvadoran grandfather, whom she had never met in real life, but whom she included in her fantasy. An eight-year-old doing a school assignment about parents' ethnicity said, "Mom, making German flags [her adoptive mother's ethnic background] will look dumb." At that moment this child was experiencing more profoundly her legacy of dark skin tone from her African-American birthfather than her white adoptive mother's German cultural heritage. She decided instead to use four flags, one for each parent—birth and adoptive. This was a mark not of identity confusion but of forming a multifaceted identity that included the various aspects of the child's reality.

In the 1960s and 1970s the strong resistance to transracial adoption predicted that these children would experience identity conflicts and confusions. Instead, research shows that these adoptees forged identities that were not experienced as conflictual and that contained ample self-esteem, even if little racial or ethnic identity as it is traditionally defined.

The transracial adoptees studied from childhood to adolescence by Gill and Jackson (1983) did not have a devalued sense of self-esteem, presumably a key component of identity confusion or diffusion. The children's racial difference from their parents, and often from their friends and neighbors, did not control their general conception of themselves, nor was it associated with any behavioral disorder.

Rather than young children's comments about differences in appearance being harbingers of identity confusion and low self-esteem, interviews with transracially adopted adolescents (Gill and Jackson 1983) showed that these adoptees experienced the most difficulty with their racial background when they were starting school. Once their friendships were established, any disparaging remarks that were made were experienced as less problematic. For the most part, older children remembered difficulty at the hands of their peers rather than adults. To put this differently, before the children were fully aware of race and the dynamics of racial prejudice, they noticed and wondered about differences, disparaging them and teasing about them. To parents this can evoke fears of racism and later injustices. Transracial adoptees, however, did not feel that they were at the same disadvantage as their same-race nonadopted peers, nor, as it turns out, did the adoptive parents of the adolescents. The reason implied—but never named—by these adolescents and their parents seemed to be class. Though transracially adopted adolescents shared the race of their birthparents, they enjoyed the social class of their adoptive parents, which most often gave them educational and economic advantages frequently denied to their same-race, minority, nonadopted peers. Indeed, studies of the effect of adoption are often implicitly studies of the effect of growing up in the middle and upper classes, as adoption occurs largely in the context of class advantage in American culture.

"Why Did My Birthmother Give Me Up?": Getting from Her to You

The children represented in the stories in chapter 4 describe in their talk and fantasy three spaces associated with adoption: their current family, being with the birthparent(s), and a transitional space between the two. The notion of having arrived at where she is now—the present, familiar, loved adoptive family—is worked out in fantasy and conversation before the child begins to wonder where she was before this arrival. In play a baby animal may be lost and then found. But the questions "lost by whom?" "given over by whom?" and "why given over?" arise as concerns only later.

Once the child does focus on her original birth situation, she may ask her birthmother's name (3:4; 4:?), what she looks like (4:?), her age (5:0; 8:3), where she comes from (4:?; 4:?; 7:11), and how long she lived with the birthmother (6:6). Because young children have little or no understanding of procreation, questions about the birthfather usually come a bit later. In our stories, however, several children mentioned their birthfathers at a very early age:

• "Is that my real daddy?" an Indian child asks her adoptive father when she sees an Indian man walking on the street (3:5).

• "So where is he, my real father? . . . Why don't you know where he is now? I don't want him to find me. . . . He'd take me away. He'd change his mind. I'd get kidnapped by him" (4:?).

• Child asks what his birthfather looks like, what his interests, race, and religion are (5:?).

Once the child begins to ask questions about "the seed," conversations about the birthfather may be imminent. "But where does the mother buy the seed?" asked one little girl, almost five. "The birthfather gives it to her," answered her mother. "Did Daddy give it to you?" "No, remember, you didn't grow in my womb, you grew in Teresa's tummy. She got the seed from her man."

It is at this stage—when the child's awareness assimilates the fact that her beginning predates what she currently knows, what is familiar to her in her present family—that she may begin to think she will run into her birthparents (3:4; 3:5; 4:3) or to feel vulnerable to being kidnapped or reclaimed in some fashion (4:?). The child may ask for the first time to see a birthparent (3:0; 4:?; 4:9) and not understand why this may not be possible. These concerns focus on the child herself and are qualitatively different from later concerns about how the birthparents are now, what their life is like, what they are like as people, and what their reasons were for relinquishment. Insofar as the child experiences a sundering between her two families, she may have fantasies that attempt to bring together in one place what has been separated in place and time: that her birthmother will attend her birthday parties (3:0), that her adoptive family will live with her birthmother in the summers (6:3), that a tent could be placed in the yard for the birthmother to live in (6:0).

Beginning at age four, some children in our stories asked why they were given up for adoption: "Why would a woman who grew a baby give that baby away? . . . Why would she give me up?" (4:0). Often when this question first arises, the child does not yet have a foundation for understanding the answer. Her thinking is still characterized by an egocentric quality; she has difficulty taking the perspective of another and is all too ready to assume that the other's behavior has something to do with her. Also, she has little understanding of the complexities of the social world that result in adoption in our times: war, poverty, discrimination by gender, the economic oppression of women, the stigma of illegitimacy for mothers and children. Thus the young child often answers her own first question (or a friend's question) about relinquishment by assuming that she was a bad or inadequate or unlovable baby.

A parent hearing this may be worried that the child is lacking in self-esteem. This is not necessarily the case. Rather, it is the only reason the child can figure out by herself. After all, the adults she cares about most sometimes distance themselves from her when she misbehaves. Shouldn't she be really good so that they too won't leave her behind? If she believes that she was left once for being bad, mightn't this happen again if she is a "handful"? When this concern arises, the parents need to reassure the child that the birthparents decided that they were unprepared to parent any child effectively at the time of relinquishment, that the relinquishment was independent of who the child was. In most cases, the birthmother made an adoption plan before the child was even born. Sadly, it usually had nothing to do with this particular child; usually there was very little or no postnatal relation between the two. Ultimately the child needs to understand that in an *emotional* sense there is no such thing as "an adoption plan." Parents do not want to surrender their children, to part with them. They do so under duress of circumstance, almost always with sadness and regret. The child is often surprised to learn that her birthmother did not even know her. The adoptive parent must begin to lay the groundwork for the child to understand some of the cultural forces that brought about the adoption, be they poverty, prejudice, oppression, or teenage pregnancy.

Children often ask the adoptive parents questions that the parents cannot answer unless they knew the birthparents well. They are asked to present the birthparents' thinking about a set of circumstances they themselves never experienced. In most cases the adoptive parents have spent years trying to get a baby. Now they are asked to explain how the birthparents could give up a child.[6] One mother put it, "It is almost unimaginable for me to think of any reason to relinquish this child." Another mother, pressed by her four-year-old daughter to explain why her birthmother had given her up, finally and with feeling, admitted,

> I've tried to give you some answers. But I really don't know all of her thinking that went into her deciding not to be your mother. It is really hard to understand why a woman would grow a baby and then give it up. You may not understand this now, but you might later on. It had nothing to do with you. It had to do with her life. I really don't know all the reasons why, but if that is something you still want to know when you are older, we can try to find her and ask her about it.

At age five this child attempted to answer her own question by imagining that she had been wanted and loved by a good mother but was stolen away by her adoptive mother. But at age nine she emerged from her early bewilderment about why her birthmother would give her up to a clear sense that *she* was not given away; a baby was. "She didn't give *me* away. She had a

---

6. In a study of domestic birthmothers, Sorosky, Baran, and Pannor (1978) found that the principal reasons for relinquishment were that the mothers were unmarried and wanted their children to have a family, wanted to finish school, suffered economic hardship, were not ready for parenthood, or were responding to pressures from parents and others.

baby. She gave birth to me. But she didn't even know who I was. She gave up a baby. She didn't give up *me*."

Adoption practice would be greatly improved if birthparents were consistently asked to provide the kind of information adoptees are known from research to want and request over time: pictures of the birthfamily, family trees for each parent (with notes about the personality, physical traits, and interests of each member), family medical history, the age of the birthparents at relinquishment, and, particularly, a letter from each birthparent explaining why the child was given up for adoption. This letter could be opened in late latency or adolescence, when the question of "why" recurs at a deeper level. Without such a practice, the adoptive parents are asked by their children to put into words what they do not fully know. It is little wonder that Brodzinsky's research shows that children have less understanding of why a parent decides to relinquish than of any other aspect of the adoption process. The adoptive parents could be helped significantly in their job of parenting if this critical decision, which begins each adopted child's life in her new family, was explained by the people who made it.

"Why Didn't She Want Me?": Differentiating Being Wanted by One's Birthparents from Their Decision Not to Parent

• "Why didn't my real mom want me? . . . I think she didn't like me" (4:6).

• "I wish I had been in your tummy. . . . Why didn't she want me? . . . How old was she? . . . Oh, ho. She was a *teenager*. If she was a teenager then, is she a teenager now? . . . Well, I love her and I want to see her" (5:0).

• "Why didn't [my sister's birthmother] want her? . . . Why didn't my mother want me? . . . How old was she? . . . Exactly how old was she? It matters. It matters" (7:10).

These two intertwined questions—"why did she give me away?" and "why didn't she want me?"—are asked again and again by adoptees. Adult adoptees interviewed by Triseliotis (1973, pp. 146–47) said that the main things they would have liked to hear in childhood were that their birthparents wanted and loved them and that they were not rejected. The child's question of why she was relinquished often obscures the more simple and important question: "Was I loved by my first mother?" It is possible to convey to a child that being placed for adoption is not incompatible with being wanted and loved by one's birthparents. Indeed, it is most often out of a sense of caring that a birthmother acknowledges that for a variety of reasons it might be better for her child to be adopted.

Brinich (1990), a psychoanalytically oriented adoption expert, proposes that the adoptive parents' task is "to change an unwanted child into a wanted child. . . . They must convey to their adopted child that, although he was born to other parents who did not want him, he is now their beloved child and shall always remain so" (p. 46). He suggests that adoptive parents must manage this transformation not only in "the mind of the child but also within their own thoughts." We argue that this transformation in our minds begins with our acknowledgment of the birthmother's reality and feelings. The testimony of birthmothers themselves and of those who have worked closely with them radically disputes the assertion that adopted children were unwanted by their first mothers. "Social workers working with unmarried mothers know what warm feelings they have for their children and how difficult they find it to part with them. It is only exceptionally that a mother, because of mental or social handicap, may appear blasé or in extreme cases abandon her child" (Triseliotis 1973, p. 147).

As adoptive parents we need to revise our outmoded and perhaps self-serving concept that these children were unwanted. Perhaps this was more often the case before birth control and legal abortions became easily available, though even then it needs to be qualified. Recent studies of birthmothers and the speaking out of women who "surrendered" their children many years ago testify movingly to the fact that many babies are intensely wanted by their birthmothers.

In Sorosky, Baran, and Pannor's (1978) study of thirty-eight birthparents, many stated that they would like their children to know that they cared about them when they relinquished them and still cared about them. In Rynearson's (1982) study of twenty birthmothers who had relinquished their babies fifteen to thirty years earlier, nineteen of the mothers had established an intense private monologue with their children before they were born and fantasied rescuing them from the situation they had been relinquished into. They had named their babies and feared, as other pregnant mothers do, that they might miscarry. All twenty experienced relinquishment not as their own desire but as an externally forced decision that overwhelmed their wish for continued attachment to their children. Millen and Roll's (1985) study of twenty-two birthmothers who later sought psychotherapy testifies to the ongoing sense of loss many birthmothers feel. These mothers imagined their children to be present, as, indeed, many adoptees imagine the presence of their birthmothers. They had a sense of loss of self, of anger at themselves and guilt for the relinquishment, an impulse to search for the child, and an identification with the child. It is important to remember that this research represents not all birthmothers but a self-selected group of women who many years later still experienced a sense of loss.

There is a critical difference between wanting to mother your child and acknowledging that you cannot at present parent her in the way you want her parenting to be done. Adoption agencies and adoptive parents have much to gain by seeing themselves as coming to the rescue of unwanted children. But the children have much to lose. If the truth were known, most of our children were wanted by two sets of parents. The child's grieving for the birthparents is often reciprocated by the grieving of the birthparents for their child. Were a child to appreciate this, her self-esteem would be less injured as she thinks about relinquishment.

Several birthmothers put it this way:

> I was a mother who gave up her rights, but not her feelings, about the daughter she gave up for adoption. I would like her to know that I didn't give her up because I didn't want her or love her. I wanted her to have something I couldn't give her at the time she needed it the most.

> If only the child I gave up could be convinced that he was loved and that he was given up due to circumstances beyond his mother's control. That she felt someone else could give him more of a life than she could.

> I have always had a desire to see her and to assure her that I gave her up because I loved her, but knew that I could not provide a home and proper relationship that I knew she deserved. I hope that my child is loved by her family and that she realizes that I too have loved her. (Sorosky, Baran, and Pannor 1978, pp. 62–67)

Adoptive parents have been cautioned against saying to their child, "Your birthmother placed you for adoption *because* she loved you," since the young child will wonder if the adoptive parents, who also love her, will also give her up (Melina 1989b, p. 83). It is important to stress, however, that being placed for adoption is not incompatible with being loved and wanted. In making a decision to allow adoption, birthparents are trying to be responsible parents because they want the best thing for their children.

The "Waiting Place": Between Birthfamily and Adoptive Family
The transitional space between the child's birthparents and her adoptive family is often a space of worry and fear. Some children imagine themselves (or their animal counterparts) as lost or alone (2:0; 2:11), taken away (1:9; 2:9; 5:0), separated from or abandoned by parents (2:9; 4 to 5), as little ones whose parents have died (2:6; 2:9), and as children left alone in a

potentially dangerous situation, crying for their adoptive mothers (3:?). One little girl (3:4) reflected on the arbitrariness of this waiting space when she imagined that her adoptive mother could have picked up a different baby from the orphanage. Another three-year-old wondered where her adoptive mother was while she waited for her at an orphanage.

One boy (6:9) asked his mother, "Hey, Mom, what happens if a pregnant woman gets sick? . . . I mean, what if she dies?" After she answered, her son particularized his concern: "What if you and Daddy hadn't been there when I came out of the lady I was born from?" The mother initially insisted that they *were* there and then, realizing that this was not answering his real concern, asked him what *he* thought would have happened. "They would have killed me" was his startling fantasy. The child's fears were eased by learning that his birthmother had chosen his adoptive parents and that if they had not been available, she would have chosen others to take good care of him. He had not been uncared for, abandoned, but was thoughtfully provided for by his birthmother.

Children in positive, loving homes equate being safe with being with their parents. Until they can understand the mechanics of adoption (relinquishment, foster and orphanage care, court systems, the adoptive work of lawyers and social workers), the intermediate space and time between families—*even if there was not a literal gap*—worries them.

Similarly, the young child who does not understand that the birthmother's relinquishment meant that adults would find her a family can blame the adoptive parents for the separation. As we saw earlier, without the knowledge that her birthmother's decision not to parent was also an intention to see that someone would adopt her, the child has few alternatives to thinking that her adoptive mother, wanting a baby, took her away from her birthmother.

Adoptive parents need to be alert to the likelihood that the young child's lack of social knowledge can lead to incorrect and sometimes frightening interpretations of the adoption process. Such interpretations do not indicate psychopathology but merely reflect the child's level of cognitive development and social understanding, a level normal to the child's age.

Some children take pleasure in this transitional space, in the fact or fantasy that birthparent(s) and adoptive parent(s) met, liked each other, or arranged together for the good care of the child. One mother says that her child "likes to remember that [her birthmother and I] met each other and that we liked one another. She finds comfort in the bridge between us and although at times she will sling out phrases like 'My birthmother would not like it that you're mean to me' (her usual response to 'go get your shoes on' or 'take your toys back to your room'), she mostly indicates that this knowing each other is a good thing." Although there is not yet research to support this, we suspect that opening up the traditional forms of adoption with a shift to some type of open adoption may be helpful in providing the child with a secure sense of transition from one family to the next.

As with any process they experience—divorce, death, birth, chicken pox, having their hair cut—young children wonder whether or not it is reversible and if not, why not. If I left one place, my birthfamily, to get to my adoptive family, will I or can I leave here to get back there? If birthparents gave up a child, can they reclaim her? If adoptive parents wanted a child, can they decide they don't want her any more and give her back?

Parents sometimes play on the young child's fear that becoming a parent is a reversible process by threatening to take the child back to "the store" if her behavior doesn't improve or to leave her in the parking lot if she doesn't come along. Such threats can be terrifying to young children, who have no rational reason to know this wouldn't happen. Some adopted children may become fearful that a birthparent will reclaim or kidnap them (4:?); others may fear that their adoptive parents will change their minds. Such children, of course, do not understand the legal and emotional permanence of their situation. No wonder so many adoptive parents in the past lied to their children, telling them that their birthparents had died, in order to forestall these fantasies.

Children Talking with Children about Adoption: Negotiating Being Seen as Different

As toddlerhood gives way to childhood, children discuss adoption with their siblings and friends as well as their parents. Sometimes a sib will ask an adoption question for the other sib before posing it for herself: "Did Maya's lady [birthmother] have brown skin like her? . . . Mom, did mine have my skin?" (3:10); "Why didn't Elizabeth's mother want her?" (7:11). Sometimes an older sib will attempt to explain adoption to a younger one. Sometimes parents overhear them trying out the hard questions among themselves, as when a three-year-old asked her two-year-old sister in a multiracial family why all the ponies in their pony doll family had different-colored skins, at a time when she was struggling to understand why no one in her family matched. One six-year-old girl cheerily announced to her ten-year-old brother that he was not her "real" brother: "You are my fake brother. We are adopted. I was born from a lady in Georgia who really loved me a lot. . . . then she gave me to Mom and Dad who adopted me and they are my fake parents. And we are a fake family." Her brother replied, "Lizzie, let me explain all this to you," and proceeded to explain why his birthmother had been unable to care for him and had found him parents. In general, it seems that adopted siblings provide solace for one another and, in particular, that the younger sibling has the advantage of entering into a family where adoptive talk is well underway.[7]

Children from nonadoptive families often appeared to adoptive parents to ask questions or make remarks that seemed insensitive:

• One four-year-old teased an adopted child from a multiracial family, "You don't match your mother. You can't match your mother."

• Four-year-old girls jeered at sisters who were Hispanic and Indian, "You two are black. You two are black."

• A five-year-old advised his adopted friend, "You don't have to listen to your mom, because she is not your real mom." The adopted child answered back, "What do you think she is, a cartoon character?"

• Another five-year-old asked the adoptive mother of a friend, "Why didn't Kathy's mother keep her?" At seven, still curious, he asked, "How old is Kathy's real mother now?"

• Another seven-year-old offhandedly asked an adopted boy, "Hey, what was your sister's name before you got her?"

Nonadopted children, of course, don't understand the complexities of adoption and the kinds of knowledge it rests on (genetic, legal, geographic, social, psychological) any better than their adopted friends do. But for parents their questions and comments appear to rupture a time when adoption talk is shared in intimacy and safety within the family. Now the child must share it with others—some kindly, some not, some well informed, some ignorant. The child can no longer be protected from the weight of cultural prejudice against adoption, for children will say to her outright what passersby and relatives have already implied: people in a "real" family match; families are more "real" and therefore better if there is a blood kinship; it is better if a child stays with the "real" parents, the parents by blood.

On the positive side, conversations with peers can help school-age adopted children begin to pull together their sense of adoption by having to explain it to someone who is outside the situation. A four-year-old said to her friend, "The way I see adoption is like this. Somebody has the baby but can't keep the baby and goes 'Wah, wah, wah. Good-bye, Baby,' and somebody who can't get a baby in their tummy says, 'Oh great, a baby.

---

7. Relations between older siblings—biological and adopted—and younger special-needs adopted children can be more problematic because the older children perceive that the parents *chose* to bring difficulty and complexity into their family through adoption. Brodzinsky, Schechter, and Brodzinsky (1986) have shown, in general, that despite increased adoptive talk younger siblings in adoptive homes have no greater comprehension of adoption than older siblings or nonadopted children.

Goody, goody, goody. Hello, Baby.' You know, somebody wins and somebody loses!"

A seven-year-old explained to his friend, "See, being adopted is better because you're chosen. There was this lady, my biological mother. She was too young and too poor to be a mom, so when I came out of her vagina, my parents were waiting for me and it was the happiest day of their lives." His friend then wondered if he planned to look for his "real" mother. He answered, "You don't understand, Richard; *this* is my real mother."

The child's beginning to talk to people outside the family should not confuse the parents regarding their own need to retain confidentiality about their child's adoption story. It is all right for a child to tell others she trusts about her origins. It is *her* story, and she should be in charge of who knows what and, further, be assured that her parents will not share the most private portions of her history without her permission. One mother reported that sometimes her child needed "to feel normal," to *not* talk about his adoption with others for a while. Age nine, she says, "was a year he felt sad about it, not glad about it," and he did not want to talk about his adoption at school as he had previously.

Children of all ages seemed heartened by the realization that some of their friends and acquaintances were also adopted. Some attend culture camps that help instill pride in their country of origin. Fellowship with adopted peers helps adopted children sense that adoption is a normal event.[8] Adopted children and their families are a minority group and profit—as do all minorities—from the support of fellow group members. Such affiliation provides not only a feeling of belonging but the clarifying understanding that prejudice and bad treatment are not an individual and private matter but a social issue.

Parents in handling ignorant and hurtful remarks by strangers, neighbors, and relatives provide a model for their children to base their own responses on when they are away from parental protection. Parents' care in thinking through the issues that are posed and the range of effective responses is a gift to their adopted children. When answering comments and questions from outside the family, the parents' most important audience is their young child. They should frame their answer in a way that is helpful and a good model for their child. If there has been an invasion of privacy, for instance, they should teach and model through their own response that the child need not talk to people about her history unless she chooses to do so.

---

8. Parents can find out about local adoption groups from their adoption agency, from *OURS*, published by Adoptive Families of America (3307 Highway 100 North, Suite 203, Minneapolis, MN 55422), or from *The Adopted Child*, a newsletter edited by Lois Melina, which provides an excellent review of current adoption research and theory (P.O. Box 9362, Moscow, ID 83843).

Beyond Early Childhood

Let us take a brief look at what is ahead, so that adoptive parents can hear how the adoption concerns and feelings of older children differ from those of early childhood and why. Latency-age children and adolescents become more interested in their birthparents than younger children are. One reason is that younger children think of a family as a group of adults and children who live together, who have love and affection for one another, but older children come to understand that families are most often identified by legal and genetic relationships (Pedersen and Gilby 1986, pp. 119–20). The older adoptee, armed with this newer, more abstract understanding, finds an importance in the birthfamily that she did not grasp when she was younger. If families are defined by blood ties, which family is my real family? Where do I belong? (see Brodzinsky 1986, p. 218). Second, the latency-age child's increasing ability to empathize with the thoughts and feelings of others necessarily results in a more pronounced immersion in fantasies about her birthparents and birthplace.[9]

One consequence of these heightened images of the birthparents is that a child may for the first time want to know what happened to her birth-mother *after* relinquishment and if she is all right now. The child may be curious about her birthparents' appearance (8:0), interests (8:3), and abilities (9:?) and how these relate to her own. In surveying the list of what older children wanted to know about their birthparents, one is struck by the complementarity of what birthparents have indicated they want to know about their children: how is the child growing up, what does she look like, is she well cared for, what kind of person is she turning out to be? They hoped their children were happy and that they knew the birthparents cared about them. Many wished their children could know how their parents' lives had turned out—being respected citizens, happily married, often with their own children (Sorosky, Baron, and Pannor 1978, p. 52).

As the child becomes more interested in fantasizing about the birthfamily, there is a greater propensity for feelings of loss and grief (see Jewett 1982). The child who was adopted in early infancy feels this grief not for the loss of birthparents she actually remembers but for the loss of the birthparents as fantasized. For the child adopted after age two who remembers her birth-parents, the sense of loss and grief is deeper and more profound. Such a child may mitigate the intensity of her grief by insisting that her adoption is

---

9. This parallels an increase in fantasizing about and understanding their adoptive parents' internal world as well. A child may now begin to understand what infertility meant to her adoptive parents. The child's fear that the parents experience adoption, and thereby herself, as second-best can be countered by awareness of the years of love and attachment that have passed since they lived through the pains of infertility.

temporary, that her birthparents will return. One six-year-old Korean boy, adopted at two, missed and worried about his birthparents. He wanted to erect a tent in his yard so that they could be near him. He was convinced that he could not join in the adoptive family's plans for the future because he would be returning to Korea. Side by side with these reunification fantasies, this boy openly and protractedly grieved for his losses with his adoptive mother and thus gradually succeeded in joining his adoptive family more fully over time. Rather than looking upon his grief as an impediment to attachment, his new parents facilitated and strengthened the child's attachment to them by sharing in his pain. This is one of the deep paradoxes of adoptive family life: that by acknowledging the losses and sharing in the pain, the family deepens the attachment in the present.

Adoptive parents may confuse this process by being unsympathetic to the child's feelings of loss ("she never knew her birthparents, so what is all the fuss about?") or threatened by fearing that the child prefers her image of the birthparents to her actual day-to-day parents. While the latency-age child is forming a more realistic image of the adoptive parents, integrating their negative and positive characteristics, she can more easily idealize or denigrate the birthparents because they are unknown. The child's belief that the birthparents are all good or all bad will pass as she grows older and comes to realize that all people have flaws and limitations, virtues and strengths. Children are great idealizers and may well compare and contrast their parents to their idealized images of parents. It must be emphasized, however, that this is what all children do, from the family romance of the so-called oedipal phase through the throes of adolescence. That is, part of the process children go through in opening themselves to a larger world than the family is to imagine themselves in different families—those of their peers, their teachers, their cousins. One often idealizes these other families. This process is an extremely important one since in our culture it is with others that the child will eventually live. Adoptive parents need not experience this contrasting of families as diminishing them if they see it as merely part of the process of making a home in the wider world.

The child, in contemplating her adoptive status and the loss of her original family, may well have negative feelings about being adopted. The parents must accept this. This does not mean that she loves or values her adoptive parents any less. Her feeling arises from a yearning we all share, a desire to have a single thread in her life, to have come from somewhere that still makes sense to her, to have, as David Kirk (1986) calls it, an "enchanted" view of her life. One four-year-old boy expressed his longing this way: "Joey is lucky because his mom is three things [his mother, birthmother, and teacher]. Why can't you be three things, Mom?"

Adoption means a confrontation—sometimes painfully early—with the difficulties of life. As parents we need to remain clear and unromantic, remembering that no life situation or story can be kept pristine, seamless.[10] There will be deaths and losses, disillusionments, regrets, times of pain and sorrow—with or without the fact of adoption. As our children encounter some of the loss implicit in adoption, it is easy for parents to lose sight of the fact that adoption is as much a positive recovery from loss as it is loss itself (Bernard 1974). We need to hold onto these dual realities of adoption, while our children grow into an appreciation of them after dealing with some of the loss.

The child's individuation from the parent begins at birth and continues through life. All children in our culture—whether they live in birthfamilies or adoptive families—seek to differentiate themselves from their caretakers and to form new bonds with them that permit their increasing individuality and maturity. This process is marked by difficult moments for all parents when the child announces her autonomy, sometimes with anger. Adoptive parents are particularly susceptible to feelings of hurt and rejection, a sense of being unappreciated, a sense of futility about their efforts at parenting when their children use their adoptive status as a way of trying to claim an inch of separation.

Just as retelling the adoption story can be a source of mutual joy when the child is feeling intimate with and close to the parents, so the fact of adoption can be invoked when there is a need for separation. One three-year-old announced, "I don't like my family, I want to live with Elaine [her day-care provider]." An eight-year-old answered his adoptive mother's statement of "I'm your mother too" with "Well, sort of." A nine-year-old said, "My real mother would let me do that" when his wishes differed from his adoptive mother's. Many latency-age and adolescent children declare at one point or another that their adoptive parents do not have authority because they are not the "real parents." Meanwhile, their agemates are just as busily undermining their parents' authority, but using other words, other tactics.

Children, like adults, intuit sensitive spots to target when they are angry, hurt, or desirous of pushing someone away. For many adoptive parents this vulnerable spot is the fear that, lacking the tie of blood, the child will not merely differentiate from the parents but will leave them in some final way. *The parents fear being orphaned by the child.* All children must differentiate themselves from their parents, while still and always needing a safe

___

10. As our children grow older, they find that many of their friends' families have suffered loss and separation, that many other children have two sets of parents and two homes. One child in our stories remarked that he was glad he had two sets of parents through adoption instead of divorce.

haven of love and care. The parent needs to hold onto the fact that adoption is forever rather than be seduced into responding on the child's level, "Well, go live with her then," or "If you are this bad and ungrateful, you should go back where you came from." The parent needs to take a deep breath and try to figure out why in each particular instance the child is making this kind of remark. Does she seek reassurance that she will always stay in this family, regardless of how she acts and what she says? Is she trying to separate from her parents in the normal way? Is she angry about something else? Is she asking for help in understanding how she could have two mothers?

As the child understands more about the adoption process and the choices her parents made, she begins to develop her own judgments about them. A seven-year-old said, "My [birth]dad is a jerk. . . . He left my mom by herself." Several seven- and eight-year-old girls struggled to decide whether other teenage girls who become pregnant should make the same choice their birthmothers did or keep their babies. A nine-year-old experienced some anger at his birthmother for drinking during her pregnancy, since this may have caused a learning disability. Interestingly, some parents who at other times gave their children space to feel their own feelings now interrupted expressions of negative judgment about the birthparent and eagerly suggested other, more benign interpretations—without ascertaining the function of the child's negativity. For instance, in one case it appeared that a four-year-old needed to think of his birthfather as bad because someone who was bad and had abandoned his child would be less likely to come back and take the boy away from his adoptive family.

Generally, adoptive parents are wise to present a benevolent view of the birthparents—among other reasons because the child will integrate the adoptive parents' view of the birthparents into her own sense of self-esteem. But just as we need to allow our children to be angry with us and try to understand the function of their anger, we need to allow their feelings toward their birthparents to evolve. The girl who called her birthfather "a jerk" was at the same moment deepening her empathy for her birthmother's predicament and establishing herself as a person who would do things differently, who would stand by a person she had been close to. Although most birthparents are careful to take care of their children prenatally and postnatally and to make adoption plans thoughtfully, some are not caring in their treatment of their babies and are therefore models that older adopted children will want to differentiate themselves from—first perhaps in anger, later in compassion, understanding, and forgiveness. Adoptive parents can help the child differentiate between anger at a birthparent and anger at the situation in which the birthparent may have been trapped—owing to addiction, abuse, poverty, prejudice, illness.

As the adopted adolescent is better able to imagine her birthparents and empathize with her adoptive parents, she may feel increasingly caught between the two sets of parents. Both are critically important in forging her own sense of identity. A major worry that frequently emerges at this time is that her adoptive parents will see her curiosity about her birthparents as a mark of disloyalty or ingratitude, a lack of attachment and love. Adoptive parents can help their child immensely by appreciating her curiosity, empathically understanding why it is important for her sense of identity and how little it has to do with them.

All adolescents struggle with issues of identity, with the process of self-questioning about who they are. Where a nonadopted child may surprise his parents by wanting to practice the orthodox religion of his grandparents, an adopted adolescent may try to braid together strands from both her families. The sense of not knowing exactly who she is or what will become of her as she leaves the family of origin plagues the adolescent and may lead her to make abrupt and startling assertions of her identity through her appearance, actions, and words.

For the adopted adolescent, this sense of vagueness about the self, the feeling of being unknown to herself can be symbolized by everything she does not know about her birthplace and her birthfamily. Again, the adoptive parents can help by understanding that loading an adolescent-identity issue onto specific adoption questions obscures what all adolescents go through—a search for self that is often painful to experience and disturbing to witness.

The adolescent gradually faces the need to come to know herself not only in the circumscribed world of family and friends but in the larger world beyond her direct experience. It is this that provokes wondering about birthparents and about whether meeting them would be helpful. For most adopted adolescents, their interest in searching out information about their birthfamilies has to do not with limitations of their adoptive families but with coming to know themselves more completely; they need to feel that they have not magically and insubstantially emerged from a fog but have come from real people with real personalities and life stories, who made life decisions that critically affected the course of their own lives.

The decision about whether or not to search for one's past and roots literally by gaining more information about one's birthfamily, meeting the birthparents, visiting the orphanage or foster parents, represents the adopted person's taking a stance with regard to the three adoption sites she has imagined and thought about in her childhood. Previously, she has been subject to the opinions of the court and her adoptive parents, living out what they felt was the best relation for her to have with her preadoptive history and origins. Parents who acknowledge the child's preadoptive reality need not see her history apart from them, her thoughts about searching, and the search itself as signs of disloyalty, betrayal, lack of love, or pathology. They are part of the process that began with the questions we are now familiar with—"Was I in your tummy?" "What is her name?" "Why didn't she keep me?" "Where is she now?"—questions reflecting the child's curiosity and intelligence. For the adoptee whose parents did not acknowledge and discuss her adoption or who gave some facts in a hostile way, thereby depreciating her birthparents, her wanting to meet her birthparents is the only way to at least partly compensate for the absence of positive information and ascertain the truth.

As adults we are often surprised by how much our childhood continues to affect us, how childhood issues still influence the way we think about ourselves, experience emotions and relationships, even the way our flesh feels to us. The adopted child carries the fact of being adopted into adulthood just as we carry other aspects of our particular histories. Whether the birthparents were married or not may affect her thoughts about sexuality and marriage, about pregnancy and abortion, being a single parent or relinquishing a child of her own. The adopted woman in her pregnancy and childbirth may wonder increasingly about the woman who carried her and the genes she received and is now passing on. Indeed, more women than men search out their birthmothers, and many do so around the time of pregnancy and early motherhood. This is, finally, an experience a woman knows she shares with her birthmother; in many cases it is the first and only one. If her adoptive mother was infertile, the experience of bearing a child naturally intensifies her fantasies about her birthmother. Once she herself has attached to her infant, the old and persistent question of how her birthmother could have relinquished her may recur more powerfully than ever. Particularly salient for adopted adults is the fact that their children are often the first blood relatives they have known. They can finally see themselves in someone else in a tangible way.

Those who have lost a parent know the intense feelings that can arise on special occasions, when we wish our parent were there to experience the joy or help bear the sorrow. This longing can occur throughout adulthood regardless of how many years have intervened since the death. Similarly, the adopted adult may suddenly and unexpectedly experience an acute longing for her birthparents at particularly momentous times—the birth of a child, the death of a spouse or adoptive parent, a child's graduation or marriage, an illness. At times of joy or contentment there may be deep feelings of gratitude toward both the birthparents and the adoptive parents for having given and nurtured life.

Adopters and adoptees are often out of phase with each other regarding worries, concerns, and pain around adoption.[11] For parents these worries and concerns surface before adoption and are often strongest during the child's toddlerhood, when the issue of beginning to talk with their children about adoption is often negotiated with some trepidation and sadness. By their children's adolescence they have often reached a deep level of comfort and satisfaction about adoption and truly feel that it was "no big deal," that it is indeed one way among several to begin a family. The adolescent may question everything about adoption and need to acknowledge and work through a host of positive and negative feelings about it. Their concerns overlap with and differ from their parents', but their preoccupations can remind us of our own earlier concerns. Each must resolve her feelings and thoughts about the significance of blood ties in family relations and personal identity. Parents of questioning adolescents can take heart by remembering their own experience before adopting when they grappled with what importance to give to blood ties as a foundation for a parent-child relationship. Just as the gradual resolution of these concerns bore fruit in the formation and empathic care of our families, so will the adolescent's issues find resolution in the consolidation of her identity and her more secure emergence into adulthood.

The theme of the orphan, severed from her roots, lost and then found, is archetypal and symbolic, appearing in the myths and religions of many countries. It speaks to all of us, not just those who have literally been orphaned, of a state of being vulnerable and lost, longing for roots that cannot be found, dependent on the kindness of strangers. At some psychic level we are all orphans. Is it not likely that adoptees who pursue their own fate, searching for their origins, are involved in a metaphorical as well as a literal search? Is this searcher so different from those of us who seek the wellsprings of our being in meditation, who visit the hometowns of our grandparents for clues about ourselves, or who yearn to go to the places from which our families emigrated in the expectation that we will experience some solemn, joyful resonance with these places? On this level, our children's searching—for understanding, information, homecoming— is something to be respected. It goes far beyond us, and we are fortunate if we can witness some of it.

-----

11. An observation made by Nancy Clayman, director of Adoption Services, Concord Family Service, Concord, Mass.

Chapter 4

Stories of
Parents and Children
Talking Together
about Adoption

Just like a baby teaches parents how to take care of him, [my young son] especially, has been my best teacher about adoption. . . . Try as I may to control his experience with my wishes, he will teach me through being open to his experience, and through his teaching I help our daughter [who is also adopted].

Talking with young children about adoption is the occasion for the unfolding of a mutual teaching. We have seen that we must help our young children come to understand the various pieces of the story that together form the reality of being adopted, that this process goes on throughout childhood and adolescence, constantly revised and reexperienced at each step of their social, cognitive, and affective development. They, in turn, teach us how they experience their adoptedness and how they assimilate our words through the years. The experience of being adopted includes all of our children's understandings of adoption—preconceptual and conceptual. It is through this mutual teaching of child and parent, this reciprocal dialogue in which each tries to understand the other, that adoptive families live together in their "shared fate" (Kirk 1964).

Let us pause for a moment and relax our eyes, our eyes vigilantly looking for adoption issues. When we do so, what we see in the stories you are about to read shows us toddlers playing around themes of nurturance and care with their parents, young children beginning to wonder where they were before they were here. We see children fascinated by being in tummies and being born like other living creatures, children happy that their arrival in the lives of their parents was an occasion for joy and thanksgiving. We see children beginning to think about all the differences around them and among them, struggling to widen their world while remaining safe. We see curious children, eager to learn all they can about their situation, their origins, their possibilities. We see children who use anger, as the rest of us do, to differentiate themselves from others and claim their separateness, children whose anger sometimes covers sadness or hurt or confusion. We see children returning to the haven of their parents' arms and grounding themselves in their parents' stories about them before stretching into more complex understandings of the world. We see young people longing for a connection to the past, struggling to clarify a sense of identity through that connection so that they can go more ably and confidently into their own futures.

We see parents cherishing their moments of closeness and honesty with their children, parents afraid of the world's power to hurt their children, to cause them pain. We see parents struggling to put aside their own feelings and agendas in order to hear out their children and understand their feelings as separate and important. We hear parents moved by their children's unexpected insights, wisdom, and intense feelings and parents surprised by their children's capacity, after intense discussions about their past, to shift emotional gears and reenter the daily concerns of the present. We see parents struggling to allow their children to be themselves, to establish their independence and their separate identities.

Indeed, we see how these adopted children and their parents are like all children and all parents. The adoptive legacy frames these very human wonderings, feelings, and desires. Through the particular language of adoption, child and parent can create together a model for sharing feelings and concerns, for experiencing honesty and intimacy, for receiving others with empathy and respect. It is a model that, once established, becomes available for a lifetime.

Teddy and Anna

Teddy: I don't want [my birthfather] to find me. He'd take me away. He'd change his mind.
Anna: You know, [in adoption] somebody wins and somebody loses.

When I initially agreed to tell some of our adoption stories it seemed so easy, and yet, as the weeks have gone by and I have procrastinated or, rather, not consciously chosen to make some time in an always hectic schedule, I have had to face the fact that there is something painful for me in the telling. For one who can stand in front of hundreds of people and tell anecdotes of the most personal nature it seems strange. But when I think about how emotional this issue is for all of us in our family I should not be surprised. My wish has always been that my children will feel normal, that they will feel that all their questions about their adoption have been resolved, and that they will experience being our children as a wonderful and natural occurrence. And so, in telling the stories, which of course often reveal what a painful conflict being adopted is for them—and this is their reality no matter what my wish—in effect I have to confront the split between my wish and reality. It strikes me as I write this that Teddy and Anna *often* confront this split. Sometimes they let me in on the pain and sometimes they do not. They—we all—need to stay aware and continue to try to find the words for this split as we stay in the reality that this indeed is *our* family.

To begin with, I was not yet prepared to adopt when our dear Teddy was born. Two weeks prior to his birth, exactly two weeks as a matter of fact, I reached the end of my capacity to continue in infertility treatment. No matter what the doctors said, I knew in my true core that I was finished with anyone tampering with my body, with being depressed and trying to force a pregnancy. For me the long process ended in a solid hour of gut-wrenching sobs on the floor of the bathroom, followed by a kind of peace I had not felt in four years. I truly handed this pain over to my higher power, not in words or in bargaining but spiritually, physically, and emotionally. I was finished with pregnancy and was ready to move to adoption. That was nine years ago, and in those nine years I've had barely a twinge of jealousy and never a regret.

Within a few days of the decision I began to network for adoption. I had never been to an adoption readiness seminar or even talked with many people who had adopted. I made two contacts, mostly to try to practice how to do it.

One week later Teddy was born at a local hospital. Teddy's birthparents had made no arrangements for his adoption and asked the hospital to do so. One of the contacts I had made was a social worker there. And so Teddy became the son of two parents who had spent a week preparing to adopt, who were about to leave for a Thanksgiving trip and would not have become his parents at all if they had not answered the phone on the way out the door to take a cab to the airport. We chose his name somewhere on the highway on the way to family court: Theodore. It was months later, in looking it up in a "Name Your Baby" book, that we realized how appropriate the name was. It means "gift of God." If we had left fifteen minutes earlier, we would not have received the gift!

I was prepared for pregnancy, and then I was prepared to deal with the adoption process, but I, *we,* were totally unprepared for the actual baby. My baby-care preparation consisted of fifteen minutes in the hospital. Our VCR came with more instructions! I was not even prepared to figure out how to keep this adorable creature alive for twenty-four hours. Bonding? I remember frantically trying to rearrange my work schedule, moving furniture, and looking enviously at pregnant women in baby departments, not because they were pregnant but because they had the chance to buy what the baby needed *before* the arrival.

Fortunately, I have learned that a baby teaches its parents how to take care of him—and Teddy has been my best teacher about adoption. Try as I may to control his experience with my wishes, he will teach me through my being open to *his* experience; and it is through his teaching that I help our daughter, Anna. In this process I also hold onto my own experience, which is, in spite of, or because of, the pain, this: I am so grateful that these are our children and that we are a family.

Embarrassing to admit with what I know now, I found out the bare minimum about Teddy's birthparents and proceeded on the assumption that he would be exactly like a birthchild (whatever that means). From his earliest age I spoke of "adoption" in glowing terms and fantasized about the day he would be old enough to ask the important questions, and Rich and I would have all the answers! Of course, these imaginary conversations would always occur around the fireplace, hot chocolate in steaming mugs, or right before bedtime, when we would snuggle together and celebrate the miracle of adoption together in a kind of love-fest of eternal gratitude. It feels embarrassing to put this on paper—my very powerful wish to save him and myself the pain of adoption.

The first experience I'd like to tell is actually the first time Teddy brought up the subject of his adoption on his own.

We were alone in the car, Teddy in the back seat. We were spending a few days alone together at a resort in Michigan. We had just stopped at a Dairy Queen, and I was pulling out of the parking lot when a little voice from the back seat said, "So, where is he?" To which I replied, "Who?" With all the righteous indignation a four-year-old can muster for being misunderstood he said, "My father!" I said, "Dad's in Chicago; he'll be up tomorrow," to which Teddy responded, "Not him, my *real father.* Where *is* he?"

I am not equipped to express the absolute desolation and terror I felt at hearing those three words, "my real father." I remember that it was a balmy day, the top was down on the car, and I had the sense that I was freezing. I couldn't see my son; he was behind me. I was in the left lane of traffic by then and couldn't pull over. Most important, I realized that I had to respond to his question, not insist that Rich was his real father. His question mattered, not my feelings. I am sure all these feelings occurred in a matter of seconds, but it felt like hours before I could find my voice. In looking back I believe it was not an accident that he chose to ask at a time when he could look at me but I couldn't see him, nor could he see my face.

I said, "Honey, I don't know where your birthfather is. When you were born he lived in Chicago."

"Why don't you know where he is now?"

"Because I don't know your birthfather and he doesn't know me, and people who don't know each other can't know these things."

"Good."

"What do you mean, 'good'?"

"I don't want him to find me."

"What do you feel would happen if he found you?"

"He'd take me away; he'd change his mind. I'd get kidnapped by him."

"You think your biological father wants to come find you and take you away from us?"

"I don't know. Maybe. Why didn't he want me?"

I don't remember what I said at this point. I felt so much pain for him I could barely think. I remember that he said something about his being a bad baby and then switched to talking about his daddy being a bad man. I remember that what seemed to help him was my staying with the absolute truth. "Babies are never bad," "parents who give their babies up are not bad people," and "I didn't know your father, but I know he and your birthmom were getting a divorce and they wanted you to have two parents who would be together and be a family." As soon as I committed to say only what I knew for certain, my feeling of panic evaporated, but I felt numb, the way I used to feel after an exhausting race when I swam competitively, as though I just wanted to sleep and sleep and sleep.

When we got back to the cottage I asked him a few questions and started talking more about his father when he told me, with perfect clarity, that he didn't want to talk about adoption any more and would let me know when he did.

And that is the way it continues. Adoption is pretty much talked about on his terms, for the length of time he decides, and that is that. Often it feels to me that we are in mid-discussion when he decides it's time to talk about Pee Wee Herman or the latest adventures of his favorite cat. And he has taught me that no matter how strong my wish to wrap up the story in a pretty pink bow it will not be that way.

Shortly after this first discussion we were again in the car and he said, "Mom, you know I'm adopted?" I said, "I know, honey, you're adopted and we're an adopted family." Giggles. "Mom, you know adoption is forever." "I know, honey, and I'm very happy about that." These few words had all the power of the sun, to hear him practice saying the words and the resolution, practicing his understanding that adoption is forever.

His fear of being kidnapped, however, has never completely gone away. It was many years before his panic about being in crowds of strangers, particularly where men were looking at him, became manageable. He's nine now, and he will still change seats in a restaurant if he catches someone staring at him. He remains convinced at some level that he could be taken back. For years he often came and slept under our bed completely covered with his blankets. He would go into an inconsolable state within seconds of losing sight of me in a supermarket. In understanding his fear I have been able to help him and see that he is not saying I am untrustworthy, but it's hard for him to believe that no one can take him back.

I am coming to grips with his wish to decide who gets to know about his adoption—with his feeling that an event that for me connotes extreme joy is for him something unpleasant, and that he wants to trust the people he tells.

One day, when I was taking several boys home after soccer practice (why is it always in the car?), one of the boys told Teddy that he didn't have to listen to me about putting on his seat belt because I wasn't his real mother. Before I could even decide whether to respond, Teddy said, "What do you think she is, a cartoon character?" He spoke in a very matter-of-fact tone of voice that clearly conveyed "discussion over."

When we got home I asked him if what Gary said bothered him, and he replied, "Gary is jealous. He doesn't have a father and I do, so he's attacking my adoption." I told him that it was really good for him to be able to figure out what was in back of someone's being hurtful.

I watch in utter awe how Teddy intuitively chooses safe people to share his story with. He and his best friend have developed long elaborate stories that contrive a way in which they might actually be blood cousins or even brothers, all in a sense of adventure and "Wow, wouldn't this be great!" I listen to him jabbering away with other adopted children or children who have adopted siblings, with an uncanny sense about who is going to be mean with the knowledge. When he has been hurt I don't try to make it all right, not any longer. I've learned from him that when someone is deliberately hurtful the key word is "ignorant."

At one point he liked to tell his adoption story; now, at nine, he doesn't. At the beginning of school this year the children were asked to bring in their baby pictures and biographies. When I asked Teddy if he wanted his adoption picture he said no, he just wanted to be "normal" this year. He said this was a year when he felt sad about it, not glad. I said I felt sad sometimes too, and in his usual way he said, "Yup, I know you do." I reminded him how glad I was that he was my son, and he said, "I know that." End of discussion.

I'm glad to have had the experience of dealing with his fear and heartbreak. This year we discovered that he has some slight neurological immaturities that are due to his birthmother's drinking during her pregnancy. As a result he needs extra help in some areas. He is relieved to discover he is not stupid, but he caught me being very careful about how I was explaining what was wrong. He said, "Does it have to do with 'them'? Were they stupid people?" I said I doubted that very much but that it might have to do with his birthmother's not doing what she needed to do while she was pregnant, and that now we had to take care of the problem by being extra careful about food, going to tutoring, and other things. He was able to say he was really mad about that, and I was able to say that, as grateful as I felt to his birthparents for having him, I was kind of mad too. More important, I was sad that I hadn't been pregnant with him so that I could have taken better care of him.

And he and Anna keep teaching me about the truth.

Anna in many ways seems to have a different pattern in dealing with adoption. She seems to have a constant need to talk about and make sense of things.

My first clear memory of her in this context is taking a walk with her and her best friend, who is also adopted, when they were both around age four. They had been talking about their grandmothers' deaths and what death means, about being gone, going to heaven, when suddenly Anna's friend said, "And my birthmother is gone too." Anna said her birthmom was gone too but she didn't think she was dead like grandmom, just gone away. Her friend said she didn't think her birthmom was dead either but had to go away so her real mom could have her (real moms in this conversation were adoption moms). They went on like this for a while, and there was obvious confusion about adoption. I stayed out of it since I wasn't included in the conversation, and then Anna, with four-year-old directness, said, "The way I see adoption is like this. Somebody has the baby but can't keep the baby and goes 'Wah, wah, wah. Good-bye, Baby,' and somebody who can't get a baby in their tummy says 'Oh great, a baby. Goody, goody, goody. Hello, Baby.' You know, somebody wins and somebody loses!"

Hearing and seeing my daughter, hands on hips, giving a lecture on adoption to another four-year-old was mind-boggling. The whole event ended with them holding hands, walking merrily down the street, dripping Popsicles in hand.

Since then the pain Anna feels in her passionate wish to have come out of my tummy, her insistence that I *did* breast-feed her, her despair over the obvious dissimilarity between her gorgeous curls and my straight hair, and her determination that we be exactly the same feel like different issues from Teddy's. Where he wants reassurance that he resembles his dad, Anna needs constant reassurance that we look *exactly* alike. By a nice accident of fate, Anna's birthmother and I do resemble each other, and when I show her the picture of her birthparents she finds this a great comfort. She also likes to remember that her birthmother and I met and liked each other. She finds comfort in the bridge between us, and also at times she will sling out phrases like "[her birthmother's name] would not like it that you're mean to me" (her usual response to "Go get your shoes" or "Take your toys back to your room"). Mostly she indicates that this knowing each other is a good thing. I wish I could provide the same comfort for Teddy.

I know at this point that when she bursts into tears and says she hates being adopted, putting my arms around her and saying that I too wish she had come out of my tummy because I love her so much is exactly what she needs. Next year, next month, it might be something different, but that's what adoption means to her at five.

●

Laura and Maya

Laura: Mommy, you're not *really, really* my mommy, are you?
Maya: Let's call [my birthmom] Forsythia.

As a one- and two-year-old Laura enjoyed looking at her baby pictures while I recounted to her how she came to be part of our family—how her father and I had wanted a baby, found out that Laura had been born in Brazil, hopped on a plane and flew and flew until we came to Natal, Brazil, where she was born. There we were met by a friend, Sonia, and taken to a small nursery with several babies in cribs. Sonia pointed to Laura, who was just sixteen days old, small and beautiful in her crib. I went over, filled with happiness to see Laura at last. I picked her up in my arms, hugged and kissed her, and felt unspeakably joyful to be holding her at last. Then I gave Laura to her daddy to hold. He was so happy to see her and be her daddy that he was crying. Laura was delighted to be the center of this story of excitement and joy. By age two she wanted to act out the happy finding of Laura over and over again, pretending to be baby Laura snuggling in her mommy's and daddy's arms.

In addition she would eagerly enjoin us to pretend that she was a bunny or other small animal in the woods, which we came upon while taking a walk. The bunny would initially surprise us, then would want to come home with us to live in our house and be our baby bunny. Sometimes the story included her younger sister as a fellow bunny to be found and loved, but more often it focused on herself. These two scenarios of being found and loved were among her favorite play scenes, enacted almost daily in some version, always with closeness, warmth, and joy. In this context of play her specific concerns about adoption first arose.

Right after Laura had turned three years old she rather frantically demanded of her father, "Take off my skin, Daddy. Take it off!" At first we were struck by her sense of her body—her feeling that parts can be added and taken off at will. We worried that Laura had become uncomfortable with her skin color, which is light tan, while ours is somewhat paler. Her father reassured her that he liked her skin and was not going to hurt it, that it was lovely. A week later, she asked me to take off her hands and replace them with my own. I asked her what she did not like about her own, or what she preferred about mine. Laura did not mention color as the important factor but size. While praising Laura's sweet and clever hands, at her insistence I pretended to unscrew them and replace them with mine. This pleased her, and she passed on to another play scene with her mommy's hands.

A month later, at a party for Indian toddlers, which Laura attended with her younger sister, a mother who did not know Laura asked her if she were from India. Laura said no, she was from Brazil. The woman then proceeded to put her fingers through Laura's curly black hair and to touch her cheek, saying something like, "There is a little girl in my neighborhood from Brazil, but her hair and skin are different from yours." Laura turned to me and, with hands on hips, said emphatically and angrily, "You are *not* my mother." The other adoptive mothers looked incredulous, unable to believe that they had heard a child of three uttering the words they were afraid they would hear when their children were in their adolescent years: "You are not my mother."

I was stunned. Despite having talked with lots of three-year-olds about their versions of all the important things in life—birth, death, love, friendship, illness, conflict, caring—I had not until this moment realized how I would be called upon to be with my young daughter in the reality of her adoptedness. I had thought she would be older, that toddlerhood would pass without this pain.

I suddenly realized that the stranger who had intrusively addressed Laura had unwittingly touched upon the area of concern Laura had been trying to tell us about—namely, that she was perceiving differences between her looks and mine, and that this was beginning to mean something about her relationship to me. She was noticing differences and she did not like them. She wanted her skin and hands to be replaced by Mommy's. I tried to approach her to talk with her, but she was preoccupied with the other children. Later, she could not pick up the thread of her proclamation. This aspect of conversation with a three-year-old I found very frustrating. I was upset by her statement, wanting to know more about what she meant, wanting to make it better. She was happily involved in her life, seemingly not giving a thought to her eruption.

A few days later I decided that it would be good to bring the baby photo books out in case there was something that needed to be worked out with her. She went directly to the pictures and asked to pretend that she was in Brazil and that I was coming to get her. We played the scene of our meeting in the usual joyful way. And as usual, we played it several times at her request. Then she asked me to play it a different way, indicating that when Sonia showed me baby Laura I should say, "It's the wrong baby." At first I protested, claiming that she wasn't the wrong baby, that we had known she was the right baby, Laura. As though to say "Of course, of course" to that, she still insisted that we act it out as it had occurred to her. Apprehensively I agreed, not yet knowing what she was getting at, but knowing that we needed to play it out to discover the meaning. I picked up the baby from the crib Sonia had pointed to, looked into the baby's face, and said, "Oh, no. It's the wrong baby." Laura directed me to put her back into the crib. I did so reluctantly. Then she popped up from the pretend crib as though to surprise me, and most cheerily said, "No, I *am* Laura." I rushed over to pick her up and show my jubilation at being united with her. She was delighted and had us replay this "wrong baby" scene twice. Then she asked about what had happened when Maya, her younger adopted sister, was a baby. But as I began to speak, she lost interest, returned to a TV program, and that was that. She seemed happy, full, loved.

Only weeks later did I understand that her intuition about the arbitrariness of how adoptive babies and parents are matched had come at least in part from the way I had presented the initial image—there had been several babies in cribs in the nursery. To me, of course, this had had no meaning, since I was enormously directed toward only one of them. But for Laura this element must have been disturbing. At four, this theme of rightness of match was happily incorporated into her baby play. She would snuggle in my lap, pretending to be a baby, and say, "Mommy, you tell Daddy, 'This is just the right baby, Daddy.'" I would, and Laura would smile from ear to ear, basking in this knowledge.

The day after this "right baby" scene we went to a farm where Laura and Maya saw a huge sow nursing her piglets. When a close friend of mine, well loved by Laura, came over later in the day Laura introduced her to many episodes of pretending to be a baby bunny, a baby skunk, and a baby raccoon in the woods. She directed Francine or me to discover "the baby" and ask her to go to our house. Then she enlisted her sister, Maya, as another baby pig, both of them nursing from Francine, the mother pig. Laura then directed me in the role she imagined for me. She urged me to take her away from her mother to live in my house. It seemed to me that she was initiating play around the theme of having two caretakers: a mother you nurse from and another you live with. Since I had not yet brought up anything about her birthmother, I was once again surprised at her intuitive leap.

I approached the mother pig and said that her baby would like to come with me to my house. I added, without Laura's direction, that I would take very good care of her. Francine added, "Do you promise?" I did. Laura had us go off happily to a pretend house and seemed in an exuberant mood. She had us play this several times, with her sucking Francine's sweater. I decided to put words to the two caretakers and said that the Francine pig was her "tummy-mommy" and that I would be the mommy she would live with for always. She seemed delighted by and interested in this. Then, after we had replayed it, she asked me to "squish" her, to hold her too tightly. I protested at first, saying, "I will never squish you. I am your new mommy and I love you very much. Also I promised your tummy-mommy I would take good care of you." But again she insisted on this scenario, so I complied. I held her tightly and said "Squish." She pretended to cry and rushed toward her tummy-mommy who jumped into the scene to protect her. Then she asked her tummy-mommy if she could come with me again to live at my house. Her tummy-mommy wanted me to promise not to hurt or squish her again. I promised. Laura again came off with me happily, seemingly without regret. Then she announced that I had to squish her again. I once again pretended to, not knowing where this was going. Again the tummy-mommy pig intervened. I apologized and promised not to squish her again. She came with me again happily, seemingly protected by this coalition of mothers, the earlier one keeping a check on the later one. Feeling protected, she went off to play something else.

I remember at the time worrying about the meaning of the "squishing" part of Laura's scene, as well as about her dealing so early with the theme of having two mothers. Later I was heartened to understand that in *her* mind having two mothers was a safe situation, one of checks and balances, of being fussed over and protected. Although she did not yet know this piece of her story, her intuition was fairly accurate—her mother had painstakingly searched for parents to take good care of Laura, had met us and been reassured that we would love Laura dearly.

Four days after this two-mother scene, we were playing at another adoptive family's house. The mother talked about how her daughter's brothers came to the airport to greet their new sister from India. Laura spontaneously wanted to replay her story of our coming to get her in Brazil, to show it to the others. I added that when we got home to Boston, her big brother, Jeff, was waiting for her at the airport, and how happy he was to hold her. She smiled from ear to ear and then settled back into making spaghetti and worms from clay.

A week later while we were watching a television program about a black family, she turned to me and said cheerily, but curiously, "You're not really my mommy." Again it seemed that perhaps seeing racial differences on television was connecting her to some sense that I was not her mom. I countered saying, "No, I am really your mommy, and I will always be really your mommy." She went back to the program. After it was over we went into the kitchen to make some popcorn. Then she smiled and said, "But, Mommy, you're not *really, really* my mommy, are you?" I gulped and said, "I was not your tummy-mommy, the one whose tummy you grew inside, but I am your mommy who will always take good care of you and love you and live with you." As though I had adequately addressed what she was getting at, she went on to say, "You know what I want when I grow up?" "No, what?" "I want to get so tiny that I can get into your tummy," she said, lovingly and somewhat wistfully. I said, "That would really be wonderful, wouldn't it?" And we gave each other a big snuggly hug.

Three days later, it so happened that I was on a family retreat with my daughters; my husband was not with us. Laura was sleeping in the same room with Maya and me, which is extremely rare. Excited by our proximity, she stayed up very late talking to me. At around eleven o'clock, as she was snuggled next to me, she asked, "Mommy, do you know who my favorite friends are?" "No, who?" I asked with interest. "Joseph, Eric, Hannah. Mommy, do you know who my favorite mommy is?" "No, who?" She threw her arms around me and jubilantly announced that it was I. She went through this questioning again and then fell asleep.

I sensed that this was the end of an intense two months in which her perception of the difference between her skin color and mine had led her to the theme of two mothers. I still cannot account for the route of reasoning she went through, since children her age do not understand the word *adoption* or genetic similarities in the way adults do. All I can say is that by age three and a half she had introduced some essential adoptive themes: looking different from your adoptive parents, the random element in adoption (the "wrong baby"), the negotiation between the mother you nurse from and the one you live with, and the problem that having two mothers makes for coming to some determination about who is really the mother and who is the preferred mother.

She fell asleep in my arms, and I lay awake in the dark, thinking about her world—happy that she seemed content about her circumstances, sad that she had needed to be uprooted from her birthfamily in order to be well cared for. In retrospect, I do not think I fully realized that this sadness was not hers but mine. Thinking it was hers at such a young age increased my own sadness and difficulty.

After that, there were three months of calm regarding adoption despite occasions when strangers made insensitive and thoughtless comments about adoption within her earshot. She occasionally had us find the baby bunny in the woods, but not as often as previously. Then for about a week, when I would lie down next to her before bedtime, she would place her head on my pelvic bone. This seemed strange to me. Then one night she wanted to pretend to be Maya. She announced that Maya was in my tummy and was about to be born. She lay her head in the exact same spot as on the preceding nights. I mention this only to underline how birth and adoption are dealt with nonverbally in many ways we do not grasp at the time. "Maya" was born, and I greeted the event with joy and snuggling. We played this again on the next night. I suspected that she had begun to think that Maya had been in my tummy and felt jealous that she had not. On the third night when she played this, I gently said, "You know, Maya was never in my tummy. I went to India to adopt her, the same way I went to Brazil to adopt you." Her body seemed to relax on hearing this, and she fell asleep.

The next night she started out with Laura's being in my tummy, then coming out and being greeted by me. She was delighted with this play and repeated it at bedtime for several nights. Fearful that her wish fulfillment would overpower her knowledge that she had not been in my tummy, I decided to enact with her how it had been. I said, "You know, Laura, first you were born from your tummy-mommy's tummy, and then Mommy and Daddy came to Brazil to get you, and love you, and become your parents." We played this out. Then she introduced a new variation. She had me ask God, "Where is my baby Laura, God?" Then she had God answer, "She is coming very soon." Sometimes she would have my tummy rumble and pretend to pop out of it. Sometimes, less frequently, she would have God say, "She is in Brazil. You can find her there." We would do so in play.

I was anxious about how often I should correct her pretending to be in my tummy with the reality. I decided to do so very infrequently. Once when I did so because of my own anxiety about her misleading herself with fantasy, she reprimanded me sharply, "I don't want you to go to Brazil to get me. God says I'm coming from your tummy very soon." I left it up to her and found that she alternated her versions, though frankly preferring the fantasy of being inside me, coming out, and happily surprising me.

Several months before she turned four, Laura and I went for a brisk November walk. As we left the house I reached out to take her hand. As I did so she said, "Some day, Mom, you should have skin on your hands like my color." "Do you like your color better?" I asked her, happy that at this moment the solution to our difference was not taking off her skin, as previously. "Yes," she answered assuredly. "I would like to have your color, because it is so pretty," I added quite truthfully. "But you know, Laura, I'll always have my color and you'll always have yours." "Why?" How was I to explain this without any understanding on her part about the permanence of bodily features, genetics, or the existence of different races? "God gave me this color when I was born," I ventured. "What is it?" she asked. "Kind of pinkish-beige with lots of freckles. God gave you a pretty tan, and Maya a deep brown." "Why?" I knew I had failed, and she knew it. She pushed on, as she was to do throughout this walk, as though she had some sense of where she needed to get to. Again I fumbled and oversimplified. "People from different places often have different-colored skins. People who come from Brazil often have tan skin. People from Texas, like me, often have this pinkish-freckled skin, and people from India often have brown skin like Maya." (Some relaxing little walk, I joked to myself.) How long might these questions have remained inside if we had not pulled away from the hubbub of the house to be with just each other?

"Mom, did Maya's nurse have brown skin too?" Since Maya never had a nurse, I thought Laura was referring to her birthmother, but I wasn't sure. "Who do you mean?" A bit impatiently she replied, "You know who I mean, her waitress. Did she have brown skin too?" "Do you mean the woman who took care of Maya until Mommy came to get her?" This was ridiculous because Laura had been too young to understand the nature of Maya's care in the orphanage while it was happening, and it had not been discussed with her since. "Yes," Laura said. "Yes, she had brown skin too, like Maya." I must have felt momentary relief that my unconscious turn away from her question had seemed to satisfy her. Not for long.

"Mom, did mine have my skin?" "Who, sweetie?" "My lady, did she have my color?" "Yes, the lady who took care of you till Mommy and Daddy came for you had your color."

We walked and I thought. I suspected that her "lady" and "nurse" and "waitress" all really referred to the birthmother, since we had never dis-cussed other caretakers in any detail. Leaping over my own resistance to talking with her directly about her birthmother at such an early age, I tried to address her questions more head on. "Usually, a baby is the same color as her tummy-mommy, the lady whose tummy she is in as a very tiny baby." "Was I?" "Yes, you are the same pretty color as your tummy-mommy. Maya is the same color as her tummy-mommy." She seemed thoughtful for a minute or two and then began to skip around mud puddles.

Again I was stunned by how strongly her color initiated her thoughts around her adoptive past. I was moved by her attempts to name this person—"nurse," "waitress," "my lady"—who had indeed nursed her and served her. By the end of her fourth year Laura seemed comfortable with and proud of her skin color and curly, dark hair. Physical differences, however, remain a frequent topic of conversation in our household. Laura associates her skin color and hair with those of her birthmother and her birthcountry. She actively looks for people who look like her and inquires hopefully whether or not they are from "my place."

She incorporates "my place" into her rivalry with her younger sister, claiming "my place is more beautiful than yours!" (This was done even before understanding what a "country" is.) One summer, these two sisters, then aged two and a half and three and a half, began to argue in the back seat of the car:

Laura: My place is more beautiful than yours.

Maya: No, India is more beautiful than Brazil.

Laura: It's my turn, so we get to visit Brazil next.

Maya: No, we're going to India.

Laura: We just visited India! I miss *my* people.

Since Laura had never visited India, I was puzzled. In conversation with her I determined that she thought India was the church where we had recently gone to an Indian gathering. Indeed, there was "missing" afoot, since we were all away from home on vacation. So indeed, birthcountries could be assimilated into sibling rivalry with the same ease that everything else is! At six, during a similar episode, she explained that Brazil and India are different "planets."

It is fortunate that she attempted to get her bearings about physical differences so early, for soon her agemates began to make comments that would probably have been even more hurtful than they were if she had not come to like her appearance and have a positive way of thinking about her differentness. At four, a close friend of hers teased her: "You can't match your mother"; three other friends teased her and her darker sister: "You two are black; you two are black." As a family we talk about prejudice and teasing, struggling to put lessons about these into words young children can understand.

Several times, when a woman stranger has shown Laura some kind attention, she has asked me if this is her mother, meaning her birthmother. The summer before her fifth birthday, Sonia, the Brazilian woman who facilitated her adoption, visited us. Laura wondered if Sonia was her birthmother.

She formed a quick affection for this loving woman. Several months later we had the following conversation in the car driving home from nursery school.

"Mom, did you know that people eat turtle eggs in China? Isn't that disgusting?"

"I don't think so. We eat chicken eggs, and I'll bet they taste just about the same."

"I ate turtle eggs in Brazil when I was a baby."

"No, you were too young. You drank milk—"

"From my mother who came to visit us?"

"No, Laura, Sonia was not your tummy-mommy. Sonia helped Teresa, your tummy-mommy, find a good family for you. Us."

"I want my tummy-mommy to come and visit us and see my school."

"That would be nice, Laura. But Teresa can't come now."

"But why? Sonia came from Brazil."

"Teresa can't come here now. But some day we could go and visit her in Brazil, if you would like."

"But I want to see her now."

"You must really miss Teresa sometimes, even though you can't remember her exactly."

Laura was sad and whimpered a bit. Maya then said: "Laura, be quiet. You make me scared when you sound like that." I suggested that it was Laura's sadness about not being able to see her tummy-mommy now that frightened Maya. She agreed. The mood suddenly changed, and the sisters began to plan their afternoon snack.

A week later, on the drive home from school, Laura was unusually sad that one of her favorite teachers was soon leaving to have a baby. Then she shared a worry that had obviously made this situation sadder for her than it might have been otherwise. "Mom, if I didn't come out of your tummy, does that mean I can never have a baby come out of mine?" "Oh no, Laura," I replied. "You came out of Teresa's tummy, and you can have as many babies as you want come out of your tummy when you decide to be a mommy." Her face lit up happily as she announced, "I want to have two babies: one girl and one boy. And they will love each other just like Maya and I do!"

A month later at bedtime, her interest in making babies intersected with adoption, as inevitably as her earlier interest in physical differences. She animatedly asked where the womb is, how a baby comes out, where it comes out, how it nurses.

Laura: Mom, where does the mommy buy the seed?

Me: She doesn't buy it. The father gives it to her.

Laura: Did Daddy give you my seed?

Me: No, remember you grew in Teresa's womb, so her man gave her your seed.

Laura: I don't want to have one mommy and then another mommy. I want to have stayed in Brazil with Teresa.

Me: Teresa was a very good tummy-mommy, but she wasn't prepared to be your day-to-day mom. It was not time yet for her to be the kind of mother I am to you.

Laura: I miss her.

Me: I know you do.

A short silence was broken by her sitting up in bed, smiling, and asking, "Well, how does the man get the seed inside the womb?" Her adoption story, her birth story, and her own fantasies about being a mother were being blended. At seven she announced further thoughts at dinner: "You know, it's not a nice thing for a man to give a woman a seed if she can't be a good mother yet. . . . I've been trying to think this out in my head."

Laura, now seven and a half, has a passionate interest in Brazil, particularly its music and rain forest. She seems more at peace with her tan skin and prideful of it, her silky black curls, and her Brazilian birthplace. She continues to want to meet Teresa, and we hope this will be possible. In her fantasy it has already happened. When asked by her kindergarten teacher to talk about adoption to her class, she cheerfully told them that each summer we vacation in Brazil with her tummy-mommy. This wish to bring the important figures of her childhood together is intense when expressed and stable over time, though she doesn't bring it up frequently.

One night, on the verge of going to sleep, she asked if Joan, her godmother, was her tummy-mommy. I reminded her that Teresa was. "I want to be with her," she stated dreamily and sadly. I acknowledged her sadness and asked if she had any questions about Teresa. "Yes. How long was I with her before you came?" "Sixteen days," I answered. "Good. Sixteen days." She calculated. "That's a long time. I miss her." She snuggled up closer to me and fell asleep in my arms.

At Father's Day this year her teacher asked her to write out her definition of a father for the card she was making. It read: "A father is like having three mothers!"

What surprises me as I recount this sequence of play and conversation on adoptive themes is the discrepancy between my internal experience during this time and hers. Often I worried about whether I was navigating this correctly, whether it was wrong that she was so involved with her adoption at such an early age. I felt sad that her first relationship had been disrupted and apprehensive about the grieving for her birthmother, in the present and in the future. Any difficult feelings Laura had always seemed to pass quickly as we played and talked, yielding to her generally lively happiness and curiosity. I would not wish on a child the need for separation from her birthfamily, but I must say that this fact *has* given Laura and me an early way to share some important thoughts and feelings, which I treasure.

In large part the discrepancy between her experience and mine is because we have not yet shared the same experience. The story I have told Laura about her adoption day is just a piece of the story she will come to know. I anticipate that just as we have shared sadness about her not having been in my tummy, we will come to share sadness about the difficulty of her birthfamily's life in northeastern Brazil. Though I have mentioned to her that many mothers in that part of the world worry about having enough to feed their children, she has not shown much curiosity about this yet.

First through stepparenting, now through adoptive parenting, I've learned that coming to love someone means making room in your heart for the other important people in their lives. With this room made, these other relationships begin to take on a life of their own, becoming gifts in their own right—despite difficulty and struggle.

Laura has brought with her into my life her birthmother, her birthgrandmother, and her young aunts and uncles. The difference is that I know them and she does not. I carry images and thoughts of her birthmother, Teresa, as I love Laura's face each day, as I remember and learn about her place, northeastern Brazil, and feel for Teresa's struggle.

The story of my meetings with Laura's birthmother and her family has been side by side in my mind with the one I have shared with Laura—the story of her adoption day. Side by side with my joy at meeting Laura has been my sadness for her birthmother's situation and my respect for her determination to find good parents for her baby so that Laura could have a different, more hopeful life than her own.

Several hours after I met and held Laura for the first time, Sonia, who had arranged the adoption, said we should leave Laura with the maid and go to meet Laura's mother because it was time to pick up more breast milk. I had known I would be able to meet her mother, and indeed wanted to do so, to make sure that her decision to relinquish Laura was freely and deeply made, and to be able to share with Laura what I could of her birthfamily's story. Yet the announcement was jarring—how could I emotionally be expected to meet the birthmother three hours after I met my daughter? The car was waiting. I handed over the baby to the maid and sunk into the familiar feeling I had had back home—that adopting entails doing all sorts of things that seem beyond one's endurance. One simply does them.

That first meeting was awkward. I was unprepared for Teresa's situation. Her employers—she worked as a live-in domestic—invited us into the living room, but Teresa was expected to stay on the outskirts of the room, ready to bring us refreshments. My hugging her appeared strange in this setting, where class lines were strictly observed. Her employer seemed protective of her, as though Teresa was younger than her years, and she managed what translated conversation there was between us. I remember searching Teresa's face, seeing it already in my baby's, fascinated to think that this image before me would be something like my child's—as though I was stealing a glimpse into the future.

We needed Teresa's birth certificate for the adoption decree, and her mother was in possession of it. So the next day, I again handed Laura over to the maid and set out with Teresa for the village where she was born and raised, where her mother, Laura's birthgrandmother, was still living with ten other children and pregnant with her twelfth. We left a spacious house, replete with pool and walled garden, and passed through the city of Natal and into the interior countryside of northeastern Brazil. This rural countryside is alternately plagued by droughts and floods. It is a countryside owned not by the people who farm it but by a few exploitative landowners, a countryside farmed not to sustain its inhabitants but to export sugar for alcohol. The vast sugar cane crop devours its workers' energy, the humus in the soil, and the competing small crops the workers eat. I knew how efforts at land reform had been largely crushed through wealth, violence, and political manipulation. And I knew that this region's sorrow came from being one of the poorest on earth.

When I returned that day, my sensibility was no longer abstract. At what closer range could I, an upper-middle-class white American professional, see this degree of poverty? On that morning it entered my family, my life, through Laura, and it has begun to change me in small ways—in how I think about, spend, and donate money; in what I think is worthwhile to teach my students; in reframing the work I want to do in my lifetime. By virtue of my privilege, the insularity of twenty-five years of formal schooling, I was ignorant. I had seen poverty at close range before, but never such extreme poverty and never in so intimate a relation to myself as now, through my child's family.

But let me tell you what I saw, because this is what I think of when Laura asks adoption questions. I feel in my stomach what she will need to deeply understand her origins. My present attempts to help pave the way seem so feeble: assembling UNICEF boxes, having her pick out food for the local soup kitchen, talking about poverty and the sadness parents feel when they don't have enough money to feed their children well. Let me tell you what I see and hear when Laura asks for Teresa's name or talks about northeastern Brazil as "her place."

We drove for several hours, over increasingly primitive roads with endless forks that confused even Teresa, our only guide to the village. Then, at the edge of a village of twenty or so small mud dwellings, I saw two four-year-old boys playing happily with a dead rat as though it were a toy. One of the boys had no clothes on; the other was in rags. Teresa indicated which dwelling was hers. Twenty feet across from it lay a sugar cane field that dwarfed everything and everyone, its tall canes stretching to the horizon. The sun was high in the sky. It must have been about 100 degrees. The road was dusty; the children now surrounding the stopped car were dusty; the air itself was dusty.

A pregnant woman, partly toothless, who looked quite old, emerged from the doorway nearest to us and embraced Teresa. I realized that she was Laura's grandmother and that the flock of children I had seen were Teresa's brothers and sisters, Laura's young aunts and uncles. A dark tan three-year-old with startling blue eyes and hair bordering on a blond Afro befriended me on sight. He was Laura's little uncle Eduard. He asked me if I wanted to sit down inside on a crate—which turned out to be the only piece of furniture I saw except for several graying hammocks strung up on the ceiling. I think I said "No, thank you," but I can't remember because of what happened next.

The "old" woman—who turned out to be thirty-eight, my age now—approached me smiling and talking. My friend translated: "She wants to know why you didn't bring the baby. She wants to see her granddaughter." The breath went out of me. I had assumed that Teresa had either brought Laura to see her mother or that her mother had traveled into town to help with or after the birth. My ignorance was profound.

The distance we had just crossed in our car in the course of almost two hours was a distance that some of the people here had never traveled. Those who had made that journey did not do so often or easily. There were no cars here, no bus, no telephone to ring up on and say, "My baby has been born." That Teresa had managed this distance, from rural countryside to the city, at the age of eighteen or nineteen was an achievement I had not yet appreciated. Nor had I yet felt the depth of her determination never to cross back on this road, never to live here again.

I would have been glad to bring Laura here, but Teresa addressed her mother directly, without uncertainty, not unhappily: "No, it is not my baby any more. It is *their* baby now." Then she turned to me, "It is *your* baby now." The moment it was said, her clarity ran counter to my sense that Laura was still more hers than mine. She had clearly taken good care of Laura in utero for nine months, careful not to drink or smoke. I had had Laura for twenty-two hours and had already abandoned her to the maid twice! Teresa's generosity in the light of these facts struck me almost physically. The rest of what I remember is almost as though it were a lucid dream, so stunned was I by her words, "It is your baby now."

Three small entirely mud rooms. No change of clothing for the ten residents. No bedding in sight. One solitary, blackened pot in the corner. A few cooking spoons. No place to store food or to keep food cool. No food in sight but the beans and rice we brought. Small openings in the walls for windows and doorway. Some relief from the sun and the heat in the dark spaces of the three "rooms." The blond boy and I winking at and liking each other. The fantasy of taking him with us.

The questions and conversation on our return trip: Teresa's father had another family as well—not uncommon, she says. They live on the other side of the village. He goes between his two wives. The children go to school several mornings a week for two years. Then they stop, because more advanced schooling is provided only in a larger village that is unreachable by foot, and there is no bus. There is also no medical care and of course no birth-control education. The water truck comes once a week, and each family fills the largest pot it has and can carry. The family's prosperity in such a place is measured by the size and quality of its pot. There is no relief from the dust, except in periods of flood, and then there is mud everywhere. All the children one sees during the day are young; the ones over five are working in the field.

Yes, we got the birth certificate. It had the wrong date on it. Had it been made out hastily by the officials, since the baby's parents could not read anyway? Or was Teresa several years younger than she thought, in a place where it didn't really matter since children were not spared difficulty or adversity or hunger?

Somehow she had gotten out of a place that she could see was a dead end, a place where you could have the joy of bearing children but then could not feed them, educate them, take care of them when they were ill. Many women named their infants "Angel" since the likelihood of a child's dying before one year of age is 50 percent in such areas.

Teresa had gotten out in one of the few ways a girl could. She became a domestic in the city. The family she worked for fell on hard times: the husband lost his job; the wife had to work nights. Teresa cooked, cleaned, looked after the children. Perhaps she was nineteen; perhaps seventeen. She was treated poorly as the household fell apart economically. Somehow she managed to leave, to travel hundreds of miles back to Natal. Pregnant, she found another job.

What did pregnancy mean to her? How could she be so clear that this was my baby now—the baby of a woman she had searched out on paper (she and her employer having managed to gain access to American home studies in order to choose what she prayed would be the right parents for Laura) but had met only the day before?

Keeping one's baby if you are a domestic maid in Natal means losing your job and traveling the long road back to the village you were born in. For Teresa, it would have meant living with her mother in those three rooms, returning to the cane fields herself. More than that, it meant watching her first child be locked into the same privations and lack of possibilities that she had as a child. It meant the very real possibility of Laura dying as an infant, the near certainty of her being uneducated, of her working in the cane fields or as a domestic. Teresa was clear that she was not going to do this kind of watching. She wrote in a letter to Laura, to be opened when Laura needs to understand why her mother chose adoption, "I do not want you to have the same sadnesses I had as a child."

Dressed in new jeans, with a bright, clean T-shirt, manicured nails, and undusty skin, she was certain that Laura's being my child and not hers was best for Laura's life and for the life she herself was now establishing away from the village, in a household where she was protected from illness and hunger.

The maid I had left Laura with was shriveled and ancient, having cared for Sonia from babyhood to her present late forties. She too led a "protected" life in this family, bringing up first one generation and then another, the children of the first. Would Teresa's life also disappear within the walls of such "protection"? My husband and I worried about this, but she seemed undepressed and unambivalent about her present situation. Was she naive or simply determined, able, courageous? Did she imagine later marrying and being a mother to her own children rather than her mother's or her employers'? Or was she satisfied for the time being simply to have escaped dire poverty?

Her clarity with us did not mean that she wasn't sad to say good-bye to her baby, my baby. When the day came, we all had tears in our eyes except Laura, who seemed happy to be held by each of us in turn.

In these six years I have written to Teresa several times, sending her pictures and news of Laura, wanting deeply for her to know how wonderful her daughter is, how much she is loved, how happy she is. Teresa never asked for these reassurances, but Sonia tells me that she welcomes them. Teresa seemed to know that she was doing the right thing. I still carry about a guilt that I have the good fortune to mother this wonderful little girl and that someone I know has had the bad fortune to have to part with her. I feel as though I have to do "it"—parenting—right, not just for Laura, but for Teresa. I have to prove she was right to be confident about me, to have chosen me for her child's mother.

I have become more involved in the politics of the region, sending money, learning about the rural land reform movement, imagining visiting there with Laura, living there for some extended time so she can learn about it. I imagine visiting Teresa with her, staying in touch with Teresa, helping her if she needs it. Then I realize my little girl's work may be in developing here the strongest roots she can. Her interests may not be development work or agrarian reform. It has been hard to realize that my experiences in Brazil need to be honored in my own life, and not projected onto Laura's tender life. We can share together some of our two different legacies from Brazil, but they will have to diverge in important ways also, ways I can't yet predict.

As I have struggled with feeling entitled to be Laura's mother, I hear this conversation in my mind, between myself and the Teresa who lives within me now:

"She is your baby now."

"I want to share her with you, Teresa."

"No, she is your baby now."

"I want to raise her close in her heart to Brazil, Teresa."

"No, she is your baby now."

"Teresa, I feel that I owe you something I can never repay."

"No, this is what I wanted for my daughter. You have helped me do what I knew was right."

She is my baby now, my daughter. Thank you, Teresa, for knowing this before I could, for guiding me in what I have needed to learn.

"She is your baby now."

"Yes, she is my baby. Thank God."

Laura's younger sister, Maya, was adopted from India at eight months of age. When she was twenty-one months old she awoke screaming from a nightmare, tears pouring down her face. For the first time she was able to tell me what she had dreamed. Rita, her day-care teacher—a woman Maya loved intensely—had taken away her dear baby bear. Maya wept over and over again: "She took my baby away. Mommy, why did Rita do that? Why did she take my baby away?" The next day she wanted to replay her dream with myself and the baby bear. I helped her say to Rita imaginally, "Don't take my baby away. I don't want you to take my baby away." Her fury came out in these statements as she tried to keep her baby with her. In the weeks that followed, Maya enacted this dream over and over again, trying to express both the sadness of having her baby taken away and the righteous anger that said "This is my baby, not yours." In retrospect, perhaps I should have just held her, weeping, without suggesting assertiveness, for the truth is that she *had* been separated from her birthmother and her ayah, her caretaker at the orphanage. But at the time, I spoke from the reality of her new home; she, a baby, will not be taken away, even by someone she loves, like Rita.

Maya had been cared for in a large institution for mothers and children in India. In all there were five hundred children and mothers, fleeing poverty, cultural censure, and the lack of a family to help them support their children. Some mothers stayed with their children; others left them to be cared for by the orphanage. I had heard from an Indian friend about how the women in her family had formed a circle and cried for the relatives killed in the partition. I wondered if the ayahs had cried in such a way around the children about their loss of family, loss of children, loss of home and hope. What of such sadness would a baby be attentive to? What of it could she understand while still less than a year old?

I will never know all that Maya experienced at the orphanage or what her baby mind and heart made of it. But it seemed to me that this dream was a crystallization of her experience: that someone quite loved (me, Rita) could take a baby (her) away from a mother (and later an ayah and an institution that was home to her), and that in this reality there was grief and fury. Even if her separations were not remembered—and I doubt they were—the fear of being taken away (now from me?) remained, displaced onto her animals.

This story came back to me over a year later, when Maya, at thirty-one months, began a piece of repetitive play that dealt with this theme. A woman friend was visiting, and Maya stationed herself between us on the couch, settling in for a long afternoon of play and make-believe. Almost immediately what emerged was the following: Maya was a baby kitty, and I was her mommy. Maya instructed my friend, Carolyn, to try to take the baby kitty away. She instructed me to protest by saying, "You can't have her. This is my baby kitty." She wished me to say this with vehemence and certitude and would add a baby-cat growl and hiss to show her assent with my position. After playing this at least thirty times, I introduced a variation, which she quickly accepted and incorporated into her play. I asked her if she would like to visit Carolyn and return to me. As long as she knew she could return, she leaped happily into Carolyn's lap and then back to mine.

The next day while we were talking, Maya claimed that I was her daddy's mother. I said, "No, I'm Daddy's wife. His mother is Nanna." She said, "I know. His other mother went away." Over the coming months this notion was repeated—that the first mother went away and was replaced by another, that the first mother died and the baby was found by another mother. Be it guinea pig, puppy dog, stuffed animal, or herself as bunny or kitty, a sad little one whose mother had died would come to see if I would be her mother. Once I said yes with warmth and enthusiasm there was great joy and expressions of closeness. I suspected that somewhere in the back of her mind she thought her birthmother must have died.

At three years two months of age, Maya initiated her first talk with me about her adoption in the absence of her sister. Heretofore, all the direct talk about adoption had been initiated by Laura, alone with me or with me and Maya. While snuggling before bedtime, Maya tentatively said, "I was in your tummy." By now well seasoned in this conversation, I answered, "No, you were in another lady's tummy, who took good care of you until I came to be your mommy." "What was her name?" For months I had been trying to find out her mother's first name so I would have it when she asked me. I felt I had really failed her. "I don't know, sweetie, but I'll find out for you." "What was Laura's lady's name?" "Teresa," I repeated a bit sadly, not wanting Maya to feel that Laura had such an important thing that she did not have. "Let's call her 'Sythia,' " Maya piped cheerily. I thought she meant Forsythia, since she and I had cut some of these flowers the day before and placed them on her dresser. "Yes," I agreed heartily, "that would be a good name for now."

Then came the repeated requests for all the stories I was used to from Laura—about the plane rides, my seeing her for the first time, my happiness, her coming home, the people who helped her—over and over. She giggled and was happy throughout, except for two spots. She kept asking me if I was sad in India, which seemed so disjunctive to me with our mood of exuberance about her story. Then I realized that she had some sadness, and I tried to match it with some of my own at that time. "I was very happy to find you and bring you home, but there were some sad things Mommy saw in India." "What, Mommy?" "Some children and families were very poor, and this was sad to see." She seemed relieved to have this piece. Then later, after much happiness, she asked, "Was I a little afraid of you at first, Mommy?" I was stunned by her insight into a baby's tentativeness with strangers, and again I wondered if she had some access to a vague recollection of how difficult it had been for her to be separated once again from all she knew at the orphanage.

"Yes, Maya, you were frightened of me. You had never met me before, and you had to get to know that I would be a good mommy to you. The first night we were alone together you slept on the other side of the bed from me. The second night you came a little closer because you knew me a little better. The third night you reached out to me in your sleep, like this, and snuggled up next to me as close as you could. You did not seem afraid after that." She enacted this coming closer and closer, and then gave me a big hug.

At three and a half, after much doll play about mothers who die, I decided to speak directly with Maya about what I thought her concern was: that her birthmother had died. I said, "Sometimes I wonder if you think your tummy-mommy died, the lady who carried you in her tummy and took care of you until I came to be your mommy." She neither assented nor objected, but looked at me curiously. I continued, "She did not die. She is well and is living in India." Though she did not respond directly or immediately, the course of her fantasies changed: her playing of mothers dying decreased dramatically, and she imagined running into her Indian family for the first time. Several weeks later, while driving through our small town, she saw an Indian man walking. She asked her father with curiosity, "Is that my other father?" We had not yet spoken of birthfathers. A few days later at a gathering for Indian children, she was upset about leaving the car. When a white woman dressed in a sari passed the car, she asked me if that was her mother. Apparently, if her tummy-mommy was not dead, then she could be anywhere, near or far. In the months that followed, Maya shared her confusion about the different kinds of mothers in her life: me, her tummy-mommy, her ayah, her Indian godmother, and her institutional mother, the Indian woman who ran the orphanage.

At a party for the orphanage director, Maya asked this gray-haired lady in a sari, "Are you my mother?" We had tried to explain to her who this was and how she figured into Maya's early life. Nevertheless, this question, logical to her way of thinking, arose. On saying good-bye to her at the end of the day, Maya seemed to understand better. She threw her arms around the older woman's neck, hugging her and saying happily, "Thank you for my sweetie mommy. Thank you for my sweetie daddy"—her endearing terms for us.

Perhaps most telling was Maya's daily fingerplay about the spider child Aranea, one of Charlotte's offspring in E. B. White's *Charlotte's Web*. Maya saw the movie version several times when she was about two years old. The mother spider, Charlotte, dies, and Aranea is cared for by Charlotte's best friend, Wilbur, the lovable pig. When she was three and four, each morning and bedtime, Maya would snuggle up with my finger, Aranea, and make up stories about her. It was a happy and warm time. Occasionally, she would mention how sad it was that Aranea's mother died, but mainly she played with and loved Aranea, taking just as good care of her as Wilbur did. Sometimes she imagined that Charlotte was still alive and playing with us as well.

At three years nine months, Maya seemed out of sorts one day when I picked her up at nursery school. She had Aranea speak to me:

Aranea: Maya is sad.

Me: Why is Maya sad?

Aranea: She wants a mommy with brown skin, not skin like yours.

Me: Why?

Aranea: She just does.

Me: Some mommies match, and some mommies don't. There isn't anything I can do about my color skin.

Aranea: You could paint it!

Me: But what if it rained? The paint would fall off.

Aranea: No, we could ask God to keep it on.

Me: I think God meant us to have two different, pretty colors. But, you know, lots of children want to match their mommies. That's okay to want and to be a little sad about.

We got out of the car at the pizza parlor. Maya gave me a big hug: "You can be my mommy forever and ever anyway!"

Although she seems to recognize how beautiful her skin is, clearly she wants someone in the family sharing her color. In particular, Aranea has explained to me, "She wants a brown mother." At times, Maya has asked me if I am a queen and has then asked what her "real mother" looks like. The other day she asked a stranger, the adoptive mother of a Korean girl who was Maya's age, if she was the child's babysitter. When I wondered if people had ever asked her if I was her babysitter, she answered yes. She did not express directly how that made her feel, but it seemed clear that her desire would be for such questions never to arise, and that would be possible only if we looked more alike.

Now that Maya is five, Aranea visits infrequently. But Aranea stories were woven through our daily life for two years, conserving Maya's sense of early loss and surpassing it at the same time through Aranea's multiple adventures with her new family and friends. She was Maya's best imaginal friend and part of our day-to-day family life—just as Maya's past and present are.

Now Maya is busily and joyfully pretending either that she is in my tummy about to be born or that she herself is about to give birth to the various stuffed animals hidden under her skirt. The theme of her being a small baby animal whose mother has died still arises from time to time. She always directs me to find her, happily care for her, and join her to our family. The newly born or found baby, she says, "never grows up and never gets a day older." She directs me: "You have always wanted, more than anything, a silver baby unicorn with a lovely blue horn. You are walking in the woods and find me." In this play she is the crystallization of some of my deepest desires and remains so forever. Being found and delighted in seem to have superseded feeling lost.

Laura and Maya in Tandem: Sisters Share about Adoption

If Maya ends up saying less about adoption to me than her older sister, Laura, has—as seems often to be the case with second adopted children—it would not surprise me. By the age of two she had already observed her sister dealing with the themes of adoption and racial differences. When they were two and three they began to share these themes in play and conversation. These sharings seemed always to be a solace to each child, playful and fun. Laura has had to work hard at being adopted. Her awareness of it has meant something positive for Maya—a household in which adoption is simply a fact, talked about and played about. The following vignette, when Maya was two and Laura three, is representative of some of their early interactions around adoptive themes.

The day after my walk with Laura when we discussed waitresses, nurses, and birthmothers, she, Maya, and I had the following conversation on the way to day care.

Laura: Why is Daddy a boy and we are girls?

Me: God decided Daddy would make a very good boy, so he made him one before he was born. [I chuckled to myself about how true this seemed, having a hard time imagining this husky fellow as a girl.]

Maya: And he decided we would make good girls?

Me: Yes.

Laura: But why did he give me black skin and Maya her skin? I like Maya's better. Why can't we have the same skin?

Me: Maya's is brown and yours is tan. They are both pretty colors of skin. I like them.

Laura: Why are they different?

Me: You and Maya came from two different places in the world where people have different color skins—Maya comes from India where people have brown skin, and you come from Brazil where some people have tan skin like yours.

Laura: But what color was my lady's?

Me: Do you mean the lady who carried you in her tummy when you were very tiny?

Laura: Yes. What color was her skin?

Me: Her skin was a pretty tan just like yours. And her hair was black and curly and beautiful like yours. And her eyes were brown like yours. She gave you your colors, which is a very special gift.

Laura: But I don't like mine. I want to have brown skin like Maya's.

Me: Once we get our colors as tiny babies, we have them forever.

Laura: What color was Maya's lady?

Me: A pretty brown color, like Maya.

They noticed some horses out the window and dropped the conversation. I had been reluctant to answer Laura's initial questioning with talk about birthmothers since Maya was present, and this was not yet her concern. I had no idea what Maya would take from the conversation. But my wondering did not have to last long. We dropped Laura off at day care and went to the market. At the checkout counter, surrounded by five women, thirty-three-month-old Maya announced cheerily, and loudly: "My sister doesn't have brown skin like me. Isn't mine beautiful!" Everyone laughed and agreed with her heartily!

When Laura was almost four and Maya almost three, they heard and saw enacted in church school the story of Moses being found in the bullrushes. The daughter of the pharaoh—the pharaoh who had ordered that the babies be killed—discovered the baby Moses while bathing in the river. Moses' older sister was stationed near the bank by her mother to watch what happened to the baby. The pharaoh's daughter asked the sister if she knew anyone who could care for the baby. Of course, the sister suggested her and Moses' mother. Thus the baby escaped death and was cared for by its own mother through the intervention of the pharaoh's daughter, with whom Moses lived when he grew up.

In the weeks after they saw this little play Laura and Maya enacted the story with me countless times—honing their own version, with elements that expressed their different adoption experiences to date. Laura took the lead in dropping the elements of the story that were not of interest to her, and then Maya added her preoccupations to Laura's version.

Two baby girls are in small boats on a river. A princess puppet—the role given to me—is talking about how she wants to have a baby but doesn't know where to find one. She goes to wash her hair in the river and discovers the babies. They are immediately her own—that is, there is no notion of transferring motherhood or of a previous mother. Laura stresses that the princess is now the mother forever and ever. I too then stress this part—forever and ever—as the princess lifts the babies from their boats and cuddles them joyfully in her arms. Laura shivers with delight to see the mother love them so much. Then she has the mother ask if there are any magic ponies to give the babies rides. Her beloved family of magic ponies—who protect one from all that is unsafe—arrive on the scene, and the babies take turns riding them. The princess, the babies, and the ponies live together in the dollhouse. The babies are tempted to do some of the things the ponies do, like stand on the roof of the dollhouse. Laura has the princess set limits and thereby protect them from harm.

We played this over and over again, with Maya participating at the edges. Then Maya reintroduced the bad pharaoh by having a magic pony on the roof spot his coming. The babies are hidden quickly. He comes and asks the women present—Laura, Maya, and the princess—if they have any babies. They all lie, saying that they don't, and send him away.

While Laura is content to play house with her magic ponies, princess mother, and beloved babies, Maya keeps introducing visits by the pharaoh in which he discovers the babies, tries to take them away, and is then clobbered by the magic ponies, who joyfully reunite the babies with their princess-mother. Here the threat of being separated from the mother is overcome again and again by drawing on the special magical powers and strength of the ponies, helpmates to the mother. For Maya—united with our family at eight months, after two separations (first from her birthmother, then from the orphanage)—the theme of babies being taken away is more salient than it is for Laura, mothered by me since she was sixteen days old.

For Maya the song "She Always Comes Back"—referring to a mother's return for her baby—is extremely important. "You always come back, Mommy," she says often as I return from work or am about to leave. "Yes, Maya, Mommy always, always, always comes back to be with Maya." "Always, always?" she queries. "Yes, always," I insist. For Laura, the important word is *forever*. For Maya it is *always*. Together they are working on and gaining a sense of permanence and continuity.

During this same period I overheard the following conversation between Laura and Maya, who were playing with six brightly colored ponies.

Laura: Maya, why are all the ponies in this family different colors?

Maya [after a long pause]: Well, Laura, everybody has to die sometime.

Laura [another long pause]: Maya, I guess you're right.

I laughed inside to hear them, each trying to talk about her major concerns with the other—Maya about separation and death, Laura about differences—and prayed that this sharing would continue throughout their lives.

●

Jeff and Melissa

Jeff: Why didn't my real mom want me? . . . I think she didn't like me.

Melissa: I was always wanted. My parents who adopted me wanted me even before I was born.

I have read, in discussions of the impact of adoption on children, that preschool children are not readily capable of understanding the abstract concept of adoption—they hear the word and may come to use it to describe themselves but do not, for example, fully realize the loss implications of their state. As older latency-age children, they will realize that for them to have been adopted, their birthparents had to relinquish them, and the impact of this awareness may initiate a grieving process. My own two children by adoption, Jeff and Melissa, now ten and eight in age, have taught me that the reality of their loss is experienced from the beginning—not with acute grief, perhaps, but certainly with moments of acute anxiety and sadness.

Jeff was a very verbal and intellectually precocious preschooler. At age thirty-four months, he was with us at the airport when we greeted his new sister, Melissa, seven months old, arriving from Korea. It was a joyous event for us all, and he understood our excitement. The plane was an hour late, and when it finally taxied in he exclaimed to the assembled adults (there were four families waiting for babies), "Clap, everybody! The plane is coming!"—and we all clapped. A week or so later, his pleasure in the new sibling had cooled considerably, and he asked me, "When are we going to take her back to the airport?"

It's a charming vignette, with obvious parallels to the child who asks her parents to return the new baby to the hospital. I did not fully realize the limitations of my young son's experience until a few months later, when I pointed out an obviously pregnant friend and asked him if he knew she was going to have a baby. He nodded and then asked, "Where is she starting?" When I asked him what he meant, he said, "Well, is she starting at the hospital or the airport?"

At about this time, my sister gave birth to a daughter. Jeff and I and my sister's son Daniel, who is Jeff's age, visited mother and baby in the hospital. Daniel was very much interested in his new sister and the whole process, and Jeff was uncharacteristically boisterous and very *un*interested in visiting the nursery and seeing the new babies. Clearly, he did not feel on equal ground with those who "started in the hospital."

I suppose I did not always feel on equal ground, either. Still, as a conscientious mother, I did not shrink from initiating discussions: "Do you know that Karen is pregnant, and that's why her belly is so big? She has a baby growing inside." Jeff nodded and said quite definitely, "Just like I grew inside you." The pangs that I felt were for him and for me as I answered, "No, you grew in another woman's tummy; she gave birth to you, and then we adopted you." His thumb went into his mouth, and his look grew pensive. "Do you feel sad about that?" I asked. He nodded. I wanted to hold him forever as I replied, "I feel sad about that, too. I wish you had grown inside me."

Melissa struggled with this, too. She was not so precociously verbal as Jeff, but when she was five or so and had asked many questions about where babies come from, the birth process, and nursing, I heard her fantasy-wish about herself. She knew she had been born in Korea, and she knew she had been adopted, and what she constructed was this: I went to Korea and gave birth to her, then came back here—and then we adopted her!

These incidents suggest to me that the young adopted child's anxieties are not so much about loss and rejection as about their awareness that a more complicated story lurks beyond the warm cocoon of "Mommy, Daddy, and me." But the darker anxiety is sometimes there, too. Quite out of the blue, when Jeff was four and a half, he asked me, "Why didn't my real mom want me?" I was startled; didn't the books say this question came much later? Very carefully, I said, "Well, what do you think?" Jeff replied, "I think she didn't like me." Quickly, I reassured him. "No, that was not the reason. She was young and unmarried, and she wasn't able to take care of a baby. She wanted you to be well taken care of and to grow up with a mommy and daddy. So she made a plan for you to be adopted." There was silence. "Have you been worrying about this?" I asked. "No," he said, "I just wondered." And that day he went to nursery school and for the first and only time, wet his pants in class.

Sometimes my children expressed anxiety about me. They knew that "something didn't work right" in my body, so I could not have babies. Did that mean I was sick? Was it contagious? Melissa, in particular, wanted reassurance that when she grew up she would be able to have babies. Sometimes their childish candor took me aback. When we took our new puppy to be spayed, Jeff exclaimed, "Oh, I see, that's what happened to you. You were *fixed!* That's why you can't have babies!"

Some adoptive parents I have talked with have expressed concern because their young children never speak about adoption. I am not sure why mine did. Perhaps their knowing that my husband was also adopted gave them permission to bring up the subject. Jeff's inquisitive, verbal nature was also a factor, and his need to "tell all" meant that Melissa had no choice in this—or many other matters. (He set her straight about Santa Claus and explained the "facts" of adoption to her, whether she wanted to hear them or not.) Both children loved to get out the photo albums and "read" about their early lives. Melissa loved the first picture we had received of her, taken when she was an infant in Korea; she expressed particular curiosity about the picture in which a woman (her foster mother) is holding her. (Was this really her birthmother?) She loved looking at her visa, with her name written in Korean letters. Jeff was thrilled, at age six, when his adoption agency had an open house as part of a centennial celebration. He wanted to see the room where we had first met him, the crib where he had slept, and the rocking chair where I had rocked him—he wanted to reenact our meeting with me sitting in the rocking chair and holding him once again.

Between his seventh and eighth years Jeff had many questions about his birthparents. He wanted to know what they looked like, what ethnic and religious backgrounds they were (he hoped they were Jewish so that he could celebrate Hannukah as well as Christmas), and what their interests were. The fact that both of them were good in math and science quickly became incorporated into his own identity. He learned that they liked animals and had expressed the wish that he would be raised in a family who owned a dog. It seems clear to me that Jeff's strong love of animals is consciously linked to them. (His current ambition is to be "some kind of scientist who works with animals because I love animals and think they're very important.")

When Jeff was not yet six, he asked me his birthmother's name. I waffled for a moment; I was not sure I should tell him, although I knew the last name from his adoption decree. A whole set of complicated feelings vividly revived. I remembered when my husband and I were searching for my husband's birthmother prior to starting our family. For most of the search, we had had the wrong name for her—"Peterson" rather than "Paulsen." Only after my husband found her did his stepmother (his adoptive mother was deceased) "happen to find" his adoption decree, which bore the correct name. And when we adopted Jeff, our lawyer had suggested that we not take actual possession of the adoption decree, so that, if Jeff ever asked, we could truthfully say we didn't know her name. We had initially agreed and then decided that we should be the "keepers of the name."

I realized, however, at the moment when my small son was asking me for the name that I had envisioned a much older child wanting that information. Should I say, "I can't tell you until you're older"? That didn't feel right, either; so I gulped and told him the name: "Gordon." And of course, nothing dreadful happened. It became one more piece of information to weave into his identity. Because he and I share a very similar ethnic background, he has raised the idea that perhaps he and I are distantly related. I happen to have a great-grandmother whose last name was Gordon, so I have joined in the fantasy.

The most interesting event around his name came when Jeff was seven. We became foster parents to a Vietnamese teenager who had escaped from Vietnam, leaving his family behind, and had come to this country as a refugee. He had lived for a month in a so-called transitional foster home, and then we brought him to live with us in what would be a permanent foster placement. The first foster family's name happened to be Gordon. With all our energies focused on helping our newest family member adjust, I was caught quite by surprise when Jeff asked, a few months later, "You know, those people—the Gordons—are they my birthparents?" (a very logical question).

Eventually, Jeff asked when he could meet his birthparents. We explained to him, with the authority of my husband's personal experience, that this was something we felt needed to wait until he was an adult, but if he wanted to search at that time, we would help him. I know there will be qualms for me when he goes to meet them, but I also know that I will not impede his search as my husband's stepmother tried to do; I understand his need completely.

As an Asian child in a Caucasian-American family, Korean-born Melissa had to face the external world's perception of her as "adopted" even before she could know what that meant. By the time she was two, she would select the Asian doll as "like me." And at three, she was clearly expressing pain over being different. In nursery school, she donned a blonde wig every day to play house. Her favorite playmate was a very blonde little girl, also named Melissa; and for Halloween, our Melissa wanted to be her friend, the other Melissa. When we declined to honor this wish, she chose to be a very tough-looking pirate. She needed that toughness to contend with the comments of friends: "How can that be your mom? She doesn't look like you." Or, "Chinese, Chinese! You're Chinese!" (said with slanted-eye demonstration). When I would take my two children out with me, others would always assume that I had one biological and one adopted child. It was not uncommon for people to see Melissa, with me ten steps behind, and ask her, "Little girl, where is your mother?" We had kept Melissa's Korean name as her middle name, and she thought that was "stupid" and wanted little to do with anything Asian.

Watching her struggle with these issues was part of our motivation for becoming foster parents to first one and then a second Vietnamese boy. We felt it would benefit her to have more Asian people within the family— and indeed it did. Soon she began emulating her big brothers and eating noodles for breakfast, and both she and Jeff became proficient with chopsticks. (Of course, one can't win; Jeff wanted to know why we preferred Asians to Caucasians!) We bought Melissa a beautiful silk *hanbok* (a Korean traditional dress), which she wore at her birthday party to the envious sighs of her girlfriends and at a candlelighting ceremony at our church, where for Thanksgiving we celebrated all of our families' pilgrimages from other lands.

The summer Melissa was seven we sent her for a week to Korean culture camp—a day camp for Korean-born children adopted into American families. The experience of being with many children like herself and of learning about Korean culture had a profoundly positive effect. She returned to school that fall not trying to conceal who she was but, instead, proud of her heritage. All year, for weekly show-and-tell, she took items related to being Korean and being adopted and gave her classmates an education on these subjects. For a while, she signed her school papers with her Korean name only. (Now she signs her full name—American first and last names, Korean middle name.) The following summer she attended another week of "Camp Pride," this time accompanied by her brother Jeff and an American non-adopted friend (whose mother worked for an adoption agency that placed Korean-born children). All three of them enjoyed learning Korean songs and the Korean alphabet and eating *mandu* (meat and vegetable dumplings).

There are, however, some clouds on the horizon for Melissa. Because she was abandoned when she was two weeks old, neither we nor the agency know the identity of her birthparents. For Jeff, we probably have sufficient information to help him locate his birthparents when the time comes. Our two Vietnamese sons correspond regularly with their families in Vietnam. Melissa has expressed her desire to meet her birthmother and to know who she is, but we cannot give her that. We can help to instill pride in her culture and promise her a trip to Korea, but these are not the same. I'm sure she will have moments of feeling alone and isolated.

But Melissa is a strong little girl. In third grade, her class was studying citizenship. Melissa readily took my suggestion that she show the class her souvenirs from the ceremony in which she became an American citizen. It was a few weeks later, when she and I were driving in the car, that she told me what happened: "You know when I told my class about becoming a citizen?"

"Yes, how did that go?"

"Well, after I finished telling them, Mrs. Lawrence asked if there were any questions."

"Yes—"

"And Jason raised his hand and asked, 'Why didn't your real parents want you?'"

"And what did you say?" (I was hard-pressed to keep my eyes on the road!)

"Well, first, Mrs. Lawrence told him that was a private question. But I answered him anyway; I said, 'Well, actually, I think I was always wanted. My parents who adopted me wanted me even before I was born.'"

I could not have said it better myself.

Sometimes it has not been clear whether a period of distress for Melissa is related to her adoption. Can it be that the felt knowledge that you are wanted by your adoptive family can lie beside worries that you might again be surrendered? One day, for example, when Melissa was ten, I was driving her and two of her friends to riding lessons. As they sat in the back of the van, one of the girls, Sharon, began to talk about her aunt, a single woman, who had adopted an eight-year-old Korean-born girl the year before. It had been a difficult year of many adjustments, but they were making it now.

Sharon said, "I have a cousin who's adopted from Korea, too. She was eight years old when my aunt got her. First her real mom died, and her dad had her, but he couldn't take care of her. So he had her adopted by another family, but they couldn't take care of her, so then my aunt got her. They had a lot of problems, but things are better now." Melissa's only comment was, "Well, is she from South Korea or North Korea? She better be from South Korea, because that's where I'm from; that's all I can say." Sharon didn't know. I commented from the front seat that I thought all kids adopted from Korea came from South Korea, and Melissa said, "Well, good, then, she's fine." End of conversation—or was it?

The next day and the day after, Melissa complained of a stomachache. By the third day she was in so much pain that I kept her home from school and took her to the doctor. He could find nothing physically wrong, and I began to wonder what stress might be at work. I recalled that conversation in the van. What if she worried that we might not be able to care for her and that she might have to go to another family?

I brought the conversation up with her. "You remember when Sharon was talking about her cousin when we were going to riding class? I've been thinking about it, and it occurred to me that it might have caused you to worry."

Melissa was loud and adamant. "No, it didn't bother me! Why should it? You get the strangest ideas."

I persisted. "Well, even so, I got to thinking it might have made you worry that something could happen and you would have to go to another family. I just wanted to make sure you know that could never happen to you. You will always be our daughter, and nothing can ever change that."

She again protested my crazy ideas, but a moment later said, "That happened to Tyler, too." Tyler is our cat.

"What do you mean?"

"Well, first one family adopted him, but they couldn't take care of him so they brought him back to the pet store, and then we adopted him."

I was incredulous. We had had this cat for a year and a half and never before had I heard this story. I thought she might be making it up, but when I checked later with Jeff, who had gone with her to pick out the cat, he confirmed the story. I began to understand their passionate attachment to the cat in a different light.

The stomachache disappeared, never to be mentioned again.

Ian and Elizabeth

Ian: How fast did you go, Mommy, to get me in the car?
Elizabeth: Then I was in Daddy's tummy!

Before we got Ian, my husband and I had many talks about how, when, and whether to tell Ian he was adopted. I could empathize with those parents who did not tell their children. I knew a couple who had decided not to— sensible, intelligent parents. I had even spoken to the mother while she was waiting for her child. She was one of the many people I consulted about how to locate a child. "Every time I sit in the subway and see an ugly-looking kid, I think, 'Is that what my kid will look like?'" I was startled, and impressed, by her candor, her ability to acknowledge her fears. Others told me later of this couple's decision not to tell their two children about being adopted. I couldn't do that for two reasons: first, how dreadful if the children ever learned by accident. The very fact of a secret would make the adoption itself something terrible, would make of adoption in general something terrible. Also, I hate secrets. I would not want to know something that relevant and not share it. So both morally and practically, secrecy seemed out of the question.

We decided several things in advance of Ian's arrival. First, we would answer every question as it occurred and would take our cues from him. We would not introduce ideas to him. We would wait. So I never said anything about adopting him in casual conversation. That worked out all right for him, but for our second child, a daughter, I used the word freely, even though she hadn't the faintest idea what we were talking about. But the word was around, and all conversations were heard by her. I think I was a little phobic about the word with Ian as I waited for his questions.

Another decision we made was that we would not talk about two mothers, the birthmother and the adoptive mother, early on. My husband in particular felt very strongly that that would be quite confusing. "You are the mom. We are parenting him." And so we developed in advance the notion that, when the time came, we would tell Ian about the wonderful lady he was born from, who could not be a mommy because (the truth) she was too young and too poor and went to find us at the hospital and gave him to us. But there would be only one mommy and daddy, the parenting ones. We held to that, and, as time revealed, so did he until he was seven and began on his own to talk about his "biological mother," a phrase he never heard from us. Our notion was that he would, of course, eventually understand that there was a mother of the body and a mother of the heart, the birth-parents and the adoptive parents, but that by the time he learned about the two mothers he would have strongly identified with us as his parents and would not be confused by the existence of another person called "mother." I often speculated that all this talk about how to put it was more important for us than for him, but so what?

The other decision we made was that we would not talk about adoption with him when we were anxious or upset, that we would have our talks when we were in good humor and our anxieties were in perspective. My husband was a great help in this because he had three grown children, all biological, from a previous marriage; he "knew" in advance that there would be no difference in his feeling for the children, and for him there *has* been no difference. His attachment and investment and connection to his two adopted children are the same as to his three biological children. That fact was, at times, a great comfort to me because I had worried about it. I remember saying to him the morning after we got Ian, "Well, how does it feel?" He said, "What do you mean?" And I said, my heart pounding, "Well, is it the same—I mean, like with your other kids?" He looked at me as though I was crazy and said, "Honey, this is my kid—I mean, this is my boy!" I went into the other room and cried my heart out with relief. For me there was no alternative, and for me this was such a miracle, this gorgeous, funny-looking, big-eyed little creature staring up at me. But for my husband it could have been different. Now I wonder whether some of my concern about his response wasn't a projection of my own doubts, which I dared not acknowledge and therefore laid on him. Who cares? I needed his support and I got it.

Ian was a passionate, happy, intense, relaxed, easy-to-be-with boy, and life went along without any mention of adoption until well into nursery school. Nursery school started at three and a half for Ian and we had a car pool. Five kids. By midfall, four of the moms, all but me, were pregnant. One day, sitting on the couch, aged three and a half, Ian said, "Mama, was I in your tummy?" I felt a sharp pain in my heart. It really was as if I had been stabbed. I remembered my decision not to talk when I was anxious, so I turned away and laughingly said, "I'll tell you all about that tomorrow."

Ian liked to have conversations after his bath at night while he was having a poop. So he was sitting on the toilet, chatting, while I was sitting on the edge of the bathtub. I said, "Remember you asked yesterday if you had been in my tummy?"

"Yeah," he says.

"Well, here's what happened. You weren't in my tummy. You were in the tummy of this nice lady who couldn't be a mommy but who kept you in her tummy for Daddy and me. And the minute you came out, the doctor called and said, 'Ian's out. Ian's out.' And we got in our car and drove as fast as we could to get you. And we got you and we took you home. And Daddy took a lot of pictures and I was so happy I was goofy and Daddy ran around acting like a nut. And it was the happiest day of my life."

That was it. The story. It was true. (A little time distortion—it was three days later that we got him—but that was not a basic change.)

He looked at me and then, very very solemnly, asked, "How fast did you go?"

"Huh," I said, having expected some anguished response.

"How fast did you go, Mommy, to get me in the car?"

Then I got it. Maybe for him the speed of driving was related to the amount of loving, or the speed of bonding or finding him. I didn't stop to think. I joined in. "As fast as we could."

"Did a policeman stop you?"

"Yes."

"What did you say?"

"I said, 'We're going to get Ian and we have to get there very fast. He's just been born and we're his parents.'"

"And what did the policeman say?"

"He said, 'I'll make sure no one stops you. I'll come along behind you.'"

Then Ian pops off the toilet seat and, naked, runs from one end of the hall to the other, starting slow and getting faster each return trip, saying, happily, "Is this how fast you went to get me?" And when he ran as fast as he could, I said, "We went hundreds of times faster than that because we were going to get you and we waited so long and we wanted you so badly." That was it.

Next day, in the car driving somewhere, he said, "So I was in your tummy." I laughed and laughed and said, "Oh, Ian, you know you were in that nice lady's tummy. And then I got you, right when you came out. Daddy used to say, 'We got you the second you came out of the oven.'"

A few more times, weeks apart, he'd say, "Remember when I was in your tummy?" and I'd laugh again and say, "I would really have liked to have you in my tummy—but you weren't. You were in that nice lady," or "It would have been fun to have you in my tummy." He never, at that point, mentioned sadness about not being in my tummy, so I did not mention it either. I began to see that this was a kid who said what was on his mind when he was ready to, and I would just wait and watch.

Several times during the next year, at bedtime when he was very sleepy and very cuddly, he would say, "Did I drink from your breasts when I was a baby like Jeremy does?" and I would say, "Yes." There had been times when he was very small and I was holding him that he suckled instinctively, which relieved my conscience about not ever lying to him. I also felt that his question at bedtime was really about being very close to me, not about bottle versus breast-feeding.

Other than these stories, repeated many times over, there were no new additions to the script. Often, out of nowhere, he would say, "Show me how fast you went when you got me." Or, "What did the policeman say when he stopped you?"

All this was before Ian was four. When he was age four and three months, his sister Elizabeth arrived. All through the pregnancies of the four moms in the car pool, as the kids talked about their impending siblings, Ian would say, "I'm waiting for my baby sister. Her name is Elizabeth. She sure is taking a long time." No one ever commented on this or on my very flat tummy.

When Elizabeth was born, it took us thirty days to get her out of Georgia. We knew she was ours on the tenth day. We knew all about her by the fifteenth, including a description by an evaluating psychologist who spent four hours with her and her cherishing foster parents. The next fifteen days were very very hard on me, but less so on my husband, who had, compared to me, infinite patience with bureaucracies. Ian listened to every conversation about getting her and every description of our efforts to speed up the bureaucratic machinery that kept her from us.

Suddenly, on a Friday afternoon, when we had been told we could not get her until the following Wednesday, and my husband was away on a two-week business trip, and I had driven three hours north to a professional meeting, I called my answering machine and heard a sweet southern voice say, "There has been a miracle. All the paper work is cleared. Call me and tell me when you are coming to get your daughter." I called a friend and said, "Get a pencil. Go to the store. Get diapers. Get bottles. Get Similac. Get to my house in two hours. Get some money. I'm coming back." And back I got, reminding myself to drive slowly, and somehow, by noon the next day, Ian and I met my husband at the Atlanta airport and we all went to get Elizabeth. Ian tells everyone to this day, "We couldn't find the right entrance and I saw her first. I saw her even before Dad, and I ran to tell Mom. She is my baby." And so she was—until he decided a week later that we should send her back to Georgia. Which we did not do.

Between the ages of three and a half and five the stories and themes described above were repeated occasionally. A few weeks after Ian's fifth birthday, we went to an island in Florida on vacation and were sitting around one day while Elizabeth was napping. Ian came up to me with his arms piled high with bath towels, four large gray ones. "Wrap me up the way you did when you got me." I immediately followed his instructions, swaddling this big, very tall five-year-old in the towels. "Now hold me like you did when you got me." And I did. "Tell me the story again. Tell me how the doctor called and you drove fast and the policeman came and you were so happy you fell against the wall and Daddy took pictures and acted like a nut." So I told him. Then he took the towels off and looked away and said, very sadly, "I wish I had been in your tummy." And I said, "I wish you had been in my tummy too. It would have been very nice." And we were sad together for a few minutes. And then I said, "You know, Ian, when you're in someone's tummy, it's very boring and you can't see out. It's after you come out, when you're born, that it gets to be very interesting." He chuckled and said, "I never thought of that." (And I thought to myself, "I never thought of that either.")

Then we kind of sat around, very peaceful (but I knew there was more to come—I sensed it), and he said, very strongly and very carefully, "Why didn't she want me?" And I said, "She didn't know you. To not want someone, you have to know them and then not want them. She only saw you for a minute and gave you to us because she was too young and too poor to take care of you. So she did this wonderful and brave and noble thing. She did it for you." And he said, "How old was she?" And I said, "Sixteen."

And then his posture changed from heavy and serious to quite light-hearted in feeling. And he said, "Oh ho! She was a *teenager*." (Teenagers he got, you see.) And I said, "Yeah. And it's hard to be a mommy when you're a teenager." Then he was very chipper and that was the end of it. I really thought it was the end of it, and I was very relieved and moved. A couple of hours later, in the middle of conversations about this or that, Ian said, "If she was a teenager then, is she a teenager now?" And I said, "Nope. She's not a teenager now." "Well, I love her and I want to see her." And I said (reminding myself that he was in a phase lately of loving and wanting *everything*), "Well, I love her too because she kept you in her tummy for us. And when you're much older, if you want to see her, we can think about it." And that was the end of that. And I had a Scotch.

Nothing more happened for a year and a half. Same themes. Adoption became part of everyday conversation. Occasional cracks like, "What's so great about being adopted?" And I'd say, playfully, "All kinds of ways to make a family." But on many occasions we would talk about families and the different ways they were created—how some people made their own babies, and some adopted them when they were born, and some adopted them later, and some families kept children with them who had parents who couldn't be with them very often. And how he had half brothers and half sisters as well as Elizabeth, his full sister. And how Becky, a teenager who lived with us for the first three years of his life, was his sister in his heart, even though she had her own family. And every time a baby was adopted by people we knew, a great fuss was made. And every time I heard of someone he knew who was adopted, I would mention it. Not a big fuss but loud and clear. And what he did see—and an observant fellow he was and is—was the wild joy in our household when people who had been waiting and waiting got their baby.

From age four on, Ian and I went out every Thursday afternoon. We still do. Saturday morning is with Dad and Thursday afternoon with Mom. One Thursday afternoon, when he was six and three quarters, we spent a particularly happy afternoon at the top of the tallest building in the city. We did all the usual things one does at the top of the world. He wanted to count all the swimming pools we could see from so high up. So we counted and we ate and we hung out. And when we got back into the car to drive home, I actually mused to myself on how easy and close the afternoon had been. I felt much less like a prison warden disciplining a six-year-old than usual.

Then Ian said, "Hey Mom, what happens if a pregnant woman gets sick?" Right away I knew that here was big trouble. "Well," I said, "she goes to the doctor." "Well, what if she's real sick?" "What do you mean, real sick?" beginning to feel real sick myself. "I mean, what if she dies?" "Well," I said, biting the bullet and wanting to get whatever was coming over with, "if she dies and the baby is close to being able to be born, they will cut her open and take the baby out and save the baby. Otherwise, if the baby is too little to live, the mom and the baby will die." Then he said, an immediate association of ideas that almost made my heart stop, "What if you and Daddy hadn't been there when I came out of the lady I was born from?" And I said, "But we were there." "But what if you weren't?" "But we were." "But what if you weren't?" By the fifth go-round, I gave up and said, "Okay, even though we were there, what do *you* think would have happened if we weren't there?" And he said, "They would have killed me."

I said all the right things. The reason I cannot remember the exact words is not just that I was traumatized by what seemed to me to be his imagined experience of that moment between his connection to his birthmother and his new connection to us—a moment in which he was, in his fantasy, unutterably, unspeakably alone, abandoned, belonging to no one. The reason I cannot remember is that all my "right" responses I knew were not good enough. I explained that we *were* there. That no one would kill him. That his birthmother hadn't died. That he was wonderful. Lord knows what I said. Also I was aware that he was perfectly cheerful throughout this. That he was in a phase of his life full of killing, monsters, chases, macho figures, mayhem. I understood that this was all normal stuff cast into the shape of being adopted. And all that understanding did not help *me* one little bit. He seemed okay, but I was a total wreck.

I slept very little that night. I felt that my answers had been insufficient and that my anguish had made it impossible for me to feel my way to better answers. The next morning, gradually, it came to me that I knew exactly what to say: the truth. The details I already had would answer the need I imagined lay behind his sense of that terrible impossible moment of no one being there.

When he came home from school that afternoon and was sitting on my lap, I said I had been thinking about his questions the day before and realized that I had lots of information that would help him figure everything out. He lay back listening and I said, "There was absolutely no way that there could have been no one there when you were born from the lady you were inside of because—do you know what that lady did?" "What?" said he. "When she was pregnant with you and in her ninth month, she came to the hospital and said, 'I have this little boy inside of me.'" Ian interrupted, obviously gripped by this tale. "How did she know I was a boy?" "You're right," I said. "She didn't know that. She said, 'I have this little baby inside of me and I am too young and too poor to take care of the baby and I want to give the baby to people who want a baby very much and who will take very good care of him.' So the social worker sent her to see Joyce, your godmother, who talked to her and got to know her and thought she was a wonderful, kind, smart person, and then she talked to Nan, our lawyer, who made sure with her that everything would be okay at the hospital. So, you see, even if we weren't there, some wonderful people would have been there because the lady you were born from was taking good care of you and making sure someone would be there when you came out."

He relaxed against me like a giant rag doll, molded against my chest, and smiling, he said, "What did she say when she saw me?" I said, "She said, 'Oh my, isn't he beautiful! Isn't he wonderful!'" Ian beamed. He glowed. He was radiant. And my inner relief was indescribable. Then he sat forward and looked at me and said, "Did she kiss me?" and I said, a little bewildered, "Should she have kissed you?" "Nope," he said, as he bounced off the chair to go play. "Only you should have kissed me because you're my parents." And I felt that that terrible moment of annihilation was gone—for both of us.

Four months later, two months after his seventh birthday, he was playing on the back deck with four friends his own age. In the baby swimming pool they were washing the plastic trays that go under house plants. They were washing them with toothbrushes and chatting and laughing and getting paid a penny apiece. An older boy, age ten, sitting on the side of the deck, suddenly said, "Hey, Ian, what was Elizabeth's name before you got her? She's adopted, isn't she?" And Ian said, "Her name is Elizabeth and always was Elizabeth just like my name was always Ian when my parents got me." And his friend said, "You mean you're adopted too?" And Ian then started to talk. He was scrubbing his trays, looked utterly unfazed, and I was listening on the sidelines. "See, being adopted is better because you're chosen. [Never heard that from me, I thought to myself.] There was this lady, my biological mother. [Never heard that phrase from me either, I thought.] She was too young and too poor to be a mom so when I came out of her vagina my parents were waiting for me and it was the happiest day of their lives." Very matter of fact. For him. For his friends. Then the older boy said, "Well, Ian, when are you going to go look for your real mother?" I was very shocked by that question. I was not ready for it. I thought to myself, "Oh my God, I'm not ready to face that one yet. He's only seven years old." And I stood there, my heart pounding. Ian continued to scrub; then he got up off his knees, wiped his hands on his pants, came over to me, put his arms around my waist, looked up at his older friend, and said, "Richard, you don't understand. This is my real mother." And then went back and continued to scrub. In a few minutes I went into the kitchen, and when I was sure no one was around I sat down and began to cry. I thought, "We did it okay. We're all okay."

For many months after this episode there were no questions or issues raised by Ian around adoption. As a person, he was more full of questions than ever: about science, nature, politics, the world. Once he said, half laughing, half apologizing, "I hope I don't ask too many questions," and I said, "There's nothing you can't ask me." The next day I reminded him of that exchange and asked him if there were any questions he had about being adopted. And he said no. In similar contexts, his father has done the same thing. Ian is now at an age where he is more likely to keep some thoughts to himself, and I feel it makes sense to raise adoption as a subject for conversation now and then to test the waters.

A few months before his eighth birthday we were driving somewhere and laughingly talking about which he liked better, Sprite or Skittles. He said, chuckling, "But do you know what the very best thing in the world is?" "Nope," I said, expecting Coke or M & M's. "To be part of a family and to love them." "Yep," I said. "I'm with you on that one." He is not a sentimental child and I was touched by his earnestness. I wondered whether his emphasis on family had to do with the work we did and all the talking about the different ways to make a family. Whatever its origin, I was counting on it as money in the bank for future upheavals.

Some months later, Ian and I had an encounter that seemed to have a different quality—of fierce intensity with demands for facts—an encounter in which I experienced some new things in myself and about adoption. We were walking to the car to drive to Ian's ceramics class. Suddenly he said, "Why didn't Elizabeth's mother want her? Why didn't my mother want me?" I said that it was the same for Elizabeth's birthmother as for his: they were young, too young to be parents; they did not know their babies in a relationship; they gave them to us to care for them after much thought because they wanted the best for them. He sat in the car and looked wretched, angry, sullen. "How old was she?" "Sixteen," I said. "Sixteen? Or sixteen and a quarter? Or sixteen and a half? *Exactly* how old was she? It matters. It matters." I gave him the exact age and he said, "What was her name?" "I don't know." "How can I find her if I don't know her name?" I said, "When you are older, if you want to find her, Daddy and I will help you." Feeling absolutely awful, I kept on driving and said, at some point as we drove in this gloom, "I'm your mother too," cursing myself for this altogether wrong, injured response. And he said, "Well, sort of." When I dropped him off, I could not drive for twenty minutes. "Sort of." I felt like a rejected lover. I felt so hurt, so disdained, and so worried. What was this anger, this fierce pain? His? Mine?

When I got home I called my husband at work, told him about this conversation, and announced that now he must get involved—I could not have conversations like this all by myself. When Ian got home from ceramics, we had to have a review of this conversation because it was so awful for me as well as for Ian. So when our now cheerful son returned home, we called him into the living room and my husband said, "Hey, Ian, it sounds like you and Mom had a heavy-duty conversation about being adopted. Why don't we talk some more?" And he beamed at us and said, "Why? Mom answered all my questions and I want to go play!" And he hugged us and went and played.

I was blown away by this—and that was just the beginning of this episode! For it was clear that he felt better, that he had dipped deep into the river of his inner life, processed something, and was done with it for the moment—but I was a wreck, and in a new way. I was angry. I was angry at his birthmother. My husband and I went out to dinner and I had a drink and, half joking, half serious, said things like, "Well, why don't the two of them just go shove it!" I was aware at the time that I was reacting like any mother who felt unappreciated or any jealous person. Or a biological mother whose kid is ungrateful and snotty that day and remembers the pain of childbirth and says, "What I went through for you, you little stinker!" But it was new for me to be angry at the birthmother, for, until this conversation, I had felt only love for her, for her gift to us, her sacrifice, her good judgment. Now I felt her as a rival for my son's affections, and I didn't want her around and I was mad.

During the night, I woke up and thought, without guilt but with a sense of having been through something very powerful, "My son really does have two mothers, and I have to find it in my heart to be generous to him and to her. I have to share him with her. I have to let her live in my consciousness. Ian has to deal with this because she really was there." And I felt much better.

Then two quite hilarious and very significant events occurred. Coincidentally I learned that two of Ian's friends, both biological children, had had encounters with their mothers that same week that were very similar to Ian's and mine—fierce, unexpected, rejecting, and leaving their mothers in pieces. The first little boy decided he wanted to run away from home because he didn't want to be there—no particular reason—and the second told his mother he'd trade her in for a dog. (He wanted a dog—she was allergic—therefore—) Each mother described feeling devastated—jealous of the dog or the "out there," puzzled, wretched—until her sense of humor returned. But neither of them had the "other" mother to use as the reason for the distancing. And it suddenly seemed to me that all three boys were dealing with separating from their mothers, with encountering the wider world, with experimenting with distancing themselves from family, all normal developmental tasks. But the extra punch was that I blamed it on Ian's being adopted and did not see, until these chance revelations of my friends, that adoption was simply my child's channel for the same struggles his friends were dealing with. And I wondered how often adoptive parents miss that fact, that adoption becomes the focus for all sorts of normal struggles of growing up that happen in natural families in the same way, with different and varying focuses.

The next night we were reading on the couch and Ian said, "Where is the blanket you took me home in?" I knew just where it was in the basement and raced to get it. He wrapped it around himself and said, "I love this blankie. I'm going to keep it my whole life. Tell me the story again about how you got me." I started to talk, delighted by his cheeriness and struck that only the day before he had seemed so miserable. Suddenly he stood up, wrapped the blanket around him, and said, "Wait, let's go find Daddy and you tell the story when Daddy's there." It was the first time he had included his father, and he climbed onto his dad's lap as I repeated the story. Then his dad said, "Y'know, your mom forgot something. She forgot how I went to the liquor store and said, 'We're getting our boy today and I want the best bottle of champagne there is.' And the manager went into the back and came out with this bottle of Dom Perignon champagne and I bought it, and when we brought you home we drank it and you even had some too." Ian laughed and laughed and wanted to know how much it cost!

Then I said, "Hey, I forgot something else. Here's what it is. Even though you were ours, and nobody could take you from us, when you were six months old we went to court and the judge and the lawyers signed all sorts of papers making it absolutely legal in all the books and rules and laws." And Ian said, very comfortably, in this quite wonderful scene, "And you know what? If anybody had ever tried to take you from me, my daddy would have killed them!" And he laughed.

Since then there have been, at bedtime, lots of questions about what he looked like when I first saw him, how we felt, how big his eyes were, how happy I was. These moments have had a quality of reverie.

After this encounter, I had a better sense of his adoption as something that would intermittently take center stage—sometimes as a metaphor for the latest conflict or growth step, sometimes as just a reality that must be directly dealt with (and who would know the difference at the time?). And just as he, being eight, was more concerned with facts and the real details that he must embrace and integrate, so I had taken a growth step myself and could now include his birthmother in my mental space, not as this ministering good fairy, but as a real person in his life, in our lives.

A few weeks later, again in the car. "Did you choose me?" "No. I couldn't make a baby in my tummy so the lady who is your biological mother—well, she sort of chose us. We were so happy to get you." "That's good, 'cuz if you buy something in the store and choose it you can return it." "Right." "Same with Elizabeth?" "Yep," I said.

Then he asked lots of questions about his birthmother, which I answered. Then he said, "I'm glad you adopted me." "Oh, yes?" "Yes. You were spared the pain of childbirth." That floored me. Where had he gotten that from? So I rambled on about pain and joy and the pain of searching for him and the joy of getting him and how life has lots of pains and joys but I really appreciated his thinking about sparing me pain.

Two weeks later, on the backstairs going up to bed after several hours of playing patience with his dad and me, half asleep he murmured, "I love Dad so much. I love you so much." And in bed, no longer half asleep, in clarion tones he said, "Mom, is it better to have adopted me or given birth to me?" And I said, "What do you think? That's a very very good question." He said, "I think it's just different." And I said, "That's what I think too. Not better. Just different." It was a very quiet and gentle moment and I continued talking. I said that I couldn't imagine him not being our son or in our family. I said that I couldn't imagine being closer to him or loving him any more if I had given birth to him. And he listened and watched very intently and said, "Me neither. Me neither. I want you for my mother." And smiled and fell asleep.

Two days later, after his sister's birthday party, he asked how old Nora was when she gave birth to Bobby, a guest at Elizabeth's party. "Eighteen."

"And how old was my birthmother?" "Sixteen." "Ah, that's younger, isn't it? Tell me some more about her." He was very cheerful and relaxed, curled up against the backseat and I told him again all I knew—that she was energetic and smart and had a good sense of humor and was good in math and science. "I'm good in math and science too. I bet I got it from her." (I did not comment on his adoptive family's talents in these areas.)

At eight and a half, a new burst. Sitting at the kitchen table, testing spelling words, he asked, "Am I Indian?" And I said, "Well, actually, we think you are part Indian. We think the man who planted the seed in the lady you were born from, your birthmother, was part Indian, maybe Mayan." He was one very excited boy. "Tell me about those Indians." So I told him all about the temples and the astronomy and the Yucatan, and he said, "Those people were very smart." "Yes, indeed." "Like me."

A long pause and then he asked, "And my birthmother, where was she from?" "Greece," I said. "A wonderful city called Salonika." "Greece!!" He was now shouting. "That's what Daddy studies!" "Yes," I said, feeling rather solemn. "You come from two great cultures that have affected all our lives." "I'm going to tell my art teacher. She's been wanting to know. I'm Indian and I'm Greek." He was very happy, deeply happy, and I was moved and impressed at what the knowing, with all its uncertainties, did for him.

We have gone over all this many times. He often can't remember. In the library one day, he said, "Hey, Mom, what am I again?" "Mayan and Greek." And then I poked him and said, "And you're ours. And you're Jewish and American and Philadelphian and You. You're completely You."

A few things are new and clear. He has a birthfather in his consciousness for the first time. Two birthparents before us. What they give him in his present thinking appears to be a sense of "real" connectedness to "place"— but "place" now means culture and body for him, and he is stirred by that. And proud. He seems to have all these pieces in his head when he trots off to Sunday school and when he looks at childhood photographs of his eighty-seven-year-old grandfather, born in Russia, light years from the Yucatan, from Greece, and from Philadelphia.

My husband and I wondered together what would come next. When it came, Ian would tell us. Of that we were sure.

For two years there were no "big talks." Ian would explain adoption to his sister; it was frequently a topic of discussion because we had friends who were waiting for their adoptive babies. There were many conversations, relaxed and informative. And then, once again in the car, out of the blue came a cruncher: "Tell me about my birthmother!" And so I did, all I knew. Did he remember the conversations we had had about her in the past? Sort of. He talked quietly and matter-of-factly, clearly now, at ten and a half, interested in information, thinking about history and lineage, not just love and family closeness. We talked a long time about what was on his mind, and I told him we would help him locate his birthmother when he was older if he wanted us to. He said he was happy she had given him to us because he loved us very much. And, as always, I knew something more was coming.

Then he said, "Okay, Mom, I know it's different for you. I really do. But this is how it is for me. You will never be fully mine. Because I did not come out of your body. Because I was not made from your egg and Daddy's sperm. That's how it is for me."

My driving speed was down from 60 to 15 miles per hour on Philadelphia's major artery, and I was proud I still had the car on the road. I felt his sadness so powerfully, and I respected his honesty so deeply. I also understood that this was the boy who a week before had half joked about still wanting to marry me, so I knew that some piece of this failure to "be his" came from the normal developmental crunch of separating from his mom. But I knew that wasn't all of it. He was telling me about his different experience of adoption.

I said to him, "You're right. That really is not how it is for me. For me you are so close that I feel sometimes that I *did* give birth to you. But I hear you. I hear that it is different for you. It's hard, Ian, isn't it, being adopted?"

There was a long silence. Then he said, "Last August, at sailing camp, that Tuesday night when I went to the social. The kids were all talking about how glad they were they weren't adopted. And I didn't tell them I was adopted because I was afraid they would tease me."

We talked some more, and I took him to his friend's house. That night he was very gay and kidded us about being so glad we had adopted him.

Since that conversation, he has been very free talking with us about his adoption. His fifth-grade class is doing family histories, and he is doing a double chart—his biological history and his family history. He and his teacher talk about how lucky he is to have a double history.

Lately he seems to be collecting stories and bringing them home: about our twenty-seven-year-old friend, a boat captain, whose father disappeared right after he was born, so that he was raised by his mother and his grandfather. Then the mother of Ian's best friend told him how her father got custody of her when she was three; her birthmother could not take care of her, and she told Ian how awkward it felt to visit her at Christmas. He also reports many stories of families constituted in nontraditional ways but filled with affection and interconnections.

His six-and-a-half-year-old sister Lizzie cheerfully announced to him last night at dinner, "You're not my real brother. You're my fake brother. We are adopted. I was born from a lady in Georgia who really loved me a lot, and she took care of me for a month, and I was her Georgia peach. Then she gave me to Mom and Dad, who adopted me, and they are my fake parents. We are a fake family."

Ian listened to this, turned, and gave me a look that said, "What are we going to do about her!" Then he said, "Lizzie, let me explain all this to you. Let me tell you about you. No, I'll tell you what happened to me. You see, there was this lady and she was my birthmother and she loved me a lot but she was only sixteen and she was too young and too poor to take care of me so she found Mom and Dad and—" As I listened to him and watched his big brown eyes staring earnestly into her big blue eyes, I could have sworn I heard my own voice talking to him years ago. Later that evening, I said to Lizzie, "Goodnight, my unfake daughter." And she laughed and said, "Goodnight, my unfake mother."

Elizabeth was always everybody's girl. Her brother still announces that he saw her first that traumatic afternoon—forty-five minutes in a mad taxi ride from the airport to a large complex of buildings all bearing the same street number in a vast southern suburb. There I stood in the 100-degree heat, loaded with bags, feeling in fact like an upper-middle-class bag lady, bags full of bottles and diapers and clothes and welcoming pictures and cameras and toys. And no baby. Ian and his dad raced from entrance to entrance looking for the name of the agency, and I stood there paralyzed with the enormity of its being the end of the searching, weighed down by the heat of the sun. And suddenly Ian came rushing out to me. "We found her. We found her. I saw her first. I was the first one. I saw her before Dad. Before anyone. Where's my picture to show her?" I staggered up the stairs, and there she was—his girl—sitting in her daddy's arms—his girl. My girl. My daughter. I had waited half my lifetime for her. I held her so tightly on the airplane all the way home that I had tendonitis for two days.

At four years she had yellow hair, cornflower blue eyes, white skin, and red lips. No one in three generations on either side looked like that! She looked like the little girl in the storybooks I read as a child, the ones with the little white dog and the white picket fence. We populated her room with dolls that looked like her, and she announced to friends and neighbors all, "This is Lizzie doll. She's the only one in the family that looks like me."

She was concerned about looking different from us. We are all various shades of middle to darker tones and all with brown hair. She announced to visitors, "I'm the only member of this family with blonde hair. My daddy loves blondes." And indeed he does. Every morning after she was dressed she told him to close his eyes. She stood before him. "Open them," she would say. He was dazzled. "Here I am," she announced. "Beautiful Elizabeth."

She was full of ideas and images and language all of which flowed into each other without regard to time or place or "reality." "Mom," she would say, "we left the blanket to dry at Frog Pond yesterday and it's ready for us to go get it." That was three months before.

She was not interested in origins. A generous child, she was very interested in babies. "When I grow up I am going to have twenty-two babies in my tummy, eleven boys and eleven girls." Always very independent, she stopped using her stroller at eighteen months. One day, when she was three and a half, she announced that she would be a baby that day, and she wanted to be wheeled like a baby to the park. I dutifully complied, and as we reached the corner and waited for the traffic to pass, she said from up front in the stroller, "Was I in your tummy?" And I said, "Well, actually, you were in the tummy of another lady who couldn't be a mommy so when you were all ready to come out, Daddy and I went to get you and you were our baby." Silence. More silence.

At four and a quarter she was happily playing in our bedroom and she announced her maternal future. "Fourteen children! I am going to have fourteen children!" "Wonderful," I replied, as enthusiastic as ever about her plans. She stared at me very solemnly with those huge eyes. "Mom, I was definitely in your tummy." "No, honey. You weren't. Just like Ian, you were in another lady's tummy." "Nope, yours. Your tummy." This little girl was not pleased. "Lizzie, Mommy was your mommy from when you were born, but you weren't in my tummy. Just like Ian." (I was clinging for dear life to her adoration of her brother.) She suddenly pulled her shoulders back, straightened up, and resonantly shouted, "Well, then, I was in Daddy's tummy!" Brutally and quietly, I said, "No. Not in Daddy's tummy either." Long silence. Then, "I'm going downstairs to check on the weather." And off she went. And no conversation.

A month later, in a crowded subway car, out of nowhere, she spoke in very authoritative tones. "I was not in your tummy. That nice lady went to the doctor and I came out of her tummy to be with you. I was *so* happy to see you!" And her moist-eyed parents said, in unison, "We were so happy to see you too!"

In kindergarten, a few weeks before Lizzie's sixth birthday, her father partly overheard another child whisper something to Elizabeth about "not in your mommy's tummy" and "you're adopted!" What he heard resoundingly was Lizzie's reply. Cheerfully and matter-of-factly swinging her yellow curls, she said, "Of course I'm adopted. Yeah, sure, I wasn't in my mommy's tummy. I was in this nice lady's tummy and she was too young to be a mommy. So I came out of her tummy, and my mommy and daddy were waiting for me, and my mom's been happy ever since." Right on, Elizabeth!

Six weeks after her seventh birthday, at a neighborhood barbecue I took a break from the party and sat for a while in the living room. Lizzie came in at one point, carrying her doll, and sat down near me on the couch. "I love my Lizzie doll," she said. "You got her for me when I was four years old. You got her because she looks like me. She has my blue eyes and my yellow hair and my peach-colored skin. You are my best mom. You are my real grand mom. The lady I was born from, she loved me a lot, but she only knew me for one day. You and Daddy have known me ever since I was a month old, and you cried every day for a month when you were waiting to get me out of Georgia. You are my real mom and my best mom." Sitting near her, I could almost hear the wheels turning in her mind as she was figuring things out—her way, Lizzie's way, as always, as it should be.

●

Mehera

Mehera: Adopting means you love a baby very much and go find her.

At twenty-five I wrote fantasies in my journal about how my life would be at thirty-five. Influenced by California surroundings in the early 1970s, I day-dreamed about a large piece of land with numerous loosely connected small houses and families supporting one another in the task of raising children. I can't remember whether or not I had a partner; perhaps I was a single parent. There were several children in my household. I believe they were all foster children or adopted.

On my thirty-fifth birthday circumstances were quite different. Now in the 1980s, back in New Hampshire, I lived in a small house in the country with my husband, Patrick. There were no communities, no children. We had been trying to conceive a child for several years, but despite expert medical assistance, no baby was on the horizon.

I felt ready to begin adoption procedures, but Patrick was hesitant. We had spent a considerable amount of time in India visiting Meher Baba's tomb and his close disciples in a community located inland from Bombay. I imagined adopting an Indian baby and remembered an old daydream of a daughter called Mehera, named after Meher Baba's close disciple, a woman who had become important in our lives.

In the spring of that year Patrick was killed in a car accident. All thoughts of babies were put aside in order simply to survive this loss. After a year or so had passed, adoption thoughts began to trickle through my mind again. I knew I would have to embark on this journey as a single parent and waited for my full strength to return. Family and friends encouraged me, and the fantasies flowered.

I remember exactly where I was standing when the decision was made, when I "knew" that I would be adopting a baby from India. On somewhat of a whim I had gone alone to a conference entitled The Unattached Child. The presenter dealt with the treatment of children who, owing to early trauma, fail to develop meaningful attachments, often causing great turmoil in their foster and adoptive families. I realized that adoption scared me when I thought about the possibility of having a child who would never be able to form a real relationship with me. I had always thought there would be nothing I could do. The presenter, however, held out great hope for these children, and I suddenly felt encouraged.

There was a single frozen moment, as I leaned on a door jamb listening to adoption workers trading stories, when I knew with absolute certainty that I would be the mother of an Indian baby. I can still see clearly the face of an Indian woman who was later to play an important role in my daughter's adoption. The smell of the coffee during the break, the light along the walls in a college classroom building, the stairs leading to another floor, the light laughter and chatter of participants' voices all mark this moment. I leaned against the door frame and knew it was time to begin. As soon as the conference ended, I raced home and began calling for information and applications.

I make an issue out of this moment because it underlines an important belief for me about adoption, one that I regularly communicate to my daughter, Mehera, now aged three and a half. Adoption is not a random process or event to me. I truly believe that this child was meant to be my daughter, and the journey to find her, part of my destiny. I realize that many people shrug or frown at such statements, and I never feel a desire to try to convince others of this experience. It is far too subjective. Explaining adoption to small children, however, seems easier for parents who believe that the match is purposeful rather than random.

As it turned out, Mehera was conceived in Pune, India, within a week or so of this conference. I spent the next nine months in a frenzy of preparation, juggling the endless forms that many adoptive parents of children born abroad remember only too well. Seals, stamps, official registers, and bureaucratic maneuvers filled my waking and sleeping mind. I prepared to go to India myself. I was becoming increasingly aware that single-parent adoption presented far greater problems than adoption by a couple. I was sure that being on the spot in India would help my case greatly.

One morning in May I woke up suddenly with something like an alarm bell clanging in my head. The baby! The baby was being born or would be born soon! I wrote and drew in my journal and picked out names. A little girl would be called Mehera. Despite some excitement, I felt quite disappointed because a baby born in May would be almost four months old before I arrived in India to start the process. I had hoped to adopt a very young infant.

Over the summer I made final preparations, obtained visas, and mentally readied myself for whatever might follow. I had a strong preference for a baby from Pune because of the city's proximity to the Meher Baba community, but I had been advised that single parents were often discriminated against by adoption officials in Pune. I felt willing to go anywhere, do anything. Perhaps I might volunteer in an orphanage, taking care of a baby I could later adopt. Friends and family were very supportive. A close friend planned to travel to India with me; another old friend decided that volunteering in an Indian orphanage touched a deep chord in him, and he made plans to meet me there later.

Mehera was born in May, and she was a little over three months old on the first day I saw her. I was not "supposed" to be the family she went to live with, but owing to various circumstances she and I ended up together. Instead of my working at the institution, a large women's shelter with a small room for babies relinquished for adoption, I was told that I would become Mehera's foster parent until her exit visa was ready and could then take her with me.

The three-month process of waiting in India to become her foster parent was filled with aggravation, but in the end I got custody of Mehera, then six months. We spent three more months in India before immigration clearance arrived for us. These last months proved to be a severe physical ordeal, but an emotional comfort. We had no stable living arrangements. Finding food, clothing, diapers, and bottles became a complex project; hot water did not come out of taps, and I had access only to malfunctioning hot plates. Sterilization presented regular problems, as did cooking and mashing up food for the baby. Diapers did not exist in the city we were staying in. We cut up pieces of terry cloth and covered them with plastic pieces that tied. Many of the arrangements struck us as downright humorous when we were in the right mood. On the other hand, we were surrounded by the affection of friends, people from the Meher Baba community. In some ways it was reminiscent of my old dream of community, although I longed for a washing machine! We had fun visiting with everyone, but my fingers sometimes cracked open from the endless washings with Indian detergents.

The story I tell Mehera is a little simpler. Most of her questions and reactions to her infancy come up when she is looking at baby pictures or hearing "the story." We have had a little post-bath ritual since she was very small. I wrap her up in a towel, like a swaddled baby, and hold her close in my arms. Since age one and a half, Mehera often asks me at this moment to tell her about when she was a baby.

I open the story: "Once there was a little soul waiting to be born. The little soul looked all around for a little body to be in so it could be born. Did the little soul want a body from England?"

Mehera shouts, "No!"

"From Italy?"

"No!"

"From New Hampshire?"

"No!"

"From India?"

"Yes!!!" (Many shrieks and laughs.)

"So the little soul found a perfect body in Pune waiting to be born. It jumped inside and in a while the baby was born in Sassoon Hospital just where Meher Baba was born when he was a tiny baby. The tiny new baby went to wait at the baby clinic for her mother to come to adopt her. The Indian women took very good care of her there. They rocked her and played games with all the babies.

"Now I was in America waiting to adopt my baby. I wanted a baby from India very much. One day I had a thought: 'My baby has been born! It is time to go looking for her!' I packed up my suitcase, took some baby bottles and clothes, and Valeria, your godmother, and I flew off to India in the airplane.

"As soon as we got to India, we drove to the baby clinic to see if my baby was there. When we came into the room, there was a very tiny baby in the back. A woman was holding her. When the baby saw me come in, she popped up her little head and waved to me! I asked Valeria, 'Do you think that could be my baby waving to me?' Then the women at the baby clinic asked me if I would like to adopt Baby Mehera. I said, 'Oh *yes*!!! I would love to adopt you!!!'

"I went to get everything ready for you to come with me. Ned, your god-father, and I came to pick you up in the taxi. You were all ready, so we said good-bye to the women who had taken such good care of you while you were waiting for me, and off we went to Meherabad. When we sat in the taxi, I fed you a bottle in my arms, and then I sang you 'Bujaawe' [a song written by Meher Baba]. You listened to every word, looking right up into my eyes, and then you just closed your eyes and fell asleep.

"When we got to the hotel we played and played on the beds, tickling and laughing. We were very happy to be together. After a while you were so tired that you fell over right on your face on the mattress and went to sleep. In the morning, I got up before you to fix your bottle. Suddenly you woke up with a jerk and sat straight up in the bed with your eyes all huge and round. You looked a little frightened because you didn't remember where you were. Then you saw me standing there and your face broke into a big grin, and you felt safe because you were finally with your mummy."

After my concerns about bonding, it seemed that this would not be one of our difficulties. Mehera seemed immediately comfortable with me and wouldn't let anyone else touch her for a couple of weeks.

"The story" has remained pretty much the same since Mehera was one and a half. Sometimes I add details, but the flavor is the same. Mehera has always loved to hear it, and sometimes I have overheard her summarizing it for others. "My mommy came to India. My mommy loves me," at a younger age, and a little later, "Adopting means you love a baby very much and go find her."

We knew a number of families with adopted children, so Mehera didn't think there was anything unusual about her situation. In retrospect, I think I was trying to create an illusion that our situation was the norm. Mehera asked if people had found their babies at the baby clinic, and when one of my friends became pregnant, Mehera thought she would be taking the baby to the baby clinic after it was born so that someone could find it!

We had a family story with no pain, no exasperations, no difference from others. Although Mehera loved it, and it made her feel happy and secure, it was rather different from the actual drama. I wasn't sure how to integrate reality and the myth. The pride I felt at having managed the adoption added to its myth somehow, as well as the fact that in the beginning we seemed to be in constant contact with other adoptive families, adoption agencies, receiving calls from prospective adoptive parents. Probably the root of the myths lay in a common parental urge to protect Mehera from the sadness of life, the confusions, the disappointments. I had been willing to show her only an India that was endlessly exciting and beautiful, not an India full of unrest and poverty.

One day a friend and I compared notes on our daughters' questions about their adoption. The girls were close in age and came from the same baby clinic. She talked about her three-year-old daughter's reactions to knowing about her birthmother, and I had a sinking feeling. She is only a few months older than Mehera, and she already knows about birthmothers! I must not be doing this right! I have been depriving her of information rightfully hers! I felt acutely the lack of a co-parent over the years, someone I would have discussed these things with. I was overcome with a sense of urgency—I had to tell Mehera about her birthmother right away—as if I had made a grave error by withholding the truth for so long. Our lovely story seemed threatened. Some magical bond we had shared was loosening, unraveling.

The issue of birthmothers suddenly presented itself as a difficult one for me, although I had not previously acknowledged it. Suddenly I remembered a time eight months back when Charlie (Mehera's new daddy) had just come to live with us. She had been very friendly toward him, very excited about having a daddy, but one night at supper she announced that she wouldn't be living with us anymore. In a very matter-of-fact way, she informed us that she was moving to her "other mom's" house. It seemed that she and her "other mom" lived alone in a cottage in the woods, down a path through the forest (rather like Goldilocks). Mehera said she would come to visit us sometimes. Her words "other mom" gave me a chill, and I had eerie fantasies that in spite of my silence she knew all about her birthmother. For a few moments I was speechless, as if believing that our connection was so tenuous, not being blood, that Mehera could simply reject me and choose a new person to take better care of her.

Finally I returned to reality and began to understand her statements in terms of her feeling displaced by Charlie's moving in. She then said that Charlie thought she was a "nuisance," a word from her favorite book. This made it easier for me to hear the hurt feelings, the jealousies, and we told her that we loved her very much and of course she would live with us, that this was her house and that there was always room for her, even if she had a new daddy. She dropped the plan of moving to her "other mom's" and we haven't heard about her since. Mehera does have a lot of imaginary relatives, however. Instead of pretend friends, Mehera has new grandmothers, uncles, brothers, sisters, and cousins.

The moment had finally come to talk about birthmothers. Mehera had seen pregnant women and their babies soon after birth, so she understood something about the process. She asked if she had been in my belly, but didn't seem too disturbed when I told her that some babies come from their mom's bellies and others are adopted by parents who make a special effort to find them. Mehera expressed regret, however, that I hadn't nursed her. She tried to get me to change my mind to say that she had had milk from my nipples instead of a bottle, but then dropped it. A week later Mehera made up a new game: sucking my nose!

At the dinner table one night recently, the story of her infancy in India came up. I asked her if she knew that she had been in another woman's belly before she was born. "Yes, I know," Mehera said in her precise manner. "She had brown skin like me," and she pointed to her wrist. She thought that her adopted friend's term "tummy-mommy" was very funny, and she repeated it laughing several times, but didn't seem to need to talk more about it. A week or so later, she referred briefly to her "Indian mom" as the birthmother, going on to talk about other aspects of the story that fascinate her, such as the taxi ride. During another conversation, Mehera told me, "My Indian mom took care of me until you could come get me." When I looked a bit surprised, she added, "You know, the one whose belly I was in!" Then she asked me where I had been.

"Do you mean where was I when you were at the baby clinic?"

Mehera nodded.

"I was in America getting ready for you."

"Sometimes I cried for you when I was a tiny baby," Mehera said, "when I was at the baby clinic."

Before adopting Mehera I had wondered what I would tell her about her birthmother. I had thought of saying that she didn't have enough food for a baby, but decided that this would only create anxiety over my being able to take care of her. If one person could run out of resources, why not another? Recently I realized that maybe there is no need to talk about reasons until Mehera wants them. I was surprised to find that at the moment Mehera not only is relatively uninterested in this business of birthmothers but has no need to know why she didn't stay with hers. Mehera's world is a place where mothers come searching for the children they want and love, and logically the children had to be someplace in order for the mothers to find them. I remembered what people always said about giving children information about sex—answer the question they are asking without flooding them with extra information. I felt a lack of guidelines in talking to a little child about adoption, but at least that principle might be the same.

This morning Mehera and I were lying on the floor playing, and she told me with a big smile that her daddy was adopting her.

"What do you think it means?" I asked.

"It means that he loves me very much and he found me!"

"It's very true," I told her. "Daddy wanted a child very much, and he was looking for a long time and now he found you. He chose both of us. He got married to me, and he is adopting you. So I guess we'll be going back to the courthouse pretty soon to let that judge know about it, and have another little party!"

Now, just when I felt sure that Mehera had the whole thing straightened out and was feeling at ease with her "story," I overheard a conversation between Mehera and her little friend Hannah (both three).

Hannah: I was born in California.

Mehera: I was born in India.

Hannah: I was in my daddy's tummy!

Mehera: I was in my brother's tummy! Then I came out and my sister came to find me. She's my mother. My sister is my mother!

Kathy and Aaron

Kathy: Who is right, Mom, my birthmom or Jane [who will keep
her baby]?
Aaron: It's okay, Mom. You have me now.

When Kathy was two years old, my husband and I took her to the zoo.
There in the elephant's cage was a baby elephant. We taught her the word
elephant. "He is brand new. He came out of his mommy's tummy. Baby
people grow inside their mommy's tummy too. When they are ready to be
born, they come out. You grew inside another mother's tummy and after
you were born, you became part of our family." We taught her the word
adoption. She was more impressed with *elephant.* Kathy does not remember
that day. But I do. I remember taking a deep breath before my short speech.
I remember how much I wanted her to know that she was adopted as a part
of her knowledge of where babies come from. I wanted to be truthful with
her as I hoped she would grow to be with me. I wanted to talk openly about
adoption to her as I hoped she could some day talk to me. If adopting and
being adopted are okay, then adoption is okay to talk about. Kathy was too
busy studying elephants that day to get much out of my speech, but it was
good practice for us. And sometime in those early years I did accomplish
my goal—years later when I asked how she learned she was adopted, she
shrugged. "I always knew."

When Kathy was two and a half, we adopted her brother, Aaron. By then
we were reading bedtime stories. In preparation for Aaron's arrival I added
books for kids on adoption and new baby brothers. We talked about the
baby's impending arrival. "A woman had a baby. She cannot take care of it.
We can, and we want another child. So we are going to adopt him. He will
be part of our family. You will be a big sister." With only a week's warning
before Aaron's arrival, I wondered how adequately we could prepare her. I
wished, again, that I could be pregnant. Before, the wish was selfish; now
the wish was still selfish, but I also wished my daughter to have more normal
preparation time before becoming a big sister.

Kathy came with us to receive Aaron. She would be able to see for herself
how she and now her brother came into our family. Bob and I went up to
the nursery and returned with Aaron. This baby, who would cry with colic
for four months solid, had the sense on first meeting to smile at Kathy. "He
likes me," she exclaimed. He was an accepted addition to our family. When
we arrived home, she ran down the block to share the news with friends.
Later a neighbor called. "What have you been telling the children?" she
asked testily. "My daughter says Kathy says you went to a baby store and
got a new baby and—" So much for careful preparation.

I love my children. In telling them about adoption, I wanted to do it right. "Right" to me meant so that they would feel good about themselves, understand the facts accurately, and know we loved them. My mental model was sex education. My parents had done a good job of answering my questions in straightforward and age-appropriate ways. When I was not asking for information they thought I should have, they usually found a way to work it into a conversation. They understood that there were many levels and that what I wanted and needed to know at age six would not suffice at sixteen. They approached sexuality with a sense of respect and privacy and humor. To them, there were no dumb questions. That seems to me a good model for discussing adoption with kids.

When Kathy was four, I realized that she was beginning to grasp the concept of adoption. About every six months since her brother's arrival, I had added a book or two on adoption to the pile of bedtime stories. Sometimes we would read one once and lose interest. Other times, a book became the theme of the week and would be reread every night at her request. Each time she asked, or I offered, a little more. "Babies take about nine months to be ready to be born." "When we adopted you, your grandmother came and showed me how to change your diapers." One day Kathy asked, "If Grandmother is your birthmother, who is your adopted mother?" I explained that some people are born into their families and others are adopted. She looked quizzical but accepted this like any other bit of information. I do not know if it bothered her then. It would later. It bothered me then, because I knew that no child likes to be different and that some day this might bring her pain. I hoped that I could teach her tolerance and appreciation for the variety of people before society could teach her that being different is negative.

At age five Kathy and her best friend darted into our kitchen for a snack. They had been helping tie up the balloons and streamers of crepe paper for the friend's aunt's baby shower. "Mom, we're going to have cake, and she has presents, and it's a surprise, and—" went the breathless excitement. "And," interjected her friend, "why didn't Kathy's mother keep her?" Kathy's face froze for just a second. This was a question she had not thought of. I tried not to let my face freeze too. This was the question that scared me; it implies rejection. "She will take her cues from you," I told myself. "Keep it brief." Aloud I explained, "Kathy's mom was young. She was still in school. She knew babies are a lot of work—diapers and all that. She did not have a dad to help her. She wanted Kathy to have a mom and a dad who were ready. So she chose us." I looked into their faces. I am not sure what reaction I was expecting, but I did not get it. "Oh, okay," said the girls matter-of-factly. "And then we are going to yell 'surprise,' and her baby is due next week," and off they went to finish decorating. The question that had held such dread for me held no such complications for them. They were just trying to make sense out of life, to get the facts. It was then that I decided to be sure I gave my kids the basic information they could absorb before their teenage years—before it was emotionally loaded; while I was still credible—so that when we got to the hard questions (those with emotional or moral overtones) we would have some foundation to build on. Little did I know the hard questions would start at age eight.

When Kathy was seven she and that same friend were helping me choose wallpaper for her room. They were in the next aisle chatting. The friend poked her head around the corner and asked, "How old is Kathy's real mother now?" "I'm Kathy's real mother," I responded. The friend's eyes glassed over as kids' do when you are losing them. Although I may have the right to claim "real mother" status and to feel territorial about it, at that moment I was not being useful to these girls. I managed to add quickly, "Her birthmother was seventeen when Kathy was born. Kathy is seven now. How old is her birthmother?" (Never pass up a math lesson.) The friend did some quick figuring and disappeared around the corner. I waited to hear the rest of the question. I am still waiting. I never learned the context of that question. It was then that I realized I would not be able to protect Kathy. I would not always have the opportunity to give cues about attitude as I had been able to do several years earlier. Kathy would be processing more and more information with her friends and, if I did not work to keep the communication open, less and less with me. Scary stuff to a mom.

This was confirmed for me a couple of months later. Walking home from the library, out of the blue, Kathy stated, "My dad is a jerk." I was taken aback. I wondered what my husband had done to generate such anger and disrespect. "He left my mom by herself," Kathy added. We were talking about her *birth*dad! With recovering calm I asked, "What do you know about him?" She had been told everything we had been able to find out, which was not much. But given the information we do have, the conclusion is hard to avoid. She had worked it out with a friend. I did not want to leave Kathy with the sense that the person from whom she inherited her considerable height, coordination, and glorious head of curly hair that makes her appearance so striking and her so self-conscious was a jerk. I suggested that given how little we knew, it might not be fair to judge him so harshly. She did not respond. I am still uncomfortable about this one. Kathy needs to know that some people are indeed jerks. When someone makes a wisecrack about her appearance, we label that person a jerk and usually discount him or her. Do we now discount Kathy's birthdad? I am sure we will discuss this issue again.

When Kathy was eight, Jane, a teenager we knew, became pregnant and planned to raise her child. "Who is right, Mom," she asked, "my birth-mom or Jane?" The hard questions had started. We talked off and on during Jane's pregnancy and the months that followed about what it takes to raise a baby. Is it all right for two people to choose differently for themselves? I wanted to teach Kathy tolerance. I didn't want her to say anything hurtful to Jane. On the other hand, I do *not* think it's okay for a seventeen-year-old to drop out of school and raise babies; I am not crazy about Kathy's thinking it might be okay. I said I was worried about the girl and the baby and explained why. I left it at that. Kathy observed astutely the respects in which the girl did and did not cope. With time I felt more comfortable, because Kathy's questions were so thoughtful. I was learning to trust her judgment.

We found Jill Krementz's book *How It Feels to Be Adopted* helpful that year. Kathy read the autobiographical stories of eight-, nine-, and ten-year-olds carefully. (Her interest waned with the older children's stories because the issues discussed were beyond her maturity.) But with the eight- and nine-year-olds, she wanted to know exactly how her own story compared and contrasted. She seemed to be working out for herself what she shared in common with other adopted children and what was uniquely hers. That felt good to me. The stories gave form to her questions and gave us common ground on which to discuss them.

That same year Kathy's class made flags to represent their parents' ethnic backgrounds. My daughter is biracial. "Mom, making German flags [my background] will look dumb." She had a point. (I had not expected to have to deal with this issue until high school biology classes, when genetics and family trees will come up.) "How about if you make four flags—two for Dad and me and two for your birthparents' heritage?" Flags turned out to be a prestige item. (Sometimes, as a mom, you luck into a great solution.) Half of Kathy's classmates proceeded to come up with a third or fourth parent because of divorce, remarriage, adoption, or whatever. That helped Kathy to view having multiple parents as not so unusual after all. Later she would comment on how lucky she was that she had more than two parents without ever having had to endure a divorce. Being adopted was not so bad by comparison. I really liked the context. It is nice to know that your kid finds you acceptable and herself not such an oddity.

That dreaded "my real mother would let me—" did not come until age nine. The first time, I treated it as a variation on "Jenny's mother doesn't make her wear boots." I said, "I am your mother now, and now you may not—" When it came up again, we talked about what makes people a family—in divorced, adoptive, and biological families. How do people take care of each other and love each other? Who had enjoyed snuggling her as a baby and listening to school Christmas concerts, and who would be there when she had children of her own some day? That conversation felt comfortable to me and seemed to make sense to her. A year later when "real mom" came up again in a similar context, I teased her that she just wanted a fairy godmother who would grant her every wish. I told her I wanted one too. That met with considerable laughter.

I did not share with Kathy until she was ten the letter her birthmother wrote at the time of her adoption. It was full of the pain of a surrender and, I decided, too complex for a young child. I told her of its existence earlier but said it was too grown up for her. She accepted that. At this writing, she is eleven, on the brink of her teenage years. Most days, being an adoptive family is irrelevant. When it comes up, sometimes it feels fine. Other times I wish I could spare her the pain or confusion, and myself too, I suppose. But she is a perceptive child and quite wonderful. And most days I am a pretty good mom. I think we will both do fine.

Telling Aaron was different. With Kathy, I had tried to think it all out ahead of time; with Aaron I could play it by ear. Actually, Kathy must have explained adoption to him, maybe while they were looking at photo albums, because I don't remember telling him. It is as if he always knew. He is the second child, and for him being adopted is normal. His sister is adopted, he is adopted, the dog is adopted ("Mom, you didn't born him either— ha ha!"). Kathy has often formulated questions for him. He would over- hear her asking something about her birthmother and request the equivalent information about his.

The questions original to him were about his birthfather. They came when he was four and thinking about what toys, clothes, and activities were appropriate for males. Fortunately, we had some information to offer about his birthdad. When we did the bedtime stories with him, he grew particu- larly fond of Sue Lapsey's I Am Adopted; the child in question is a boy with a tricycle like his.

Because his learning about adoption was merged with Kathy's, or per- haps because I was more relaxed, I recall fewer specific conversations with Aaron. I do have one distinct memory. When he was in preschool, he asked, "Why did you adopt us?" It was 7:00 A.M. and I am not a morning person. He was munching breakfast; I was curling my hair and putting on makeup in rushed preparation to leave for a seminar I was presenting. "Why now?" I thought. I began with a quick explanation. "Dad and I wanted kids. But my body does not work right for having babies. So we could not born you. We really wanted you. So—" Aaron had come over to where I stood and was patting me on the back. "It's okay, Mom. You have me now." Aaron was not a particularly empathic preschooler. I had thought the pain of infertility and the longing were settled. Apparently, not completely; he had heard it. I gave him a big hug. He scooted happily back to his breakfast. I had to wash off tear-streaked makeup and try again. Years later when I came across a copy of David Kirk's book *Shared Fate* I thought of how useful it had been to Aaron to understand that we needed him as much as he needed us.

Aaron is eight now. We have read a few autobiographies from *How It Feels to Be Adopted*. He would like to know if he is going to be bald some-day. He was surprised and not a little annoyed to learn that I could not just call up his birthmother and ask if baldness runs in the family. But by and large, he is much more interested in sports and Scouts and anything mechanical than in the issues of adoption. In this he is quite different from his sister, but he is an equally wonderful kid. He, too, will be fine.

●

Daniel Joo Bin: Family Lost and Found

Daniel: You're Oma. That means "Mother" in Korean.

Daniel Joo Bin spent the first five years of his life as an only child, living in Korea with his biological parents. At age five he was relinquished and subsequently lived for five months at the Holt Reception Center in prepara-tion for his final journey to the United States. Waiting for him was his new family consisting of my husband, John, myself, and our biological children, Matthew, age nine, and Jennifer, age seven.

Becoming a member of our family would require Daniel to undergo huge changes in every facet of his existence: identity, culture, language, role within the family, habits, and relationships. He was to enter an Ameri-can family that had well-established sibling and parent-child relationships and rules and routines that had developed over a period of years. Daniel would be forced to assimilate and accommodate at a time when he was also experiencing intense feelings of loss.

During the two years that Daniel has been with us, the issues of loss and integration into our family have been major themes for him and for all of us. In looking back at the significant incidents, it seems that Daniel has progressed through several stages in the past two years, and that each stage has been marked by his work on the themes of loss and integration. In telling our story for others we hope to share some of the understandings that Daniel has helped us to reach, realizing that every child and family will experience the process of adoption in their own unique way.

Daniel's first six months with us was a time of great vulnerability, a period when his need to be accepted often felt overwhelming to us and most certainly to him. In recalling the May night when he climbed smiling into our car at the airport for the drive to his new home, I am again and again struck by his incredible courage, his tenacity, and his desire to triumph in a situation that most adults would find devastating. All of Daniel's energy in the earliest few days focused on pleasing us. We remember how he emerged from his bedroom the very first morning completely dressed with his bed made, how he ate every morsel of the strange foods we presented him with that first week, always smiling, struggling to communicate despite his total lack of the English language.

Soon, however, the needs began to surface, and by the end of the first week Daniel required my constant attention. He was an extremely competent five-and-a-half-year-old with unusual independence skills; yet he wanted me to do almost everything for him. He often regressed to what felt to me like the emotional level of a toddler, physically hanging onto me, needing to be held for long periods of time, once mimicking the feeding behavior of an infant. Without having experienced an early history together, this bonding process was difficult for both of us. I understood that Daniel could not tolerate any rejection from us, yet it was exhausting and truly impossible to meet his every demand. I found myself feeling resentful and angry that he should expect so much from me. The many conflicting emotions sometimes led to a sense of guilt that I wasn't a good enough mother.

The days filled with Daniel's loud shouts of "Mom!" and since we had so little shared verbal language, every interaction had the potential to be long and eventually frustrating for both of us. Daniel wanted to control every-thing, from setting the table to buying certain foods in the grocery store, many of which he later wouldn't eat. Tantrums with crying, screaming, and door slamming became frequent and often intense. But just as difficult to deal with were the angry, sullen periods when Daniel refused to make eye contact or to interact with anyone. John and I felt it was important to have consistent and realistic expectations for Daniel's behavior, as we did for Matthew's and Jennifer's, but his neediness and newness to the family made us question our expectations and methods of discipline as we never had with his older siblings.

Perhaps for me the most painful part of Daniel's first months with us had to do with how his presence affected Matthew and Jennifer. Daniel did not want to share me with the other children and would on occasion try to block me physically from interacting with them. He was extremely sensitive to any attention I gave them. Matthew had some trouble dealing with Daniel's desire to possess me but coped well most of the time. For Jennifer, however, Daniel's presence was often devastating. She had lost her position as "baby" in the family to what she perceived as a demanding, in-trusive stranger that we had actually wished upon ourselves! She had hoped for a cute, fun little brother and was furious with the disappointment and the injury we had inflicted upon her. Matthew's relationship with Daniel progressed more smoothly as Daniel tended to look up to and admire his older brother from the beginning, but for Jennifer, Daniel's integration into the family circle was a slow and painful one, with many wishes to "send him back."

Daniel acquired English with astounding speed and in fact had forgotten most of his Korean language after about three months with us. He frequently talked about his life in Korea when he came across something that reminded him of a particular incident. He drew pictures of his Korean house and shared some memories about his "Oma" and "Appa" (mother and father). We were surprised by his matter-of-fact way of relating and his apparent absence of pain.

It was not until he had been with us for six months that Daniel's grief and mourning for his tremendous loss began to surface. In retrospect, it seems that during the initial critical adjustment period Daniel's survival was dependent upon having his immediate demands for love and acceptance met. Only after he had attained some level of integration and security within the family was he able to begin to pay attention to his feelings of loss for his Korean parents and the world he had left behind. This time of grieving, which was to last for about a year, seems to us to mark the second stage in Daniel's development within our family.

Although most of Daniel's days were marked by his exuberant approach to life, during this long year it seemed that Daniel was often withdrawn and sad, especially when he was not involved in a structured activity. It was difficult for him to spend any time by himself, although we knew that he had previously enjoyed many solitary activities. He was seldom able to articulate his feelings, but it was clear from his facial expressions that he was dealing with a good deal of anxiety and sadness.

During this year Daniel experienced a number of intense grieving episodes. He would cry for long periods of time and was truly inconsolable. Although John or I would hold him as he cried, he appeared to be unconnected to us, totally involved in a very private world of pain. On several occasions, either just as the crying began or when the tears were subsiding, he was able to tell us that he missed his parents or that he worried that they wouldn't survive without him to help. Being with Daniel during his grieving was very difficult for me. It seemed that I was little comfort to him; his pain was beyond my reach. It was frightening for me to feel the intensity of his loss and disappointing for me not to be able to take his pain away.

After some time it became clear to us that although we couldn't console Daniel or change what had happened to him, we could help him by bearing his sorrow with him. It seemed important for him to know that no matter how desolate he felt, he would not be destroyed by his sadness and that we as a family would continue to be there for him. As time went on we tried to help Daniel put some boundaries on his sadness so that he could stop crying after ten or fifteen minutes. We hoped that eventually he would learn how to deal with the feeling of being overwhelmed and would develop coping skills that would give him some sense of control over his life.

Daniel had many reunification fantasies and wishes during this period. He often talked about returning to Korea and finding his home there. He told us that he wanted to have his parents come and live in a tent in our backyard so that we could all be together. He once dictated a letter to me to send to his parents that told them how much he missed them and worried about them. Even though I told him that we couldn't send it because we didn't know how to locate them, and though we repeatedly told him that he would be staying with us and could return to Korea only when he was a grown-up, Daniel persisted in his belief/wish to maintain his contact.

In retrospect, it seems that Daniel's fantasies contributed greatly to his belief that he wouldn't be staying with us permanently. Although he was frequently frustrated that he didn't share a history with us (as when his siblings would say to him, "Oh, that happened before you came, Daniel"), he also alluded to the belief that he wouldn't share a future with us. While visiting Disneyland, Daniel was very disappointed to have to leave at the end of the day. When my husband told him that we'd come again when we next visited our close friends in California, he forlornly said that he wouldn't be with us then. Despite our many reassurances and even the formal adoption proceedings, Daniel persisted in projecting disappointment and loss into his future.

Daniel's fragility continued during this time. He was extremely sensitive to any comment he perceived as critical and was very upset if anyone corrected him in any way. He always wanted to be first, found many situations unfair, and wanted to control his siblings in a parental way. Obviously these attributes were not popular with Matthew and Jennifer, and discord frequently arose. It wasn't at all unusual for Daniel to become suddenly extremely angry, to burst into tears and run into his room, slamming the door behind him. Despite our attempts to help Daniel verbalize his feelings and work through difficult situations rather than fleeing, he continued to struggle with these issues.

It is most important to note that amid his inner turmoil Daniel achieved a tremendous amount of growth. He attended school and with the help of a very nurturing teacher experienced a most successful kindergarten year. Not only did he develop friends at school, but he became very popular in the neighborhood and developed a great deal of independence and autonomy. He excelled at every new sport he learned and became an expert at six-year-old jokes and games. Daniel appears to have dealt with his world in a very systematic and successful way, working on the difficult emotional issues at home and focusing his energy on appropriate developmental tasks in the community.

Also during this year we sought counseling for Daniel and for ourselves. We were concerned about his intense grief and anger and often felt confused and unsure about how to respond to him. Daniel's issues had stirred up many feelings in me. At times I was frightened by and resented his neediness and was disappointed in my lack of ability to satisfy him. The counseling we received was extremely helpful to me in gaining an understanding of the process of Daniel's bonding to our family and in reaffirming my self-esteem as a mother. Daniel also seems to have benefited from his relationship with our psychologist; some of the intensity in his interactions dissipated and the grieving process appeared to reach at least temporary resolution.

There has been a definite change in Daniel during the past six months, and his work on loss and integration into the family has taken on a new tone. It appears that we have reached another level in the development of becoming a family—a third stage in the process. This stage might best be described as one of acceptance: acceptance of what has been and acceptance that we will continue to deal with these important issues for Daniel.

For myself, the recent months have brought a sense of relative relaxation, a feeling that a period of crisis within our family has passed. Daniel's presence in our lives has promoted a good deal of growth and change; we have reorganized in a new way, one that we hope better accepts and nurtures individual differences and a greater range and diversity of emotional expression. With the support of family and friends I feel more comfortable in struggling with and acknowledging many conflicting emotions. I now recognize that Daniel will undoubtedly work through his feelings of loss and acceptance throughout his life, but I feel more confident that as a family we'll do the best we can to support him.

During this current stage anger continues to be an emotion that Daniel experiences often. He now holds great expectations for what we can do for him and is frequently upset when he doesn't get what he wants. He seems to be testing anew what is possible, to be trusting more, but also to be more open to disappointment. Better able to verbalize what makes him angry now, he is especially sensitive to the inequities of the world and is compelled to tell us about them. Although we experience periods of calm, sibling rivalry continues to be an issue, especially for Daniel and Jennifer. We are trying to meet Daniel's outbursts with a sense of acceptance and understanding that he must work through his angry disappointed feelings. But we also have a sense of expectation that eventually he will develop a more reasonable method of coping.

Daniel is giving us strong messages now that he plans to stay. He attached a good deal of importance to his becoming an American citizen, a process that seems to have as much or more significance than adoption for him. On Father's Day he signed his card "Your son, Daniel" and wrote a story about his family for his class newsletter. Also in school, he recently wrote a very touching story about his trip from Korea to this country and his new family. He appears to view his journey with a sense of history and acceptance. Future events and family plans are now approached with much more anticipation and excitement.

We have also noted differences in the quality of Daniel's affection. Although he has always been very demonstrative, in the past much of his physical attachment seemed to stem from his great sense of neediness. More recently, he seems able to give of himself, a quick kiss or hug on the run, a sign of his affection. We often find little love notes from Daniel that he leaves for us at bedtime. Recently, when I was with Daniel and a friend of his, he called me "Oma." He then repeated it: "You're Oma. You're Oma." He asked if we knew what that meant. I told him I did and he announced proudly to his friend, "That means 'Mother' in Korean."

●

Virginia and Jonathan

Virginia: Mom, why would a lady who grew a baby give the baby away?
Jonathan: I so sad I didn't grow in your uterus, Mommy.

Faith: When we were first planning to adopt, and went through some group meetings and adoption orientation, and did an awful lot of talking about adoption, I was uncertain. It was not something I had ever planned to do, but we went ahead and put our name on an adoption list. When it came time, I was ready to adopt and to fully accept that as a choice. But what I had to do to become ready was to grieve not having a biological child and what that meant *for me*. I think it means different things for different people. And when I really had done some resolution about not giving birth to a child, it was clear that the next task was that I had to separate from my image of the child I had imagined having, in order to have an actual child. And I said to Tony, my husband, I think that that is the work all parents have to do, whether or not they are biological or adoptive: they have to separate from their image of who and what the child will be, whether it is that she will be skinny or athletic or whatever. I think that my work was in separating from the image I had for my child. I realized that whoever the child was—whether he or she came by birth or adoption—I was going to have to separate from that image because the child was not going to be an extension of me. That was the hard work I had to do. I feel that I have been really free to let Virginia become who she is going to be. And I probably would not have been this free if I had had a biological child, because I would not have been forced to realize this so early in the parenting process. I was really aware of learning that. The child needed to be free to become whoever it is he or she is going to become.

Mary: Can you talk about how Virginia's story unfolded and your feelings along the way?

Faith: As my children have gotten older I have forgotten some of their exact words, which at the time I thought I would never forget. Each time we talked it seemed like such an "aha!" experience! But over time as I've told the experiences they have lost some of their impact.

The first time she brought up birth she was about twenty-seven months old. She was very precocious verbally and spoke her first words at about nine months. She was in the bath playing with her baby doll and asked her first question about how babies get here. My answer was that a daddy puts a seed in the mommy, and it joins with an egg, and the egg grows into a baby, and that is how babies get here. Then three or four months later she was sitting in her room, playing with a doll. I was in the room making up the bed or something, and she said, "Just where does a baby grow?" "Well, it grows in the uterus of a lady."

I did not use the word *mother*. I had a lot of feeling about using the word *birthmother*. So I called her *the lady*. It sounds a little cold to me now. But at the time I rationalized it—not calling her a *birthmother*—because I did not want to impose on Virginia any connection between mothering and the woman who gave birth to her. *Mother* has so many connotations. I wanted Virginia to be free to name for herself what this woman would come to mean to her rather than have someone else ascribe maternal status to her. I wanted to leave the slate as clean as possible so that Virginia could ascribe maternal yearnings toward that person or not.

Mary: What had you told her about her adoption story at that time?

Faith: I hadn't really told her, except that from day one she heard that she had been adopted and had come to live with us at fourteen days of age. So when anybody asked me I would say she was adopted, in large part so Virginia would hear, and then at some point after that, she would ask more.

Now this day when she was playing, she said, "Well, then I grew in your uterus." I said, "No, you grew in another lady's uterus. And Mommy and Daddy adopted you when you were born." She seemed all right about that at that point. She did not ask any more about that then or say much.

I said to her, "Mom has said you are adopted when people ask. Children come into families in different ways. Sometimes the person who grows the baby becomes the mother and sometimes that person does not become the mother and so the baby is adopted." That was at about two and a half years. She did not ask any more.

Then at her third birthday, we had set up her party in the backyard. As we were walking over toward the guests, Virginia asked me, "Well, is she coming? Is my lady coming?" "Which lady?" "You know, the lady I grew inside of. It is my birthday, isn't it?" "No, she isn't coming. We didn't invite her." I explained that someday she could come, but not today.

Mary: How old was Virginia when Jonathan was born? Did his adoption seem to have an impact on how she understood and talked about adoption?

Faith: She was three. She was really excited to go to the agency. I called it the "waiting house," because foster homes have so many connotations. The waiting house was where you waited for your adoptive family. She was excited because Jonathan's worker was the same adoption worker she had. The social worker remembered what Virginia had on as a baby, remembered lots of Virginia's stories. She really liked that. She knew that the birthmother for Jonathan was different, but just coming from the same place provided a way for her to bond to him. What was hard for her was that after we had told her we would be adopting a baby and that he would be coming home in a week, the birthmother changed her mind. That went on for three and a half months. She really grieved, as though the baby had died.

Mary: How did you explain to her the change back and forth?

Faith: I told her this: "Sometimes when ladies grow babies they know that when the baby begins to grow they are not prepared to be mothers, and they know that right away. And they keep to that decision even when the baby is born. Some mothers think that is going to be true for them, and then when the baby is born, they think, well, maybe they would like to give it a try. And that Jonathan's mother was having an awfully hard time being a good mother to him. That some of the thoughts and fears she had about the kind of mother she would be were coming true. So sometimes she thought Jonathan should be given to someone who could really be a mother to him and other times she thought that she wanted to be that person."

And then finally the social worker called and told us that the birthmother said she would be back on Wednesday to sign adoption papers. But when the birthmother arrived she had changed her mind again and said she would return Monday morning for the child. When she came back on Monday with the father, she had decided to sign the adoption papers. The social worker called again and said that the birthmother was now 100 percent sure. She also said, "I'm so glad you were home." I turned to Virginia and said, "Virginia, I told you it was over, but remember how I told you some mothers can't make up their mind if they will be a mother or not. Well, Jonathan's mother finally made up her mind that she can't be a mother, and we need to go and get him." She was excited, but the whole process was really hard for her.

She had a real connection that this was the lady who gave birth, that this was Jonathan's birthmother. She understood that she was trying to be a mother and couldn't.

She was tentative in her bonding with Jonathan. When he had been home for two weeks, and I was trying to feed him, she kept coming in and, in essence, saying we should get rid of him. He's crying too much. I wasn't at that point connecting it with adoption. I suggested that maybe it was hard for her because she wanted me to spend time with her, but I really had to take care of him.

She went downstairs and got out the colander and one of our best cooking pots, one that I made her favorite dishes in. Then she urinated in the colander and the cooking pot. She had been toilet-trained for over a year. When I came downstairs, she was sitting on it, just smiling, and she stood up and said, "See what I did?"

"Yes, I think you know this is for cooking food and maybe you are trying to upset Mom. Your brother is never going to upset me enough to make me go away. You are never going to upset me enough to make me say you should go away, either. I am your mother." I explained that once you adopt a baby you are the adoptive mother for good. That's it, you never go away. I said to her, "I'm not sure we will cook your favorite dish again in this pot!" But after that there was never any issue about my giving her or Jonathan away. She might say, "I wish you would give him away, because he is too much for me." I would simply say, "I understand your wish, but that is never going to happen."

That year, from three to four, she was in a little nursery school. She was always complaining. She did not wear the right clothes. She lived too far away from the rest of the group. And she really began to think about not belonging and not being accepted. It was really bothering her.

Then we were driving home and had gone out shopping for her fourth birthday. We were coming home, and she asked, "Why would a woman who grew a baby give that baby away?" I said, "Well, sometimes a person who grows a baby is young, or she really did not plan to grow a baby. Perhaps the woman would really like to be a mother, but realizes that she is not prepared to be a mother." Virginia persisted, "But *why* would a mother give up a baby?" I said, "I've told you several reasons." "But I want to know why." "Maybe you want to know why the lady who gave birth to you decided not to keep you and become your mother?" "Yes, why would she give me up?" I replied, "I've tried to give you some answers. But I really don't know all of her thinking that went into her deciding not to be your mother. It is really hard to understand why a woman would grow a baby and then would give it up." She said, "It's awfully hard." And then I said, "You may not understand this now, but you might later on. It had nothing to do with you. It had to do with her life. I really don't know all the reasons why, but if that is something you still want to know when you are older, we can try to find her and ask her about it."

That was it. Her birthday came and went. Her birthday was not happy for her. She was really irritable. She had us plan a humongous party. It became more and more elaborate, and we tried to accommodate as many of her wishes as we could. But when it was over she said it wasn't enough. She felt really deprived. My thought at that point was that she was feeling a loss, and no matter how much we did, it couldn't solve that sense of loss. I didn't talk about that. I just said that it was okay if it didn't feel like enough. That you can't fill up something that feels empty. That it was okay.

Mary: At this point how were you doing with her sense of loss, and her wondering why her birthmother had not kept her?

Faith: My real wish was that it not be so significant, because it was bringing her some trauma, some pain. But I always felt that this was her history, and that she has a right to the pain of that separation and sense of loss and to as much of the information as we can get her, when she is ready to get it. I have told her that the social worker did meet the birthmother and talk to her. That we really should wait until she was a little older, and then we could get a lot of her questions answered. I think it is just a sadness, that she has had to go through this pain. I felt bad that she was so sad.

My husband really felt bad. He has never talked to her about adoption at all. She has never initiated talk about adoption with him. His feeling—and it was so from day one—has been that the records should be closed; it should be over; it never has to enter her life again. We differ here. He doesn't object to my talking to her about it. And I think at this point, since the children have asked so much, he says, "I think Virginia will want to know what is in her records, but not Jonathan." I say, "I think you are identifying with Jonathan such that you feel it would be all right to let Virginia go a little bit now and have that, but you're not so sure about Jonathan." He says he does not feel a threat about it now. That he really feels they are his children now.

And then Virginia, between ages four and five, went on this crusade of saving all these baby animals. For months, we had little wicker cups and she tied them with string to the car handle to toss them out in case they were needed to rescue a baby animal whose mother had left it. We would bring the stray animals home to adopt them. She had toads, newts, salamanders, guinea pigs, all kinds of creatures. She was really interested in procreation. She wanted to mate them, be there when they gave birth, separate the babies from the mother, adopt them out. She went through a lot of work in these rescue operations. She used the term *adopted*.

Then came her fifth birthday. Around this time Virginia was just awful with me. If I made breakfast it wasn't what she wanted, and on and on. Mothers were awful, terrible persons. Then finally one night she couldn't get to sleep. It was ten o'clock, and I finally said "Virginia, something is really bothering you and has been bothering you for some time. Let's just sit down and play and maybe it will relax you." She got all her dollhouse characters out and explained in no uncertain terms, "Now you do what I say." We played till about one-thirty in the morning.

What she came out with eventually—and I used to remember what the play was step by step—was this. She gave me a doll and told me that it was a wicked, mean lady, and she had two other dolls: a lady and a little girl. There were other people around too. But what ended up happening was that this kind, wonderful lady was a mother to the little girl. They were happy, playing, doing lots of nice things. A mean, wicked lady, who did not have a child, in essence came over and snatched the little girl away and said the child would be hers now. The little girl was screaming, "If it hadn't been for you, I would be with my real mother."

When I heard this I said, "No wonder you have been so angry at me lately." I suggested that maybe she had been so angry at me, fighting with me over so many things, because she had been thinking if it hadn't been for me she would still be with her birthmother and wouldn't have to be wondering about her and why she was given up. And she said, "Yeah, if it hadn't been for you, I would still be with her. You came and took me away."

I said, "Well, it didn't really happen that way." I tried to explain that the birthmother had made a decision not to keep her when she was pregnant, long before I came along. If it had not been me that had come to adopt her, someone else would have. But that I didn't take her away from someone who had decided to be a mother. In essence, she was saying, "If you hadn't adopted me, she would have had to keep me." I told her, "It's hard to understand that that is not the case, and you will understand that better later on." I urged her to talk to me whenever she felt angry at me about it, and said I could understand her being very upset and angry that someone would give her up, someone like her. But that that would never happen again.

And then six, seven, and eight have been fairly calm birthdays. In first grade, Virginia had some troubles, which the teacher thought stemmed from her being adopted. But the teacher had an adopted child of her own and had her own issues with adoption, which she was confusing with Virginia. What she brought up at seven and eight was no longer around birthdays. When we were alone, she would often talk about teenagers who get pregnant and have babies. In her mind it is okay for a teenager to have a baby. We talk about how our values differ. She thinks that a teenager who has a baby should keep it. I talk a lot about how teenagers need to be more free to go out and go to parties. I have never said directly to her that her birthmother was a teenager, nineteen, but she has probably overheard that, when other people have asked me how old her birthmother was.

Mary: She thinks she would do it differently than her birthmother.

Faith: I ask her if she thinks a teenager should get married. She doesn't think so necessarily. She thinks it would be nice to have a baby and to keep the baby. I hope I can help her work on this before she is a teenager.

Mary: You can see the seeds of this so early in her rescue play with the animals, trying to be a good mother in the face of the abandoning one.

Faith: Yes, she has really worked at that. Until age nine, however, she never worked this out in doll play. She displaced it onto her stuffed animals and multiple pets. I gave her dolls, but she never let them be in her room; she never dressed or fed them.

One day recently she asked me if we could stop to buy some diapers for her doll baby. I agreed, and she seemed very grateful to have these diapers. On the car ride home from the store she began to ask me why her birthmother had her birthfather plant the seed that was to become her if she wasn't able to be a mother. I tried to explain that when a man and a woman do this, it is very pleasurable for both of them, and that often one has the man plant the seed just for the pleasure of it.

Then, as though speaking from a place inside herself where she is now assured of her own unique individuality, Virginia said, "She didn't give me away. She had a baby. She gave birth to me. But she didn't even know who I was. She gave up a baby. She didn't give *me* up."

I said, "Nobody could have given you away if they knew you."

She asked how a mother can *not* grow a baby if the father plants a seed. "What happens if the lady doesn't want to grow a baby?" I explained that she had heard a lot recently about abortion, and that many women decide for different reasons that they can't be mothers at a particular time and so they have an abortion.

Virginia replied, "I guess it's really good that she chose to let me grow. She was my mother while I was growing in her uterus, and you are my mother since I was born. You know which is the harder job."

Sure she would say mine was harder, I nevertheless asked her what she thought.

"My birthmom's, of course, because having a baby is so painful."

I laughed inside, surprised by her answer, and then lightly defended the hard work of being a day-to-day mother. At the same time though, I was glad that she knows how wonderful it is for me to be her mother—that, indeed, it is not just a "hard job" but a joyful one.

Mary: How did Jonathan's understanding of adoption unfold?

Faith: Jonathan had no questions about where babies come from until he was a little bit over three. Then he became very interested in how all sorts of things are made. One day we were coming home from a grocery store, and we passed a factory, and he asked, "What's that place, Mom?" I said it was a factory, a place that makes things. He asked what this factory made. I said it makes baskets. He said, "That factory does not make baskets." And I said, "Why do you say that, Jonathan?" "Because it makes babies. That was where I was made."

And I said, "Oh, honey, babies are not made in factories." "Well, where was I made?" he asked. "You grew inside a lady. A man gives a seed to a woman and the seed becomes a baby that grows in a lady's uterus." "So, Mom, I grew in your uterus." I said, "No, honey, you grew in another lady's uterus. Not all babies grow inside of their mother's uterus. They may grow in someone else's uterus, and then their mother adopts them. Virginia was adopted and so were you." He didn't say any more.

That night he couldn't go to sleep. He was up and down, up and down. I went upstairs and sat with him, and after a while he said, "I was made in a factory." I said, "No, honey, babies aren't made in a factory. You grew in a uterus." He responded, "I grew in your uterus." I said, "No, honey, not in my uterus.

You grew in another lady's uterus, and then we adopted you." "I so sad, Mommy." He began to sob. "What are you sad about, Jonathan?" "I so sad I didn't grow in your uterus, Mommy." I said, "Yes, honey, I'm very sad that you didn't too. I really wanted you to grow in my uterus, but that wasn't the way it was. I understand your sadness. We both missed something by your not growing in my uterus." He sobbed for a while; then he felt better and went to sleep.

Now he is six. Only one other time has he initiated talk about his adoption. One day he asked me, "When did you come to the hospital to get me?" I said, "I didn't." He asked, "Well, where did I go?" I answered, "You were in the birthlady's house for a while, before you came home to me." He said, "Oh, I thought you got me at the hospital." "No, we picked you up at the office of the lady who helped us adopt you." There have been no more questions about babies or adoption since then.

Mary: Would Virginia talk about adoption in front of Jonathan?

Faith: No, she usually talks to me privately about it. I watch for Jonathan's concerns or thoughts about adoption, but I don't see or hear them.

Mary: How do you think the two of them differ regarding their feelings about adoption?

Faith: Virginia really perceives a rejection. It was a rejection she was able to deny initially, thinking I had stolen her away from a birthmother who wanted her. She was able to get angry by thinking of it as having been my fault for taking her away. With Jonathan, it is just the profound sadness of not having been inside me. That was a loss for him. For him it was not so much connected with the other person as it was the loss he felt in relation to me. For Virginia it was another person, and that other person is not available. I think it has been harder for her. So far it has been easier for Jonathan to deal with because he is dealing with the person with whom he had the loss rather than with someone who is unavailable.

Mary: I wonder if Virginia felt she could more easily be angry with you for the separation from her birthmother—since she knows you love her and allow her anger—than she could be angry at someone she never remembers having met, and who she feared might have rejected her?

Faith: Yes, I think that that was probably the case. Virginia, now nine, can differentiate between her birthmother's experience and Jonathan's. One day she said she felt sad about Jonathan's birthmother. I asked her why. She said that while her birthmother had not wanted to be a mother, Jonathan's had. That Jonathan's had tried to be a mom and couldn't do a good job taking care of him. We agreed that this was different from her birthmother's situation.

●

Nora

Nora: Some kids have lots of mothers.

When I decided to adopt a child, I had plenty of time to think about what it meant, since more than two years elapsed between the time I started the application process and my daughter Nora's arrival from El Salvador at age eleven months. During the time that I waited I did a number of things to prepare. I went to several large regional conferences on adoption, I joined an organization for "single" (that is, not married) adoptive parents, and I talked extensively with two couples I knew who had adopted children. Each of these resources was helpful in its own way.

Much of what I thought about were the ways Nora would be different from many of the children she would grow up around: she would be adopted and would have spent the early part of her life in a very different culture; she would have a Latina heritage, be part of a minority group in our country; and she would be raised by two women.

I wanted Nora to have a vocabulary and experiences that would affirm the positive aspect of her "differences," but overall I wanted to help her feel "normal" in most aspects of her life, more similar to than dissimilar from those around her. I didn't want to push ideas until she was concerned herself or ready to take them on. Intuitively, I thought she wouldn't understand much about adoption until she understood reproduction. I had less certainty about her comprehension of or reaction to racial-ethnic differences or a nontraditional family.

The strategy we settled on with respect to the latter was to try to have Nora have regular contact with other children and families who were different—that is, not only white two-parent families with biological children. This was relatively easy—we live in a community that is quite diverse in terms of race, ethnicity, and family constellations.

Already we had friends with different family configurations, and through the long waiting period of the adoption we had made and kept contact with people adopting foreign-born children. Nora was in a family day-care setting for two years with five children. One child was half Puerto Rican;

another had no father in his life. When we transferred her to a larger pre-school day-care program, we chose one that had a strong commitment to a racially mixed group and a multicultural emphasis in the curriculum. (It also had three adopted children out of fifteen.) Next year she will begin kindergarten in a public school bilingual program in which half the children are from native Spanish-speaking families and half from English-speaking families.

One aspect of Nora's differences that we felt we had some control over was defining who would be her official mother. We decided it would be simplest for Nora to have one mother in her daily life—me—and that Jenny would be called a "parent." We felt strongly about this since we assumed that at some point the knowledge and figure of her biological mother would take on importance in her concept of her self, and to have to incorporate and explain a third mother seemed too much to handle.

Although this solution has posed some problems in introductions, Nora and everyone around her knows who she is talking about when she says "my mom." Most surprising has been our experience that children, who often ask Jenny the question, "Are you Nora's mother?" are very accepting of the explanation: "No, I'm not Nora's mother, but I am her parent. I live with Katherine and Nora and help take care of her." In both day-care settings Jenny was identified by the children as "Nora's Jenny."

We have very little information about Nora's family background or her life in El Salvador. When we accepted the adoption agency's assignment, we received a one-by-two-inch picture of her and a health report that gave height, weight, and head circumference and said, "This is a well-nourished, three-month female with no physical abnormalities." The birth certificate that accompanied her on the plane eight months later also gave her birth-mother's name, age, occupation, and residence. That was it.

Because of the dearth of information we felt that it was very important to try to remember and record the details of Nora's arrival and early life with us. She loves the story. "You came with two little boys, twins, who had the exact same birthday as you! You looked at all the lights in the ceilings of the airport. When we got into the car you showed us all your tricks: you said, 'Ta, ta' and clapped your hands, and the next morning you saw the cat and said 'gato.'"

We also began to collect pictures of our family life in albums. "Nora's albums," as they have come to be called, begin with the tiny photograph of her as a three-month-old, then jump to her arrival eight months later, and continue from there. The album, until she was about four, was the main vehicle through which we could talk to Nora about her adoption history. Any other attempts were met with noncomprehension. For example, "Your friend Elena is adopted too" elicited an incredulous response: "Elena's a doctor!" When I said, "Myles [on "Sesame Street"] is adopted too," she changed the subject: "Can I wear my red shoes today?"

The first indication that Nora had taken in anything about adoption came when she was about two and a half. Her day-care provider reported that the children had been telling each other stories as they lay on their mats for rest. For several days Nora had told the same story, which was quite popular among the children. That story was the one we always told accompanying the early pictures in the album: "When I was a baby I took a long, long plane ride all the way from El Salvador and Mom and Jenny and Mimi [aunt] came to get me at the airport." The listeners' question: "Did you eat things on the plane?" Answer: "Chicken and rice and I threw my bottle down the aisle." (All true.)

During the summer after her third birthday I observed Nora "nursing" her favorite stuffed animal. She must have learned about breast-feeding by observing mothers at the playground, for we had never discussed it at home. She was matter-of-fact about it. "Scotty Dog is nursing from my breast."

Several weeks later she began a new preschool. On the first day, during snack time, the children were talking about milk and where it came from— cows. Nora announced to the group, "When I was a baby I drank milk from my mother," and proceeded to describe the process of nursing to the group. Since she had never mentioned this at home it came as a total surprise. What did it mean? Was this separation anxiety on the first day of school? Did it have anything to do with her understanding or feelings about adoption and her infant experience? I decided not to say anything to her since she did not directly tell this to us.

For about ten months after starting preschool Nora developed what we came to call her hobby—baby equipment. She seemed to be obsessed with the details of equipment: she pored through catalogs that sold baby supplies; she knew all the features of most kinds of strollers; she could spot a backpack from a long distance; she looked longingly at any baby's pacifier or bottle; she insisted on going very slowly past the diaper display in the supermarket. She had little interest in baby dolls or most doll equipment and seldom played house at day care, but when alone she played extensively with her stuffed animals, a real child backpack, and a large, folding doll stroller. The stroller, however, had the "wrong" kind of foot support, and there were many tearful, frustrated moments as she (or we) tried to adapt various straps to create the right kind of footrest.

During this period Nora would ask about her own experiences with various kinds of infant equipment, and then look at us in disbelief when we described her apparent lack of interest in or outright rejection of different items at that time. We tried to place our descriptions or explanations to her in the context of the adoption—that she was not a tiny baby when she came to us and was probably not used to the equipment; that this was probably why she spit out the pacifier, was scared of the jump-up seat, preferred crawling or riding in the stroller to being carried in a backpack, and so on. We also tried to incorporate what she did do. "You knew how to drink from a cup, but you also liked a bottle," or "You didn't like the big bathtub, but you would sit in the little wash basin and pat water on your face and body. We think you probably sat in a basin like that in El Salvador."

Still, we puzzled over Nora's intense interest in or nostalgia for babyhood, since even those representations of young childhood that she did have— bottles until she was about two or diapers until she was daytime trained at about thirty-two months—had been given up by her easily and without apparent emotional distress. What did this all mean? Had our apparently happy, adaptable child been pushed too fast? Did the interest in infants and baby equipment reflect some recognition (though unarticulated) that the much loved albums did not have pictures of her first year? Was she trying to remember early caretakers or experiences in El Salvador? (When Nora was almost five she said to me, "You know, it's funny. I don't remember anything about the plane trip from El Salvador.")

Or was the involvement with baby paraphernalia simply reflective of her being an only child, when many of her playmates had younger siblings and thus access to the equipment and vicarious experiences of babyhood? Or perhaps she is simply a child with intense interests. This summer she is obsessed with pools: wading pools, above-ground pools, in-ground pools, pools with ladders, pools with steps, with and without diving boards, and so on.

Sometime around the time she turned four Nora's interest in babies waned. Her dramatic play started to be about children in school or on playgrounds rather than infants at home. What we were left with were questions with no clear answers and an understanding that even if there were no direct traumatic or dramatic experiences for us or her around adoption, we would carry with us those nagging questions: "Is this normal development?" "Is this problem not adoption-related or is it adoption-related?" "Are we going about this thing in the right way?" "Is this going okay or not?"

When Nora was about four she said to me "I wish I had a dad." I (probably jumping in too quickly) said, "Yes, it would be nice for you to have a dad, but there are all kinds of different families. We know other children without dads too. There's Elena, Amelia, Carlos, Conor—" She interrupted me, "Yes, but that's unusual." About a month later we were at a child's birthday party where there were a number of foreign-adopted children and parents (mostly mothers) present. When we left the room where the party was held to use the bathroom, Nora said to me, "Some kids have lots of mothers."

I thought this indicated some kind of understanding or acceptance of our family situation, although Nora has never seemed confused or unhappy about having two female parents. When other children have asked about her two mothers, she explains, "Katherine is my mother and Jenny is my parent." It has been striking to me that in her imaginative play the domestic scene she creates is usually of one parent (mother) and children—no father, no other parent.

During the year after she turned four Nora seemed to become more aware of people's skin color and hair texture. She would typically ask, "What do you call my skin?" I would say, "I think your skin is the color of coffee with milk in it." And she would respond, "Your skin is pink." Or she would say, "I have shiny black hair and you have orange hair." There seemed to be no value judgment for her in these observations (except when she told the parent of a curly-haired, blonde child, "I don't like her kind of hair").

Around the same age, Nora also began to show interest in her Salvadoran heritage, looking at books with pictures, showing souvenirs to guests. There were two other children of Salvadoran background in her preschool, a boy with a North American mother and Salvadoran father (not actively part of the boy's life) and a child with two Salvadoran parents who were immigrants. When Nora took in that the three children shared something in common, she then assumed all of them were adopted. Although we would explain the differences among the three families—biological versus adopted parents—she would repeatedly make the error. On the other hand, her closest friend at the school is an adopted (white) boy. Yet as far as I know their adoption is not part of their bond or closeness.

A few months before her fifth birthday I bought Nora a book on reproduction that has bright graphics and pull-out flaps, and places conception and reproduction in the context of family life and growth through the life cycle. She was fascinated with the book and seemed particularly interested in a section on inherited traits, which I adapted: "Sarah [in the book] gets her blonde hair from her mother, her curly hair from her father, her nose from her grandmother. You get your shiny black hair from your Salvadoran father or mother, your pretty neat nose from them," and so on.

Several weeks after we acquired the book, Nora asked in the car riding to school, "What is Salvador's name?" (She has consistently referred to her birthmother as "Salvador.") I told her the name. She then said, "Does she have those lines [stretch marks] on her tummy like in the book?" I said I didn't know. I said that for some women the stretch marks went away after the baby was born; for others they always had the lines. She said "Oh," and changed the subject. She has asked nothing about her birthmother since. What was her question really? Was it "does she remember me?" Or "did I hurt her in some way so she didn't want me?"

Recently her preschool sent home a sheaf of Nora's drawings. Around the same time she had asked about her birthmother, she had drawn a picture for which a teacher had written out Nora's description. It said: "This is a picture of me and Max [her best friend] and my grandfather who lives in El Salvador." We were taken aback by this. When she had mentioned grandparents in the past, we had told her that she didn't have a grandfather because both our fathers had died before she was born. Yet she had expanded her concept of her family and heritage to include people in El Salvador she had never seen or talked about. It made us realize that our own concepts of her birth heritage began and stopped with her birthparents.

As Nora has become more interested in El Salvador, we have been faced with a dilemma we didn't anticipate: how to present El Salvador to her in a way that is accurate—that it is a very poor country in the midst of a terrible civil war—but also in a way that is not frightening and is affirming of the people and culture. Children, of course, have their own ways of balancing information. Recently, Nora came into a room where the television news was showing footage of the bombing of a Salvadoran village. She said, "Mommy, look at all the volcanoes exploding. El Salvador has beautiful volcanoes!"

But Nora has also asked why soldiers have guns and shoot people in El Salvador. We try to explain it in terms of social justice and fairness. People there need more food to eat, better homes, clean water, and some people aren't letting them have it, so they have to fight to make it fair for their families. We explain that is why we have sometimes gone to demonstrations here to say we want life to be safe and fair for the people in El Salvador. I think she is able to understand this in part because her preschool did a unit on Rosa Parks. Her telling of that story: "Rosa Parks was tired and said 'It's not fair I have to go to the back of the bus,' and she sat down. And she was taken to jail, but people came to visit her and help her and she went back home." She also thinks it isn't "fair" that the Charles River is polluted and we can't swim in it.

I imagine Nora will some day feel some pain about her adoption and the conditions in El Salvador because I do now. Every year her birthday brings up for me how her birthmother must feel on that day. It is almost unimaginable for me to think of any reason to relinquish this child. Yet I also wonder what Nora's life would have been like if she had stayed. Would she be doing hard physical labor? Girls often begin carrying water long distances at about her age. Would this happy, vital child even be alive? El Salvador has a 50 percent mortality rate among children under five.

After Nora arrived I developed the idea that her birthmother might have come from a middle-class family. We had been assuming poverty, but what did we know? Her birthmother had found and dealt with a competent lawyer and had been available to go to court twice in order for the legal work to be completed there. Perhaps she had lots of supports and resources. I maintained this fantasy for some time despite information I had gotten that the area where the woman lived (listed on the birth certificate) was a part of San Salvador marked by particularly terrible poverty and violence—gunfights nightly, different streets controlled by different factions, and a tremendous number of people arriving who had been dislocated by the war in rural areas. I realize now I didn't want to face the likelihood of harsh life conditions for either Nora or her birthmother. Still the thought recurs occasionally— maybe it wasn't so bad. If I have such an elaborate and fluctuating fantasy life about Nora's birthmother, I am sure that some day she will too.

In general, the way Nora has related to her adoption has gone pretty much as I imagined and would have wanted—she doesn't actively deny it or seem to be distressed by it. She asks occasional questions and seems to accept the answers, but overall that she is adopted does not seem to be a major factor in her self-identity or to affect negatively her self-esteem. Yet I expect that she will feel pain at some time—about the absence of much information about the circumstances of her birth or about either parent, about her birthmother choosing not to raise her or have contact with her, and about the war and poverty in El Salvador. By the time Nora faces these kinds of questions and unknowns I hope she will have a complex enough sense of people and appreciation of differences that she will be able to live with the ambivalence that will almost inevitably come.

●

Max and Lani: Twins in an Open Adoption

Max: Okay, Sis, first I'll marry our friend; then I'll marry you, and one can be the birthmom and one can be the adopted mom.
Lani: I wish I had been in your womb.

Premature twins? Did I want them? Or did I want to see them first? What strange questions from the adoption agency. But they couldn't have known that I had always dreamed of having boy-girl twins. We were already bonded. I felt that Max and Lani had entered my life long before their birth on August 17. My husband and I had dealt with infertility for more than six years. So I dubbed them my special "back-order babies."

Here lay our dreams in a crib. As I stood there reading *Why Was I Adopted?* I realized that we had left behind the problems of infertility for the complications of adoption. Stories of the agonizing searches of adoptees for their birthparents, the pain of unanswered questions, combined with normal identity crises, have led us to believe that truth is necessary from the beginning.

Many adoptive parents have believed in giving their children factual information about birthfamilies, but that wasn't enough for me. By September 3, I was already questioning the system. During an adrenalin surge after a 3:00 A.M. feeding, I sat down to write to my children's birthmom, whom we knew only as "Michele." I didn't know it at the time, but this was the beginning of an unconventional relationship, drawing us closer together while straying further and further from the traditional adoption scenario. My emotions swung high and low, as if they were part of an adoptive post-partum syndrome. I wrote of wanting to share the joy she had given to me. In those quiet moments I wrote that "our" children were surrounded by love.

By November, those feelings had intensified. In my second letter I wrote Michele: "I just spoke with Kathy [the adoption agency maternal case worker] to see if there was anything you needed to know from us. And, as I hung up, I began to cry. I'm not sure just how to explain this—they seem to be combination tears. They are tears of sheer exquisite joy and happiness about the miracle that we are living, and yet hurting and painful tears that you cannot be sharing all this with us. As I look into their beautiful faces, and lock eyes all during feeding time, I wonder and think about you. I wonder just what traits they have inherited and what they will take from us. I wonder whose eyes, hairline, mouth, nose, or body type they will resemble. Already, as we go out and about, people stop to ooh and ahh and say, 'Oh, they have daddy's coloring and mommy's smile.' We smile, say thank you, and think of you. I hope it makes you feel glad that we are all fitting together so well. I want to tell you so much and yet I'm so aware of the pain you must feel as I bubble over. My heart aches for you and your family and I can't begin to explain how much love we feel for you. Whatever we can do to make life any easier, we would be glad to try—just let us know.

"After having so many people stop us and ask their names and how old they are, I realized that it's quite possible that our paths may cross. . . . Some people have expressed the fear that they would always be looking over their shoulder in terror that their adopted child would be taken away, but as I wrote before, we all love these incredible babies and want nothing but love to touch their lives."

We continued to exchange letters, photos, and gifts through the agency. My letters were mostly filled with descriptions of the babies' development.

Michele's were chatty, never questioning our position as Max's and Lani's parents.

In June, I wrote of a dream: "I was at a party, sitting on a couch, holding Max. A lady sitting next to me made some rude remarks about adoption. Suddenly, I felt Michele sitting right next to me, and our body language was such that we both just leaned forward and wrapped our arms around Max to protect him. Awakening, I felt so warm and comforted, knowing our babies were sheltered by both of their mothers."

We had exchanged photos, and I placed Michele's pictures in our family album so that, as the children paged through it, they would have opportunities to ask questions. Also, I didn't want her to seem a separate, hidden part of their lives, locked away in a safe deposit box.

Finally, frustrated by the hide-and-seek of our communication going through the adoption agency, I proposed that we eliminate the secrecy and meet. Trying to keep emotions under control, we took a giant leap forward in February. Max and Lani, one and a half years old, were too young to grasp the significance. They were safe in Mommy's and Daddy's loving arms, accepting whatever we presented.

We introduced Michele and her parents to the children as Mommy Michele and Grandma and Grandpa Ferrara. This came about instinctively, perhaps because of our previous foster-parenting experiences and, again, our need for truth. After all, Michele is *not* an aunt, *not* a "friend of the family." She is Max's and Lani's biological parent (we will have to deal with the unknowns of the biological father). We felt that if we presented facts in a comfortable, natural fashion as part of our daily lives, the pieces would fall into place.

Pictures of that day and subsequent meetings have been inserted chronologically in our growing family album. One of the children's pastimes is to review all our photos, identify the people, reminisce about the past, and ask questions about what they were like when they were little. In a Mother's Day card shortly after our first meeting, I let Michele know that Max and Lani had gotten into a batch of unsorted photos, including some of Michele and her parents. In a most unusual gesture, the children kissed each of their photos.

Visits with Mommy Michele and her extended family have become normal, happy events. We share a Christmas holiday meeting, try for an annual birthday celebration, and usually manage about two other get-togethers a year. Comfortably juggling schedules, we arrange visits with no formalities, no rules, no set dates. In-between we chat on the phone and catch up with news.

Max and Lani have included everyone in their growth stages. They've gone from being shy, wanting only Mommy and Daddy, to being politely cute, to running into Mommy Michele's arms. Now they are making requests that we all get together. They can't wait to spend the night with Mommy Michele, and they tell us we need a night out soon so that they can visit.

The adoption experience has evolved parallel with the children's developmental stages. Just after Max and Lani celebrated their fourth birthday, their best friend, Rebecca, found out that she would become a big sister the following spring. As Rebecca, Max, and Lani were made aware of the ongoing miracle of birth, questions of "where do I come from?" naturally evolved.

Max and Lani matter-of-factly announced that *they* had been in my tummy. Matter-of-factly, I just said, "No, you were in Mommy Michele's womb." I quickly sorted out thoughts suitable for their grasp, trying to figure just how far this was going to take us as we plunged into a discussion of adoptive versus biological families. Our family motto, "We don't do things the easy way," popped into mind.

The time for real truth arrived as Max blurted out an indignant, "Why?" How could we explain infertility without getting too anatomical? As four-year-old boy-girl twins, their preoccupation with their body parts and functions was already intense. Even though I expected this conversation, Max's timing caught me off guard.

Shrugging, I just said, "Mommy's body wasn't able to have a baby growing in her womb, but Mommy Michele had two babies, only she knew she wouldn't be able to take care of them. So she searched for a daddy and mommy who would help those two babies grow up well and love them very much. After she thought about it for a very long time, she asked us to be your mommy and daddy."

With minor variations that's as much information as the children needed for a time. One day, as we curled up together to watch "Sesame Street," Lani snuggled into my lap and asked, tentatively, if she had been in my womb. It was odd coming from her because she is usually a no-nonsense individual who never forgets. Gently I said, "You were in Mommy Michele's womb, remember?" Okay, I thought, that's clarified, back to Ernie and Bert. Then came the magic melting moment that will get me through all the later "you're not my real mom" moments. She nestled right onto my stomach, almost burrowing, and said, "I wish I had been in your womb." Oh, I wished that, too, Lani. But however it happened, I'm glad you are in my life.

On the other hand, a moment of fear concerning the good judgment of our open adoption came from Lani when Michele and Grandma Ferrara met us at a mall to take the children to a family Christmas party. It was their first time visiting without me, at age four years four months. The Ferraras returned the children at 7:00 P.M. after a busy day of photos, presents, and fun. Everything seemed perfect. The biological family was happy, Max and Lani were sleeping, and I got my last-minute shopping done. When I was transferring the children to my car, Lani woke up and started crying—no, sobbing. Once we were alone, heading home, she announced in no uncertain terms that she was not to go alone to see Mommy Michele *ever again*. Fearing all sorts of things, I was glad it was dark and she was in the backseat, so she couldn't see my eyes widen in shock. What could possibly have happened? Gently, I asked, "Oh? Why?"

"You can't go shopping without me! Max can go visit while you and I shop!" she exclaimed. Here I had envisioned a traumatized relationship when perhaps the only problem was a little girl who was born to shop and miffed at a missed opportunity. Or perhaps she was feeling insecure without me. I was firmly directed never to do that again. The next meeting was a joint one.

It seems that most of our questioning begins with some variation of "Was I in your womb?" Max opened a dialogue with "Was I in Mommy Michele's womb?" Since I've learned to listen and respond with an open mind, I simply mumbled, "Uh-hmm," while wondering what was going on in that little mind now.

"And Lani was there, too?" he asked.

"Yes, you're twins. You were both in there together."

There was a pause, a look of intense thought, processing the whole concept, and suddenly that "Eureka!" look appeared on his face. "Oh," he said, "like a camel!" It was very difficult not to collapse with laughter at his vision of Mommy Michele with two bellies like the dromedary he had seen on an exotic animal farm. With a big hug, we sat down to explain how they were curled up close together.

So far, none of the questions have had to do with Mommy Michele's decision not to parent. In this stage of egocentricity, the children want to know only where everyone stands in relation to them. They know that Grandmama is my mommy, Daddy and Mommy are husband and wife, they are brother and sister but are also son and daughter, and Mommy Michele is their birthmother.

They are just now, at age four years nine months, beginning to assimilate the term *birthmother*. They announce to all that they have a birthmom and that they were in her womb and that I am their adopted mom. They never ask about a daddy, but we have heard them trying to sort out relationships.

Max exclaimed that he was going to marry his friend Rebecca, and Lani started crying, wondering why he wouldn't marry her (even though we've explained the rules of who can marry whom). Max, wanting to comfort her, said, "Okay, Lani, first I'll marry Rebecca; then I'll marry you, and one can be the birthmom and one can be the adopted mom." Overhearing this, I chuckled, but decided not to step in with facts just then, realizing that comfort and acceptance were the foremost needs of that moment. But I must admit that I did worry about the harem concept—perhaps it goes along with the camel image.

Max is working hard to process the concept of "birthmom," but he is at the stage where he wants to marry me, so this mom stuff is very important. While we were out one day, he saw two pregnant women and called out to me, "There's two birthmommies!"

Our birth-adoptive family bonds keep strengthening. Michele has just asked that the children be in her upcoming wedding. Perfect timing! Lani has been fantasizing about being a flower girl, and much of their play centers about weddings and marriage.

On our part, after great thought, we asked Michele if she would be second in line after my mother as legal guardian for the children if anything should happen to both of us. Shortly after we proposed that to her, I overheard Max tell Lani that, if Mommy and Daddy both died, they would go live with Grandmama. I was able to snatch that moment to add, "Why, yes, that's right, and if Grandmama wasn't able to care for you, Mommy Michele would. There will always be some adult around who loves you very much."

They just replied, "Oh, yes!"

After four and a half years of agonizing indecision concerning guardianship, I was struck by the timing of the conversation. Neither they nor I had ever brought up the idea of Mommy and Daddy not being there. Yet, within three days of our asking Michele, it became an important topic for Max and Lani. Interestingly enough, the children have never mentioned the subject again.

Having Mommy Michele, Mommy, and Daddy answer small questions at the time they arise we hope will reduce big traumas later on for all of us. Because we continue on the course of open adoption with comfort, conviction, and love, there is a great sense of security.

Just tonight, after not touching the book for nearly three years, Max brought out *Mommy, Why Was I Adopted?* As we read, I asked him, "How does it feel to be adopted?" With a smile that must have started at his toes, he spoke for all of us when he said, "Great!"

Paul and Steven

Paul: Joey is lucky because his mom is three things—his mom, his birthmother, and his teacher. Why can't you be three things?
Steven: When will I ever see my sister again?

From the time he was four days old, Paul has heard me tell other people that he was adopted. He started asking questions about adoption at around age three and a half, the time he began to ask questions about everything. By that time, I was used to talking about adoption in front of him. I had the vocabulary that I needed to express my relationship with him, his relationships with the people in our family, and his relationship with the woman who gave him life. Since he had heard all of this before, I don't think any of the answers were threatening to him. Now, at age four and a half, Paul seems to be very comfortable with all aspects of himself, including the fact of adoption.

My husband and I are also comfortable with the fact that we have adopted our children. I recognize that we have been fortunate in having a family that has given us support and approval for our decision to adopt. We have not had any experiences with other people putting a negative connotation on us or on our children for being adopted, and that has made it easier for us to be as open as we have. But the fact of our having adopted our children instead of giving birth to them is something of which both my husband and I are continually reminded. Other people, often unknowingly, set up situations that remind us of the adoptions; the children themselves refer to it; watching the children, I wonder what they will look like as adults, where their skills and interests come from. All this causes feelings in me, feelings that are quite strong. Before I write any more, I want to be sure to write that I love my sons. In my eyes, they are perfect and perfectly wonderful, the standard against which all other children are seen (others are too pale or too thin; they walked too early or don't like balls and fishing enough).

The first time I told anyone besides my husband and lawyer that we were hoping to adopt this newborn baby was when I told my mother that a baby might be coming in September. This was the third baby we had hoped for, and by this time I did not want to have any baby things in the house to remind us if he did not come. (I also did not want to have to answer any questions that our two other children, foster children, aged sixteen and two, might ask about what those things were doing here.) I asked my mother to have things at her house so that if a baby did arrive, we would be ready. I also told her that I didn't want to make any decisions about what she might choose to get. It was too painful because of the uncertainty. My mother was blessedly understanding. She must have had a lot of fun shopping for the layette, thinking about my taste, because everything she selected turned out to be perfect. The question of whether these things were a gift to me for the baby or whether I had said I would pay for them was never brought up. To this day I have been afraid to ask. I think it must have been very important to me that these things be a gift from my mother to my baby, because I never could bring myself to ask her how much money I owed her.

In the three weeks before the baby was born, my in-laws came to stay with us, partly to see the other children and largely in hopes of meeting this new grandchild. I honestly do not remember what I said to them about the hoped-for baby; in any case, they had to return to their jobs before he was born.

The baby was born three weeks later than expected, and my husband had to be in Japan, so my mother and I went to court with my sixteen-year-old to finalize the adoption. I knew I was too excited to drive, so my mother came along to drive. I also wanted her with me so that I would know that I had her support and approval for what I was doing. The judge said, "And now you can go get your baby," and I cried. I had never seen the child—I just knew that he was a healthy boy—but the fact that I finally was going to have a baby was so powerful that I couldn't not cry. My mother drove us to the hospital, and all I wanted to do was get the baby and leave. I was so afraid that something would change their minds about it. But the nurses did give me the baby. The head nurse told me that when she had adopted a baby herself from this same nursery she cried so hard she couldn't see him. I wondered why I wasn't crying then too, but I knew that I needed to get out of the hospital quickly before something happened to ruin this. So they *finally* gave me my baby, and my mother put him and me in the backseat and we drove away.

Later I would remember many things that the nurses told us. My son had been held constantly since birth by the nursing staff because they felt sorry for him because he wasn't being kept. My son was perfectly healthy. The hospital gave us a trunkload of formula, diapers, and clothes because they didn't know if we expected a baby. My baby could go outside if he wore a hat. My baby had an envelope containing a religious medal from his birthmother. My baby had six cousins, and they were all girls. My son's birthmother's family had all come to see him. But what I remember most vividly is needing to hurry and get my baby home. That night, I sent a telegram to my husband in Japan: "Paul is home."

At that time, we had sixteen-year-old Lenore and two-year-old Steven living in our home, both foster children. Lenore came to court and to the hospital with me. I think she wanted to see what it was like. That day, I was so happy that it seemed as if everyone I knew could and should share my joy in actually adopting a baby. For years afterward, though, I have wondered if it was wise to let Lenore come. Did it make her feel more transient and unlovable to see a new baby being greeted with such unreserved joy? Did she wish that I felt that way about her? How much jealousy do siblings feel when parents decide to add another child, either by birth or adoption? My two-year-old alternately ignored or was delightfully fascinated by the new baby—or so it seemed to me at the time. Again, in retrospect, I wonder how he felt about the sudden addition of the baby.

Still, for six weeks, with my husband in Japan, I had a newborn, a two-year-old, and a sixteen-year-old to care for alone. If the two youngest ones went to sleep, the teenager was awake and wanted to talk. I must have been exhausted, but I was so euphoric that it didn't seem that way. I have heard from other people who adopted babies that their joy also carried them through the first year of no sleep.

It took a *lot* of work to find our son and adopt him. Although it was an experience I could have done without, the time we spent looking for children was very positive. We got support from literally everyone we talked or wrote to. People we did not know wrote to us from as far away as England and the Philippines, and we definitely felt that ours was a human search and that we were treated humanely. We did get a baby as a result of our efforts, and we also gained a sense that adoption—being adopted oneself or being an adoptive parent—was much more common than we had known before, and that it was nothing to hide or not discuss. After spending several years talking openly with everyone we knew or met about wanting to adopt children, it was quite simple for us to continue talking openly about having adopted a child. In fact, I do not know how we could have kept the fact of adoption a secret. It would have involved having to lie or refusing to answer questions from other adults in the normal course of conversation too many times. So our son has heard from the time he was four days old that he was adopted.

But—there is a big difference between a sleeping five-day-old baby in a Snuggli overhearing you say he is adopted and a four-year-old's wondering why he can't see his "birthday mother" after his foster brother has returned from a visit with *his* birthmother. The situations have had different effects on my children. They have had different effects on me. So far, my children (now aged five and seven) are unjudgmental about adoption—it is a given. But all the givens about themselves are constant topics of discussion. They daily make reference to the givens that they are boys and not girls, five and seven years old, taller or shorter, older or younger, brown-eyed and brown-haired, fair and dark. They love to define themselves, and part of their definition of self is the fact of adoption, so they make reference to it quite often. So far, it hasn't seemed to bother them, but the questions about adoption crop up regularly enough that I know it's fairly constantly on their minds. The fact of adoption is often on my mind, too. If the boys do not bring it up, someone else will.

The very first time I took Paul to the park in a front pack, at age five days, was so the two-year-old could play. I was sitting on a bench in the sun, watching Steven run around. I felt for the first time how it feels to have a baby sleep on my chest, curled up and quietly breathing and occasionally moving the tiniest bit. I felt peaceful for the first time in several months, happy, quiet, joyfully content, warm. Another mother, also with a baby in a front pack and an older child running around, looked at me and the baby with a practiced eye and said, "He's pretty young. How old is he?"

"Five days."

A perceptive woman, probably happy at the thought of having a conversation about birthing techniques and postpartum matters, she said, "You look pretty good for having given birth five days ago."

"He's adopted."

"Oh." End of conversation.

It is interesting for me to realize that I still resent her for reminding me, the very first time I took my son out, that he has a past apart from me, that I truly cannot just pick him up and take him as though his life began on day 4 when I met him for the first time. It has never occurred to me when situations like that arise to just let them go and not refer to the adoption. It may seem in this essay that I harp on it too much or too often, but the fact remains that in normal conversations there are often times I would have to lie or refuse to answer questions if I did not choose to talk about adoption. I do not introduce Paul as my adopted son, but many of the people I meet do know he is adopted.

One of the things that I like about Paul's being adopted is the story of how he came to be our son. Paul has heard this story, but he has not been especially interested in it. One day, though, I suspect I will tell it to him as a bedtime story when he suddenly needs to know more about himself.

I was teaching grade school at the time my husband and I decided to adopt. Because it was a decision that I cared deeply about, I told the children in my class that I had decided to try to find a baby to adopt. Two girls in my class—one adopted and one her sister—took the statement quite calmly, but a boy who had been in my class for two years became quite agitated. He remained unusually restless at school for about a month. One night, his father called me at home and told me that his son had been adopted as a baby and had asked him to find a baby for me, too. The father wanted to know if it was true that I wanted to adopt a child, and I said yes.

About a year later, this father got in touch with my lawyer—and Paul came into our family. I will always feel grateful to this eight-year-old boy for finding me a son. Partly to show my gratitude to him and partly because I felt Paul's birthmother would want it, we had Paul baptized with this boy standing up as his godbrother.

One of the other great helps that came to me from my work as a teacher was being familiar with the vocabulary used to explain adoptions and understanding the need children have to label the adults in their lives. In that same class were two children who were siblings as a result of remarriage. Their parents (all four adults) had made a conscious effort to give their children nonjudgmental labels for all the adults in their lives so that everybody in the family would know who they were talking about. Even though I had no children at the time, I recognized that children needed someone to call "mother" or "mom." I was also aware that they needed some way to talk about the other mother in their lives, and I knew enough to realize that very few adults would be comfortable being called a stepmother—the connotations of the word are too "wicked." This family had a system of "blood mothers," "blood dads," and "blood brothers" along with plain "mothers" and "dads," which worked well for them.

As we talked with social workers and lawyers before we adopted our children, we became comfortable with the labels "birthmother" and "birthfather." It has helped us to talk to our children about who they are, who we are, who other people are. It is interesting to me that my five-year-old has as yet asked very few questions about his birthmother. He has asked me her name and smiles when I tell him what it is. He has not yet asked anything about his birthfather.

He is a child who likes to understand relationships. He spends a lot of time asking questions: Who is Dad's mom? Who is Uncle Paul's brother? Who is Grandma's son? So the question "Who is my birthmother?" isn't out of character for him or threatening to me—especially since I know the name and can tell him. If I didn't have a name, I think it would be harder on both of us. Occasionally, he will exasperate me with his questions. When he was about three and a half, he realized that I was a teacher, but not *his* teacher. He also realized that he had several friends whose mothers were their teachers. We had several conversations like this:

"Gloria is Joey's mom, right?"

"Yes."

"Gloria is Joey's teacher, right?"

"Right."

"Why can't you be my teacher?"

"Because—" and I begin to not want to explain all the becauses, but he doesn't stop there.

"Gloria is Joey's birthmother, right?"

"Right."

"Joey is lucky because his mom is three things—his mom, his birth-mother, and his teacher. Why can't you be three things?"

How do I answer that one?

I'll never be able to have been his birthmother, but he's probably not even asking that now. Probably he only wants to know why I'm not his teacher, but I do feel somehow helpless not to be all things to him anymore.

When Paul was four, we adopted his older brother, Steven. Paul had lived with Steven all his life—Steven lived with us before Paul was even born, so it wasn't as if we were adding a new person to our lives. Paul is the one of our children most like a barometer; we can tell from him when storms are brewing or changes are coming. Steven is more private and doesn't reveal his feelings as much. As the time came closer for Steven's adoption, Steven himself did not ask any questions about it—no why, what, when, how. But Paul became very agitated. I'm not sure if he was jealous or curious or upset or threatened, but he was definitely worried. The thing about his brother's adoption that Paul chose to focus on was his name! Until now, there had been three Copes and only one Anderson in our family. Now there would be four Copes and, as an added insult to his four-year-old sensibilities, his brother would have four names (we decided to add our last name to his original three names), and he, Paul, would have only three. Paul would not be comforted with the idea that he could be Super Paul David Cope or some such thing; he wanted to be Paul David Cope Cope so he could both get the same last name as Steven and maintain name number parity. There was probably more to it than that, but I felt that if I heard one more complaint about "but then he'll have four names and I'll only have three" I would scream.

We finally decided that Paul was upset enough that we should talk to the lawyer who was doing Steven's adoption (coincidentally, the same one who helped us with Paul's) and ask if he could say a few special words for Paul before Steven's adoption ceremony began. To our surprise and relief, the lawyer said that of course he could—they would just do a double adoption ceremony. And so Paul got to dress up in a suit and tie and go with his brother to get adopted again by the same judge. It was beautiful for us to watch the two boys standing in front of the judge, answering questions be-fore a court, being served with warrants. It satisfied a need in Paul, for he was now much more willing to be plain old Paul David Cope. It probably helped Steven to have his brother there, too, on the theory that we might let something bad happen to him but not to his brother.

It was the first time in my dealing with social workers, lawyers, legal systems, judges, and courts that I felt someone was actually looking at the immediate needs of my children and was able to respond to them. I suppose many children react as Paul did, and that is why the lawyer and judge both knew that having a double ceremony would help Paul. And as a parent, it makes it infinitely easier to answer any "How was I adopted?" questions. Since both boys are old enough to remember it, I can just answer, "Remember when we went to the court and the judge said—?"

Once the actual ceremony was over, I took the boys to a restaurant for lunch and to the toy department in a department store to see Santa Claus and buy literally any toy they wanted. (I hate to spend money, so this offer—that they could spend any amount for whatever they wanted—is an indication of my own joy.) I was surprised and touched that they chose the same things—a Paddington teddy bear (which they both still sleep with) and a red toy car.

Sibling rivalry does bring up several adoption issues in our family, although not, thank heavens, "I'm adopted and you're not" because they both are. (Interesting that I put it in that order—they probably think more children are adopted than are not.) Because they came from different families at different ages, my younger son has never seen his birthmother or birthfamily, but we have all met the birthmother, sister, and grandmother of my older son. Paul will sometimes wake up crabby and say, "When can *I* see my birthday mother?" or "I want to see my birthmother 'cause Steven saw his." Usually when he is in that kind of mood he is not too persistent. I will answer, "When you're eighteen, if you want to then." Sometimes he asks, "But why not now? Steven saw his birthmother." And I'll repeat, "You can when you are eighteen." So far, that has ended the conversations.

Car pooling is not one of my favorite activities, and I usually try to ignore any conversation that goes on around me. Today I tune in and hear:

Adam: I'm going to New York to visit my grandpa for Passover.

Steven: Well, we are going to have a trip, too, to Washington.

Adam: Well, so, I used to live in Washington. My mom and dad used to live in Pittsburgh and then they moved to Washington and a tiny baby came pop out of the tummy and it was me.

Steven: Well, I came out of the mom's tummy in Pittsburgh.

Paul: I came out of Maria's tummy and Steven came out of Monica's tummy.

Steven: Well, so, you came out of Maria on "Sesame Street."

Paul: No, not that Maria—my different Maria.

Steven: Ha, ha! Nanny nanny boo boo. You can say, "Hey Maria—I want to come to Sesame Street."

Paul [upset]: No. My Maria is from the country of—Mom, where is it?

Me: Steven, people get very upset if you tease them about their moms. Paul, your birthmother is from Mexico.

Paul: And my birthfather is from the other place.

Me: Ireland.

Steven: When I was born, Patti was there too at a fair.

I realize that Steven has gone off on a fantasy trip, and it's noteworthy that he has a terrible day at school after this. The exchange of facts in the conversation doesn't bother me. I am startled by how quickly Paul is upset by teasing about his birthmother. Adam, listening, doesn't mention the conversation at all, and I wonder what he thinks about it.

My son has stayed home from nursery school with a cold; he is watching one of his favorite movies, *Robin Hood,* on the VCR for what seems like the one hundredth time this year. I am reading the newspaper.

"Mom," he says to me, "when Robin Hood wins he'll be king with King Richard and then they'll be brothers, right?"

"No," I answer. "Robin Hood will never be a king or a prince because his mother wasn't a queen."

"But he's a good guy, so he'll be a brother for King Richard, and his brother is a king, so he can be too."

My four-year-old is persistent in his logic. I want to read my paper.

"No. Robin Hood can't be a king because his mother wasn't a queen. You have to be born into royalty to be a king."

I start wondering how much British history we are going to get into; I don't want to discuss royal bloodlines and abdications and the peasantry. It turns out that my son doesn't either.

"Well, then, Robin Hood can be King Richard's brother because they are good guys and they act together." The child is persistent. He would be content to leave it at that.

Without thinking, I say, "No. They have different mothers [I'm still thinking about royal bloodlines], so they can't be brothers."

"But Mom—" and he wanders off looking slightly pained but also deep in thought.

It takes me a minute, but I realize he is being quiet. Too quiet. What I have just said doesn't match his life experience. He knows that he has a brother, and he also knows that he and his brother have different birthmothers. Although he hasn't said anything further, I know from his posture—shoulders slightly hunched—that he is uncomfortable. I give up on my paper.

"Hey. Are you worried because you and your brother have different birthmothers? Are you worried you can't be brothers?" This time I know I have listened to him appropriately, because he nods and relaxes. But I realize, too, that sooner or later we will have to continue this discussion because he says, "But lots of brothers have different birthmothers, right, Mom?" And it makes me tired at one-thirty in the afternoon. I don't want to go into statistics with a four-year-old about how many people are adopted, and I know that's not what he wants to hear. He just wants to know that he's in the majority, that he is normal. So I just answer, "You and Steven are brothers now" and hold my breath, hoping that the conversation will end, and it does. But he turns off the movie (maybe because it has a threatening element in it for him now?) and asks to read a story while he sits on my lap. I am so glad that he is still cuddly and physically affectionate. We both need to hold each other close.

Paul is standing on a chair in the kitchen, flicking the lights on and off while my husband and I are eating breakfast and unloading the dishwasher. He is four. He wants attention. He is basically understanding, but he is also basically not hungry in the morning and does not sympathize with our need to eat before noon. When we merely ask him to move into the hall to flick lights, he tries something else for attention. He picks up his karate belt and wraps it all around his arms, tying them together. He loves his karate classes and views his teacher with awe, respect, devotion—his first male teacher and his first case of real live hero worship. Finally he says, "Sensei has lots of foster kids," referring to the two teenaged boys who assisted in his class yesterday. (This is true; at least we think so, because another parent of some-one in the karate class has said so.) Everything about Sensei is enormously fascinating to Paul, so the fact that Sensei has foster children, as do we, is definite food for thought. I think Paul also realizes that any time he says anything about foster or adopted children, he gets my undivided attention. I look up, finally alert and paying attention to him, and he adds, "Sensei has a lot of adopted kids too" (something we do not know). He wanders off, apparently content with making contact with us before I have had two cups of coffee. I am left wondering at how he remembers the foster-to-adopted transition.

Three months ago we learned that Paul has juvenile rheumatoid arthritis. There we were in the doctor's office, and the doctor asked about family history. "Paul is adopted," I said. "But don't you know anything about the birthmother?" he asked. Paul said, "We know lots about my birthmother. Tell him, Mom." So I told the doctor everything about the birthmother except what he needed to know, which we don't know.

"And does he look like your husband?" It was the first time we had visited the home of Evan, Paul's new friend. Evan's mother, her racial awareness probably heightened by her own Chinese-American marriage, asked the question. "No, he is adopted," I answered automatically. "And your other son too?" "Yes." These questions do not particularly bother me anymore, although I am so used to looking at myself and my son together that I feel we look alike, natural, as if we belong together. But then she said, "Bless you for doing it." That hurt. I certainly don't have my children because I am trying to right a wrong in the world. I have my children because I need them. If anything, I thought, she should bless them for filling a need in my life.

I didn't think anything more of the conversation, but hours later that afternoon Paul asked me, "What did the man with the tie say about me?" It took me a while to figure out that he was referring to the lawyer who talked with me and my husband when we adopted his brother. He wanted to hear again the story of how we adopted him for the second time so he could have four names too. So I told him the story and it satisfied him.

That night some old, by-now familiar thoughts came back to me: Paul is so beautiful and perfect, the standard by which I judge all other children. What would it be like to live with such a measure of beauty who also looked like me or my husband, the way some of my friends' children look like my friends? Perhaps a biological child would also have the same kind of reactions as me or my husband. I still feel sad that I don't have a child who looks like me, although I honestly believe that I want such a child in addition to, not instead of, the ones I have adopted. It makes me wonder, too, how much my son wonders about the whole adoption issue. These questions reverberate hours after an overheard conversation—at age four.

The Adoption of a Foster Child

As part of a writing project for his first-grade class, Steven dictated his story to another child three weeks after we adopted him. Steven had been in foster care for six years; he had lived with us for five of those years. It was kind of nice to have a seven-year-old tell someone else what happened when he was adopted. He called the story, "Why Steven Gets Adopted," proudly adding, "It's by Steven Cope." He was very proud of changing his name and would no longer answer to the name "Anderson." Steven said:

"Once upon a time Steven went with his mom and his dad. They were going to get Steven adopted. His new name was going to be Steven Douglas Anderson Cope. When we got inside we saw the man and the man was our person. He was a great person. We went up the elevator to the person's office, there were toys in the office. Mom and Dad talked to the man. It took a long time to get adopted. Finally we went into a big room and had to touch the paper. I said 'Bippity, bippity, boo.' We went back into the room, we took the elevator. And there were the toys and we played again. And then we went into a big, big room where there were a lot of people watching us. We finally got adopted, and Paul got adopted too, but he has three names. We got a sucker from the big room from the lady and then we went to see Santa Claus. The End"

> Susan: Steven was a year old when you got him?

> Nancy: He was two when he came to live with us as a foster child. He'd been in foster care in a number of homes for a year before that.

> Susan: And he lived with his mother for a year?

> Nancy: After Steven was born, he lived with his birthmother and birthfather till he was ten months old, and then he was placed in foster care for a year. At the end of that year there was a routine court appearance during which his mother was judged rehabilitated and Steven was, therefore, returned to his mother on his second birthday. Three days later she walked out, leaving him at her mother's house. The grandmother said that she already was caring for Steven's sister and could not manage two children, and she returned Steven to the welfare department at which time he was placed in our house.

> It's not quite as simple as that, but that's a rough outline of his legal history. Steven came to live in our house when he was two. Depending on who you talk to, he had been in either four or six or eleven different foster homes between ten months and two years. No one seems to be quite clear. Three years after he had come to live with us, when he was about five and a half, his mother's parental rights were terminated by the state, meaning that at some point he would be legally free for adoption. In this state foster parents are allowed to adopt foster children; this is not true in all states. My husband and I did want to adopt Steven, but even though he was technically available to be adopted, it was a year and a half before we were able to do so. His mother had also filed an appeal of the termination decision, so that, for a time, even though he was adopted, it seemed that his adoption might be overturned. That is no longer the case. Her appeal was turned down. So Steven knew for about a year to a year and a half that he was going to be adopted by us. And it was hard for him to wait because no one could give him a date when this would happen. It was very hard for us not to be able to say, "Steven, when you are seven we will take you to court; we will adopt you, you know, change your name." No one knew when this was going to happen, and Steven would have liked to have known.

To go out of time sequence for a little bit, Steven has always been kept in contact with his birthfamily. He was a foster child, and birthparents are legally entitled to visit their foster children, usually not in the homes they're living in but in a somewhat more neutral place. It's up to the birthparents to exercise that right or not as they see fit.

Steven didn't have any contact with his birthmother for the first eight or nine months that he lived in our house. But about nine months after he had come to live with us we got a call from Steven's social worker saying that Steven's mother wanted to see him. And that upset me greatly. I viewed it as a threat to my existence, a feeling that as a foster parent I should not have. I mean, that's just part of the job of being a foster parent. But I was definitely upset by the situation. And I was also relieved when his birthmother didn't show up for this meeting. I had taken Steven to the place where we were supposed to meet her. I just told him we were going to an office where he would see his social worker, as he was used to doing every month. I'm sure he knew I was upset, because it would have been hard to miss. We got there and waited for about an hour and a half, and the birthmother never came, so we came home.

Susan: But he didn't know that he might be seeing her—you protected him from that?

Nancy: No, he didn't know that he might be seeing her. A month later, she called up the social worker and again requested a visit, and this time she came and it was actually a fairly cordial visit. The social worker was there, Steven was there, I was there, and Paul, the baby, was there. And it was a situation to all intents and purposes where three adults sat around in a room and the two children were there, and the two children played and then they went home. After that, Steven started having visits with his birthmother in the social worker's office about once every two months, and they gradually increased to about once a month over a period of about a year and a half.

It occurred to me after a while—and this may sound funny—but it occurred to me after a while that Steven had absolutely no idea why we had to truck downtown, sometimes in blizzards and sometimes in the rain, to do something that didn't seem to make any sense. I mean we would go, we would sit in this room, his social worker would always be there, and sometimes this woman would come, sometimes she wouldn't come. Sometimes she would come and spend an hour talking to the social worker about who knew what, usually about her apartment, or trying to get a job or the fact that she needed a new medical evaluation. Sometimes she would come in and swear royally at everyone in the office; sometimes she would come in and try to play with Steven. But no one ever seemed to explain to him that this woman was visiting because he was her son and she was his mother. And after a while I thought, you know, the social workers haven't told him this, his mother doesn't tell him that she's his mother, his mother calls me his mother, and it doesn't make any sense. I decided that I should at least tell him point-blank, "Steven, we are going to visit Monica because she is your birthmother." I still think it's funny when I remember that I decided to tell him all this on a bus! Steven was looking out the window at Christmas decorations, and I said, "Steven, do you know why we go to visit Monica?" Steven said, "No, I'm Dorothy going back to Oz." This was his technique for dealing with these visits! They were so unpredictable that he would just be Dorothy going back to Oz, with his magic ruby slippers. I said, "Steven, we visit this woman because she's your birth-mother. That means that when you were little you grew in her tummy and when you were born you came out of her." He said "Oh!" like, "Who cares? I'm still going back to Oz." He didn't want to have anything to do with it, but I at least felt a little better or more honest about what was going on to be telling this child who was supposed to go back to live with this woman again why she wanted to see him or why he might want to see her.

Steven also has a sister and a grandmother who live in our town. Since part of the goal of foster care is to try and keep families together, the social workers decided to set up visits with his sister and grandmother in addition to visits with his birthmother. We have had three of these that I remember. Steven loves the fact that he has a sister. It's very important to him that he has a sister, and he will ask where his sister is, if she's okay, how old she is, what she's doing. He will tease his younger brother for not having a sister because this is something Steven has. Steven has never tried to "go to Oz" to avoid the fact of having a sister. I don't know if this is because it's not threatening to him, or because he likes it, or because it makes him the only one in our family like this.

The visits with his sister were very pleasant. His sister also did not know theoretically that her birthmother was her birthmother, although she did know that Steven was her brother. So I don't know how the sister and grandmother were dealing with labels or names. Those visits were quite good.

Susan: How come you didn't have more?

Nancy: We didn't have more of them because when Steven was five, his sister's adoption was finalized. She and the grandmother had been living with Steven's mother all the time, although they were legally not supposed to be doing that. The grandmother adopted the sister, at which point she decided that they no longer needed to have any more contact with the welfare authorities, and they did not wish to continue visiting. Steven occasionally asks where his sister is or when he will see her, whether he will ever see her again, and those questions bother me because I don't feel like saying point-blank, "Steven, they don't want to see you; that's why you're not seeing them."

Susan: Is the mother still with the grandmother and the sister?

Nancy: As far as I know. It's tricky. Before her legal rights to Steven were terminated, she asked me if we would still let her visit him after we adopted him, and I said yes because I thought that it was totally reasonable. I mean, Steven remembers the woman, and she remembers him, and it seems to me less anxiety-provoking to have a reality to deal with than to have a myth.

Susan: Especially when you've known the person.

Nancy: Well, he has seen her a total of at most twenty-three hours in the last five years, but it's twenty-three hours that he remembers, and it's twenty-three hours that I don't want to try to take away from him or erase. But since after her rights were terminated, she filed an appeal of that decision, I figured it was not a final adoption, so I wasn't ready to initiate visits myself and she has not done anything about requesting visits either. The grandmother and the sister know where we live because they have visited us in our house, but they have not made any effort to send Christmas cards, birthday cards, or anything at all. So I think at this point that I'm not going to make an effort because his birthfamily doesn't seem to need or want to see him.

When Steven began to register for nursery school, camp, and after-school activities, he first noticed that he had a different last name than we did. This would be around the age of five. He was Steven Anderson, Steven Douglas Anderson, his brother was Paul Joseph Cope, I was Nancy Cope, and his father was Richard Cope. At about that time he started asking questions like "Why do I have a different last name?" The answer to that was "Because your birthmother is Anderson and you are named Anderson." "Well, why isn't Paul named something else? Paul has a different birthmother." And the answer to that was, "Well, Paul is adopted. You are a foster child."

For about a year that was fine for Steven. It was a statement of fact; he didn't seem to need any more. At about the time his mother's legal rights to him were terminated, we could tell him if he asked why his name was Anderson, "Steven, we are going to adopt you just like we adopted Paul. We will change your name when we can, and then you will be Steven Cope."

My husband and I both felt strongly, though, that when we adopted this child we didn't want to take any of his family or background away from him, so instead of taking even part of his name away from him, we would add our name to it, which is why he is now Steven Douglas Anderson Cope.

Steven was very proud to be able to change his name. But Steven, I think, is very troubled about the whole issue of mothers and who his mothers are. It's hard for him to remember which mother has done what to him in his life, partly because he hasn't had just one or two; he's had a whole succession of them. At the moment Steven and I are in therapy because he has what is called an "attachment disorder." He has not fully attached to me as a loving, caring mother because he has me very much mixed up with all the other mothers who have ever dealt with him in his life. So a lot of the adoption questions or mother questions he asks are threatening to me because they're accusing me of doing things to him that I've never done. This is a seven-year-old child who can still scream bloody murder if I'm fifteen feet ahead of him on the sidewalk and he can clearly see me. He's screaming because he's been abandoned by a series of mothers. And he's screaming at me, the mother, for abandoning him, and I never did that.

Susan: He's screaming *to* you about them because he knows you are there for him.

Nancy: Perhaps—it's hard to make that distinction all the time. A lot of the questions Steven has are threatening to me because a lot of his reactions are threatened reactions. He's not a happy child, and a lot of the questions he asks about adoption are not happy questions. He has never yet asked why his birthmother doesn't live with him any more. I suspect he knows, but he has not yet asked me to verbalize it, and his therapist has done something about trying to get Steven to verbalize it for us. But Steven has not been interested in getting me to tell him why he had to be adopted or why he's not living with his birthmother.

One of the things I think has made our family situation easier than it might have been is that Steven's problems and fears basically have to do with women. He's afraid of women because, in his mind, he's been mistreated or abandoned by a series of them. In fact, I don't think the series of foster mothers he had were anything but caring for him, but he did have to leave their homes regularly, so he would view that as being abandoned by a whole succession of mothers. But he has never had any major problems with men, and at the moment he gets along much more easily with men than he does with women in any setting. This means that all the problems he has with me—me and adoption, or just me and the issue of mothering—don't carry over to the relationship he has with his father. If Steven and I get totally embroiled in this bad mom, good mom, kind of merry-go-round, my husband can take him and do something with him, and Steven will be able to relax and have a good time. I will at least get a break from it, and when Steven and I see each other again, he will go right back to it midsentence from where he left off. But it does give our family a way to diffuse the tension that definitely builds up in our household. Steven is basically not a happy child.

Susan: Does he ever have a good time with you?

Nancy: Yes, since he and I have started going to therapy weekly or biweekly, our life together has definitely improved. It's a lot more relaxed and consequently the whole house is a lot more relaxed. But it's kind of sad because every once in a while, like once every two months, Steven will manage to forget that he is an upset human being and will become just totally, wonderfully normal and be able to have fun, and it's really wonderful to see. It's kind of sad to watch him then revert to being a damaged child again. So we do occasionally have fun with each other. I love him. I don't want him and all the problems that he causes out of my life at all.

Susan: Can you tell me anything about what happened to Steven before he came to you?

Nancy: I truly do not know what happened to him for the first twenty-four months of his life, and there doesn't seem to be any record of this anywhere. I think this is true for a lot of other kids who are adopted not from birth but later. No one knows exactly what happened to them or why they react the way they do because no one has any way of knowing what they have lived through, whether it's been good or bad or indifferent. And the children very often can't tell you or won't tell you or don't remember or don't know how to remember. I don't know why at his first eagerly anticipated slumber party, he called at eleven o'clock to come home. I don't know why Steven screams every time he hears a fire alarm. I don't know why his automatic reaction to someone with his hand up is to cower in a corner.

Our situation with telling Steven he's adopted is hard for us because we want to be as reassuring as we possibly can and say, "No, you're not ever moving again." Even before his birthmother's appeal was denied we said that. Now we can say it honestly. You know, he's moved a lot, he remembers moving, and we wanted him to know that he's staying right where he is. That was hard for us as adults to do because there was always the possibility that he *would* move again. That's something we had no control over. When he asks the adoption questions like "What's my name now?" we always give him the same answer. "When will I ever see my birthmother again?" "Well, when you're eighteen, if you want to then, you can see her again." "When will I ever see my sister again?" "That one I don't know, Steven. That one is not up to us." "What's my birthmother's name?" "Her name is Monica Anderson." He's never asked what his birthfather's name is, but I do know that, so if he ever needs to know I can tell him.

Paul, our younger son, has never asked why his birthmother couldn't keep him. He asks for her name, but he never asks why she gave him up for adoption. Steven has also never asked why his birthmother gave him up. Again, part of this is because he lived with us as a foster child for years. Since the goal of foster care is eventually to return the children to their birthmothers, you cannot afford to be at all negative about who the birthmother is or what she has done to him in the past or why. You truly need—especially if you're visiting the woman once every four weeks—to have some kind of positive relationship, and I don't want to destroy anything we managed to create just because we have now adopted him. In order to get on with his life Steven does need to come to grips with the fact that he was not treated well by this mother. It wasn't me that mistreated him— it was another person who did that—and it wasn't his fault either. But those are issues that bring problems when you change someone's legal status as gradually or slowly as happens to foster children. I think children who go with one parent as opposed to another as a result of custody battles or divorce have the same situation. Sometimes one parent will try to blame the other for something, but the kids still have to be able to get along with both parents. So no, we have not made a major effort to look into his first two years.

At times, I have definitely wished that Steven were able to act differently. As a parent one of the things I have done is spend time with my friends telling them about Steven and his back-ground, trying to explain to them and to myself why he acts the way he does, why he is sometimes kind of antisocial. "Well, this is what Steven did. He did it because this has happened to him in his past life." It's interesting to me that now that we are in therapy I no longer have the need to say to people, "Well, yes, he has no best friend. This is because—" I can let it go at "Yup, he doesn't have a best friend." And I don't feel so threatened by things that I view as weaknesses in him. I'm starting to be able to let him stand as a human being in his own right. Which is good.

But I keep thinking, "If I had been able to adopt him when he was four months, or four days old, he wouldn't have these prob-lems"—which of course is not necessarily true. But I do have the feeling as a parent of this child that I want him. I've always wanted to have him—I just wish I could have gotten him sooner! I would guess that most people who have adopted older children have felt the same way, that if only they could have gotten the children sooner life would have been much easier for everybody. Which may or may not be true, but it's definitely a feeling that I have and I know my husband has.

Susan: How do Steven and Paul do together?

Nancy: Steven and Paul do absolutely wonderfully together. Being brothers is, I think, the central point of Steven's life. Paul is the only person who's been stable throughout Steven's life. If anything, the little brother is more important to the big brother than the other way around. They still want to sleep in the same room. Big Steven views little Paul as protection from the monsters. You know, the monsters would eat the fat, short one first! The older one is dependent on the younger one. They truly love each other and I remember at about the time Paul was a year old and Steven was three and a half, I remember actually getting scared because these boys had bonded to each other as brothers. I remember thinking consciously, "My God, what if Steven has to leave? Not only will I have to go through the pain of Steven's leaving, but Paul is going to lose his brother."

One of the things we have tried to do for the boys is let them know that they aren't unique in the world by showing them other kids who had been in the same situation, either adopted or foster and then adopted, or adults they knew who had been adopted. Every time we found out about a famous person who was adopted, like Greg Luganis, the Olympic diver, we would say, "Hey! There's an adopted person!" We would meet with total blanks from our kids—they couldn't care less! "Gerald Ford! He was adopted. He was president of the United States!" It made absolutely no difference to them if someone they didn't know was adopted. Adopted was kind of like an adjective; lots of people in the world shared it. When they found someone they *did* know and like, though, it was important to them to find out that they shared that same adjective. As an adult I've been totally amazed to find out how many people seem to have either been adopted themselves or know people who are adopted or have adoptions in their families. The fact that many people are adopted has been comforting to me, helping me know that my kids are not unique in the situation that they're in.

Addendum: One and a Half Years Later

It is six years since Steven moved in with us as a foster child. We adopted him two years ago. Each winter with him has been difficult. He and I go into therapy each January and are done by May. The therapist says that Steven has a hard time with an anniversary date around the end of January. He thinks that Steven remembers, at some preverbal level, something or some series of things that happened to him in the winter. Last year he was on antidepressant medication for several months and it helped, and by May things were again tolerable. This year, the therapist decided it was time to try to work it out. It is clearly more than what is called a "seasonal mood disorder."

As a parent, I am incredibly grateful to our social worker who originally set us up to receive help. She made sure that we went through the twelve-week testing and evaluation procedure that made him eligible for psychiatric care and made that care a part of his adoption subsidy from the state. More important, she got us connected with a truly wonderful therapist.

By the time things get unbearable in January and I recognize that it's time to call for help for us both, I have the phone number ready and waiting in the address book. If I didn't know who to call, quite frankly I wouldn't have the energy to try to locate anyone. I'm too busy just coping with our lives. Living with a depressed and angry eight-year-old is hard work.

Let me describe one of our latest sessions. The therapist sat me and my son on a rug and gave my boy a lot of the cardboard blocks that look like bricks. "Build a wall between you and your mommy," he said. Steven complied, complaining that this was "baby stuff" and that he didn't want to do it. When the wall was finally built, Steven and I were to play peek-a-boo over the top of the wall. I was willing to look over the top, but my son was only willing to be found. He could not make himself look over the wall. The therapist then showed Steven how to put windows in his wall, so that we could play hide-and-seek through the wall. Steven moved away every time I found him; when it was his own turn to be the peeker, he moved around so fast that I couldn't keep up with him.

"And now, take down the wall between you and Mommy." Steven slowly started taking the blocks off the top, stacking them around himself. As the wall got lower, the piles of bricks began to surround him in a semicircle. He worked slowly, and finally there were only two courses of bricks left in the original wall. As Steven reached for a brick in slow motion with his right hand, his left hand drew back in an involuntary volley ball serve and he crashed a brick directly into my face, nearly breaking my nose.

After six years of living with me, my son still is not able to relax the defenses he has created to keep himself safe from possible hurt. Six years later, he is still not able to let down his guard enough to let himself be loved. He can't let go of his walls.

●

Margaret and William: Adoption as "No Big Deal"

Adoption has always been an accepted part of my life. It isn't something I had to make a great decision about as an adult when my husband and I wanted to have children but seemed unable to have them. I was adopted as a newborn, and I have a brother born to my parents three years before my adoption. I never felt any different from my brother, nor was I ever treated differently by my family or relatives. I resembled the rest of my family physically in that we are tall, slim, and fair; matching was part of adoption forty-five years ago. Adoption was seldom mentioned in my family. The only mention I can recall—and, in fact, it was told to me by my mother years later because I don't recall the actual incident—was that I asked her some questions about my birthmother. My mother replied, "She must have been a wonderful person because she had you." In my memory that is the only conversation I had concerning adoption. Over the years when people would comment on the resemblance between my mother and myself, we would just look at each other and smile, but nothing was ever said. In a way, having that physical resemblance overcame some awkward situations and made for an easy fitting together of that family. Whatever other insecurities I might have had growing up, adoption was not one of them because I truly forgot about it and only occasionally would be startled to realize, "Oh, yes. I'm adopted." It was just never a big deal in my life or anyone's around me. I was the only girl on both sides of the family and felt unique and treasured as such.

During much of my life I have wondered from time to time about my birthparents—did they have pointy elbows and fat thighs and dislike bread crusts like me? Real major concerns! I know almost nothing about them except that one of them was artistic. My mother must have mentioned this at some time. Nothing else was ever volunteered. Curiosity was never enough motivation for me to bring up the subject of my background. My parents were the best in the world. In fact, I tear up as I write this because several years after her death I still miss my mother. I had a wonderful, secure, happy life, thanks in great part to my parents—I never think of them as adoptive parents. I read the Dear Abby letters and I know there are many good and bad stories about seeking out birthparents. I would not upset a very good life just to relieve my curiosity. Although she never gave any indication of feeling this way, I also felt it might hurt my mother if I undertook such a search, as if I wasn't satisfied with the life she had given me. I would never want her to feel that way. But this is just my own opinion about searching for birthparents and not one shared by everyone, probably including my daughter.

My husband and I both enjoyed working with children and in the late 1960s, as he was finishing a residency in pediatrics and I was teaching grade school, we decided to start our own family. We thought we wanted a large family, and when I wasn't pregnant within a few months we turned to adoption. We had already decided it wasn't right to have more than two children ourselves, so adoption was already part of our plans. We hadn't planned to start our family by adopting, but it wasn't a problem in our thinking. When I wasn't pregnant, we plunged right in with phone calls to agencies in the last two months of 1968. Our experience here was unique, even for those years. As we expected, several agencies said "No" or "Long wait," but one said "Yes"—that they were expecting several births in early 1969. We quickly completed all the necessary paperwork, and our daughter, Margaret, was born on March 27, 1969. My husband received the call from the agency on April 1, and I truly thought it was his idea of a joke when he called to tell me of her arrival. Our request had been for a healthy newborn. We went to the agency two days later to "meet" her. It was our choice to accept this child (as if there was any question!), and we brought her home. I was so excited I couldn't even dress her and my husband had to rescue us.

Friends and family were all thrilled for us. The only reaction I could call negative was that my in-laws were hurt that we had not shared with them our disappointment in not having children ourselves. Since there never was any disappointment on our part, their reaction surprised us. We hadn't discussed my doctor's visits with them, nor were we ever told that I couldn't have children. We looked forward to having children in our family whether by birth or adoption. We sent out regular birth announcement cards at this time. I probably should have indicated the adoption in some way on the cards because for years afterward people would say, "Oh, I didn't know you were pregnant." Lots of explanations could have been saved.

In July 1970 we adopted a second child, William. As I said, our situation was unique and we knew it. This agency was unusual. When our daughter was six months old, we had asked the agency about a second child. They said, yes, they preferred a second child in a family—that it was better than having an only child. We said we were leaving for military duty in the summer of 1970 and would a second child be possible before then? No problem, we were told. Research no longer said that the best spacing of children was necessarily three years apart. It sounded good to us! They even said they would try to honor our request for a boy. Having a healthy newborn was our first priority, but when you're writing the script, why not put in your preference, we thought. Our son was two weeks old when we "met" him at the agency. We also met the foster mother who had cared for him, which was especially nice for us.

In March 1972, just as our daughter turned three, I gave birth to a son, Michael. As I recall, the older two took this addition in stride, much as any children would. I did arrive home from the hospital on our daughter's birthday, so the emphasis was on her, not the baby.

I had always read a lot to the children, and one of our books was *The Chosen Baby* by Valentina Wasson. It was through this book that we told the children of their adoption. The book was always out with their other books and was just a natural part of our lives. There was never any Big Announcement. They absorbed the fact of adoption and/or natural birth in a family gradually as they grew up. Neither child has any specific memories of being told. Our daughter says it is something she always knew, although she didn't really understand what adoption meant until some time in grade school. But both children say it was no big deal—exactly my goal!

As in my own childhood, we have not talked about the adoptions much with the children. We've told them the few details we know of their mothers —age, schooling, ethnic background. Our daughter has brought up the subject more frequently and has said that as a teen she wants to find her birthmother. I would not be upset if she pursued this. Our daughter is confused about her ethnicity. My husband and I both come from German origins. My daughter's birthmother had English and French in her background. When asked to research her background for a foreign-language class, she didn't know if she was German or French-English. For myself, I only knew the German background of my parents and grandparents and was surprised by her thoughts. Of course, I now see her confusion. As I recall, we talked about it and settled on Germany for the class project.

William indicates no interest in adoption—in fact, he seems a bit bored by her curiosity. We've offered him what we know and that seems okay with him.

A greater reaction has come from Michael, our youngest. I'm afraid we overdid the "chosen baby" story. When he was small, he must have felt he wasn't as special as his brother and sister. He said, "I want to be your best boy," as though he had to compete with the "chosen" two.

And certainly to reassure Margaret and William we did tell them they were chosen. As the agency said, we did not have to accept either of these babies! There was never any question in our minds when we held them in our arms—we would not have said no. But the choice certainly was there. It was all so easy we couldn't believe our good fortune.

With three infants so close together, our thoughts of a large family of six or seven quickly changed. Perhaps we should have reassured Michael that he was as precious as his brother and sister. We were delighted to have had a birth of our own. We have always kidded that he was the straw that broke the camel's back—three were enough. We have never wished for more or regretted for a moment having the three.

There have been many differences between our family now and mine as I grew up. Because I lived in the same community until I left for college and because I resembled the rest of the family, I suppose people either knew or didn't know of my adoption, but the subject would not logically have come up.

With my husband and three children, we've moved often and our children do not all resemble each other. People don't know our family background and frequently make comments about our appearance. We either smile and say nothing or say with pride and a big smile, "Some of the children are adopted." It isn't a subject I talk about a great deal. I was just happy not to be set apart from the rest of my family as a child, and I assume my kids feel the same. I continue to think adoption is No Big Deal. The children are all very different from each other not because they were adopted but because they are themselves with their own characteristics, strengths, weaknesses, likes, dislikes, talents, and so on. I understand one of my natural parents was talented in art. I also know my father designed many fine houses and won many awards for his watercolors. My mother was an interior decorator for thirty years. How would I explain my own interest in art, color, design—genes or environment? Does it need an explanation? I don't think so. I would not use adoption to explain or excuse something about myself or my children.

With that logic, I don't worry about my adoption and I hope my children aren't overly concerned about theirs. I had great parents and I hope I've done as much for my own children.

We have several friends and relatives who adopted children after us. They have approached us with questions, and we have been pleased to talk. We've shared our thoughts and experiences, but everyone brings something different to the situation. Some people have had to work through not giving birth to their own children and seemed forced to consider adoption. Others want to celebrate the day the child was brought home from the agency as though it were a second birthday. Both of these ideas go against my thought of "why emphasize the adoption?" It's a fact—now get on with life.

●

A Birth and Adoptive Father

Richard: Where the kid came from seems sort of bookish, abstract.

Susan: You have four biological children and two adopted children. I would like you to comment on your experience as a father because you have been both a biological and an adoptive parent.

Richard: Let me preface this by saying that because my father died when I was very young and my mother never remarried, I had no experience in my childhood of a father in the house. So I have always had some difficulty fathering or trying to understand what that meant. And much of what I know I learned from books—*War and Peace,* novels like that, not psychology books.

But despite all that, in reflecting on my experiences in my second family with my two adopted children, one of the things that has struck me very powerfully is—though it's a little hard to put it fairly—my basic sense that there is no significant difference between fathering adopted children and fathering one's own bio-logical children. As I think about it, my sense of these children is that they are just as much mine in just as full and complete a sense as my biological children. Now it's true that we adopted the two of them when they were both very young—the older one at five days and the younger one, my daughter, at three weeks. So in getting them, my experience was very, very close to my experience with my biological children.

But I don't think the way you get them matters very much. Much more important for me than that is the sense that once you get into the daily routine of parenting, taking care of an infant, reordering one's life—all the stuff that goes on in taking care of a newborn—or when you get a second child, all the difficulties and complications that go on with the older kid in relation to the newborn—in that context technical questions of where the kid came from and things like that just seem unreal. They seem sort of bookish, abstract; they don't have any substance to them. The day-in, day-out business of being a parent is what really seems to matter. And then as the child begins to grow there are all the things you begin to notice about the way he begins to mimic you, to pick up your characteristics, hand gestures, body language, facial expressions, all those things. I saw and felt all that very powerfully with my son.

Susan: Yet he doesn't look like you, and your biological children, I gather, look exactly like you.

Richard: I haven't particularly noticed that. I don't think men look at themselves in mirrors very much. I don't think men know what they look like anyway. Women know what they look like a lot better than men because they spend a lot more time in front of a mirror. But I do think men (and women, too, for that matter) do have a sense of how they appear to others, what their facial expressions convey. I don't think it's the physical features that count; it's your actual expression, the way you talk, your voice, your hands, and all those things. And, of course, these are exactly the things that kids imitate; these are the things they notice in you, the things they pick up and reflect back to you.

My biological children were born when I was much younger, my first child at a point in my life when I didn't have a job. I was a graduate student just getting out of the army, and I found my-self with a baby. I used to lie awake half the night, every night, wondering whether the poor little thing was going to starve because I couldn't put food on the table. I was very nervous about that. That's not an issue for me now; I have a job, I have a tenured position, I have a career. I have a sense of who I am, where I am going, what I'm doing. And the result is that I find parenting much pleasanter and more satisfying. Now that may be due to being older and more settled, but the fact is that my feeling of ease in parenting my adopted kids is a much more real, much more present reality for me than the fact that they're adopted.

Then there's something else that I think is enormously important. How do I put it? Men don't go through being pregnant and giving birth. Apart from some anticipation, parenting really begins for a father when you bring the baby home from the hospital. And when the baby finally gets there, it's not because of anything that the father is particularly conscious of having done. With my biological children, the way in which my wife got pregnant was just that we stopped using birth control.

Now one of the things that is peculiar about adoption is that it normally happens for most adoptive fathers after a long, frustrating, unsuccessful period of attempting to get your wife pregnant. It seems to me that for most people there is a lot of unnatural activity preceding the adoption process: attempting to get pregnant, charting your temperature, potency work-ups, fertility work-ups, lots of doctors, risky medical procedures, and so on—all kinds of intrusive, embarrassing, unpleasant stuff. That's a very unnatural, discomforting situation, and actually I was glad when we stopped it because it made making love and all of that less attractive and comfortable. But when you finally give up on getting pregnant and get into the adoption process there is also a lot of intrusive stuff—social workers, agencies, filling out forms, answering questions about very private matters, legal stuff—that sort of creates a public setting in which the adoption takes place and adds to its unnaturalness. I think this whole process of attempting to get pregnant, failing, and then struggling, usually for a very long time, with adoption procedures has got to be extremely dispiriting, depressing, demeaning to both men and women. I don't see how anyone can go through all that without feeling like a failure, a helpless, passive pawn, and finally a frustrated, angry schmuck. And, frankly, that's not a real good state of mind in which to begin parenting.

Now it seemed to me that because I had already had biological children I was simply able to ignore a lot of that stuff and not let it get to me. I remember saying over and over to myself: "This is something we have to go through. I don't like it, and I wish we didn't have to do it. It's like those disgusting premarital blood tests to find out if you have syphilis." And I remember saying to my wife that as soon as it was over and we got our baby, we would try to forget all that junk and just focus on the child and start being parents.

My sense is that if you have not previously had children, biological children, and gone through the whole process of becoming a parent, then you don't have anything against which to compare the experience. For most adoptive parents, who haven't had biological children, the unnaturalness, the artificiality, the making public of things that are meant to be private, the attempting to do deliberately things that ought to come spontaneously, all of that necessarily gets to be part of becoming a parent. To be blunt about it, I think this pollutes, distorts, disarranges the whole process of becoming a parent, particularly since an awful lot of adoptive parents, by the time they get around to adopting, have discovered for themselves and officially been told by all sorts of people that they are biologically defective, that the husband does not have enough sperm or the wife has blocked tubes, but whatever it is something is wrong with them. To become an adoptive parent almost always means that there is something wrong with you. But in my case I didn't feel that there was anything wrong with me. If I'd wanted to have more kids, I could have had more. Well, it didn't work out biologically with us, so we had to go through all this crap. But then when it was over, it was over, and then I just started being a parent. And it seemed to me that it was very important to keep that stuff to a minimum, this whole matrix of unnatural, distorting activities, to keep that to an absolute minimum, to allow the ordinary and everyday activities of taking care of a newborn baby to take over as quickly as possible, just to forget the whole adoption process and focus on the child.

And in fact when that happens I think all the differences between having a biological child or adopting one actually begin to disappear. For me there's been a kind of amnesia about all the crap we went through to get our two kids. I've heard that women have a kind of amnesia about the pain of childbirth, that the presence of the new baby lets them forget how painful the labor was. I think I've done something like that about adoption.

So for me there are no real differences about the way I feel about my adopted kids and my biological ones. And if there are differences at all, it is probably because I've had two sets of children at different stages in my life, and that is much more significant than the fact of adoption per se.

Susan: Do you ever think about the birthfather?

Richard: What do you mean, "think about the birthfather"?

Susan: Well, your son and daughter each have a biological father different from you. Do you ever think about him?

Richard: No! I mean it occurs to me that my son's biological father is probably a lot taller than I am and my son is probably going to be taller than I, and I guess I have the fantasy that Mark probably looks like him, although I'm not sure. How do I know?

Susan: Does that bother you in any way?

Richard: No.

Susan: This gets to the question that is important to many adoptive parents. These children, close as they are to you, are not "yours" in the sense of "flesh of my flesh," and that's very important to some people, though perhaps not to others. Would you comment on this?

Richard: I think it is important, but in a purely fantasy way. I have four biological children. They are very, very different from each other and from me. So that any notion that a child simply replicates you is pure fantasy. It is true that my biological children are all like me in some ways; I don't have any question about that. All four of them, for example, have a slight dimple in the middle of their nose that they get from me because my nose is something like that, but they are also unlike me in very, very different ways. I don't have a sense that every one of my kids is a clone of me. Furthermore, it is strange to see how your kids, your biological kids, are like you in unexpected, surprising ways. Raising children, watching children grow into independent adults, is a very mysterious business; there are all kinds of ways in which you suddenly recognize yourself in them in ways you hadn't recognized yourself before. There are moments when you suddenly see something familiar in a child, and you realize it is familiar to you because you are like that, and you never knew it. Sometimes, of course, they are like you in ways you are familiar with. Then, when they get older, children take a certain amount of pleasure in being different from you, in revolting, in defining themselves in opposition to you. So they do that too.

It seems to me that we are talking about raising children over a twenty-year period—parenting is, at minimum, a twenty-year commitment, and remember that during that period the parent is changing almost as much as the child. So the developing relationship of parent and child, with all the similarities and differences, is enormously complicated, incredibly individualized. It is extraordinary the way those babies turn from little five-pound nothings into real people, the way they reach out into the world and find out about it by exploring various dimensions of your own being and working off you and your life. That kind of thing is so individualized, so different for every child, that I cannot honestly say that my adopted children are more different from me than my biological children. In some respects, it seems to me, my adopted son is more like me than one of my biological sons is. How do you gauge these things? What's the standard by which we measure our impact on our children anyway?

And then, to complicate matters more, as one gets involved with a child, at least it was so for me, the experience is one of falling in love. And when you fall in love with and become passionate about a child and respond to him and he responds to you, a relationship develops. Along the way you may notice similarities and differences between the two of you, but the real energy, the real action, is in the developing relationship itself, a relationship that is difficult and delightful, troublesome and rewarding, passionate, infuriating and illuminating, always engrossing. Against that, all the other stuff you're asking about seems mere theoretical chatter about sperms, eggs, where they come from, what they're like, what's heredity, what's environment—that kind of thing. All that comes from biology and psychology textbooks, but for me it doesn't carry an awful lot of weight as against the concrete reality of my son or daughter there before me, the one I'm dealing with.

My wife tells me that perhaps I deemphasize or ignore the realities of adoption more than I should. That may be true. I'm not sure. But so what? If someday adoption becomes an issue with my son or daughter, then I'll have to deal with it. But why assume that will happen?

Susan: Let me ask you whether your son or your daughter has ever talked to you about being adopted. Has that happened yet?

Richard: My daughter's still very young and she hasn't talked about it at all yet. My son, who is eight, has done almost all of his talking about adoption with his mother. She is much more sensitive and concerned about it than I am, I think, because she is essentially an adoptive mother; she hasn't had biological children. I have raised the subject with my son several times, but he doesn't have much to say to me about it. He's a very sensitive kid, he's got terrific emotional antennae, and he may be picking up that I don't have a lot to say about it. So he doesn't ask me much about it. I suppose we've talked a couple of times about it, but not in detail, not at great length, and not with a hell of a lot of affect or passion involved.

Susan: I gather that he does not yet focus on having a different biological father, that for the most part he focuses on having a different biological mother.

Richard: That's right. I don't think that it's ever occurred to him that there was another man involved in his life. I mean, he's aware that there's another woman from whom he was born, who carried him. No, I don't think he's aware that there was ever another man in the picture. He hasn't put that together yet. I do want to say this, however; if my son says to me, as undoubtedly he will at some point, when he gets angry or whatever, "You're not my father!" I'm not going to get real pissed off at that and it's not going to upset me terribly much, because the fact of the matter is, I know I *am* his father. I don't have any doubt about that! For better or worse this kid has *me* for his father. I'm the only father he has, the only father he ever will have, the only father he's ever going to know. If he ever tracks down his biological father, he'll find a man who had something to do with him—there's no question about that—but there's no relationship with that guy. And whatever he has with that man, it's not going to be a relationship with his father because I'm his father.

Susan: How do you feel about not being the recipient of your son's conversations about adoption?

Richard: Well, there are a lot of things I do with Mark that I report back to my wife about. I find these conversations he has with his mother about adoption very moving, but I think I am mostly moved by my wife's account of them and her responses. I find them touching because I think they represent her process of working through her own feelings about being a mother and an adoptive mother and what the significance of that is. She has a powerful drive to be absolutely straight with our son and at the same time to help him deal with his feelings while she tries to cope with her own feelings about adoption. I think the simple truth is that I personally don't have an awful lot of feelings about these things. I worry about the kids. I think I'm a somewhat nervous and anxious parent, but not about this kind of stuff. And though I have a lot of sympathy for my wife's feelings, I don't experience those feelings in the same way. If Mark should ask me about his biological father, I would tell him what I know, which is practically nothing. But in telling him, I don't think I would feel any particular ambiguity about who his real father is.

Susan: What would you feel if he talked to you about wanting, when he's older, to go look for his birthfather and meet him?

Richard: My wife and I have talked about that, and my general sense is that when Mark is eighteen—I think not before then, because I would want him to be old enough to be able to handle something like that—if at eighteen he wants that, I would do whatever I could to help him find his biological father or find out about him. I'd be perfectly happy to do that. However, I think I would be anxious about it because if he goes that way he's bound to have some disappointment. After all, apart from a few trivial facts, all he'll have is some fantasy about his biological father, and the reality cannot possibly match the fantasy. So there is bound to be some unhappiness for him. And I think that may happen. As I think about it, it feels like watching your kids go through their first serious failure. Every kid goes through it, but it's very painful for parents to watch their children not get something that they want. One thing parents can do is help a child deal with deep disappointment as best they can. But now that I think about it, that's going to be a hard one.

Susan: Would you comment on the adoption process?

Richard: Yes, I'd be happy to because I have very strong feelings about it. I think that many of the people involved in adoption have little awareness of the degree to which their behavior, their procedures, their whole way of dealing with prospective adoptive parents, have profound effects in feeding into, supporting and exacerbating all of the worst fantasies and beliefs of adoptive parents. This is especially true for those who have not previously had biological children. Everything—procedures, attitudes, atmosphere—reinforces the infertile parents' sense that there is something wrong with them, that they are in some way defective or abnormal. The result, I think, is to exaggerate the significance of adoption. Instead of making it simple, quick, easy, uncomplicated, it's made something special. All that ordinary people have to do to become parents is go to bed together; if the woman gets pregnant, then a baby appears in nine months, whether you want it or not, and you're a parent. Adoptive parents, by contrast, have to justify, have to rationalize, have to come to terms with their own inadequacies. They have to make choices: is it to be an interracial baby? a foreign baby? a boy or a girl? an infant or a toddler? or how about a child with some birth defects or who is retarded? Biological parents don't choose any of those things; for them having a baby is like a lottery— you take what you get. But for adoptive parents all these issues are options, features that can be chosen, that are subject to some sort of rational choice. Of course, even if the adoptive parents somehow choose the particular features they want in a baby, in actual fact they get their child the same way everybody else does: it's a lottery, you take what you get, though you won't know what you've got for twenty years or so.

The point I'm trying to make, a point that I think is very, very important, is that by magnifying the adoptive process, by emphasizing the parents' defects or deficiencies, by deceiving adoptive parents into believing that they can in some sense choose their child, the whole process of parenting is unnecessarily but seriously distorted. I've seen this in families with adopted children where the parents are so intensely conscious of being adoptive instead of biological parents that everything gets related to adoption. And in actual fact, as I've said, I don't think it's all that important. I'm not for ignoring it, and I'm not for denying it; I don't want to do either of those things. But I think there are a lot of things that go on between parents and children, adoptive or otherwise, that have nothing to do with how the kid got there. It's a mistake that is reinforced by all these legal and social service agencies to make adoption more important in the consciousness of the parent than it actually is. And since children pick up their sense of reality from their parents, if the adoptive parents think that adoption is the overwhelming fact in their relationship with their children, then the kids will inevitably feel the same way. And I think that that is very unfortunate.

Roughly speaking, I see adoption as a fact, perhaps a disturbing fact, that a child has to cope with. There are a lot of children in the United States today who are growing up in split families because their parents are divorced. There's no question that divorce is not good for children, but nonetheless children of divorced parents have to cope with it. Some cope better, some worse. Much of the responsibility for whether the children cope better or worse with divorce has to do with the way in which the parents handle the situation. Other children grow up with a physical defect or with a sick or disabled parent. In my own case, my mother was widowed as a young woman, so I grew up without a father. I was raised in a single-parent family not because of divorce but because of death. Until a few years ago that was very common since a lot of people died young from diseases that are now easily curable, as was the case with my father. I'm not saying that it was better to grow up without a father than with one, or as good, but it was simply a fact of life with which I had to cope for better or for worse. I think I did reasonably well.

I don't see that adoption for a child is any different from that. Of course, the child will cope well or badly depending on how the family deals with the situation. If the family of a deceased parent remains forever melancholic and endlessly mourns the lost parent, then I think the children are going to be profoundly affected by that. They cannot help but be. On the other hand, if the death of a parent is a very sad, very painful, permanent loss that a child and the surviving parent mourn together, a loss that they don't either deny or exaggerate, then I think it becomes for the child just that—a loss, a pain, something to be coped with, something to come to terms with.

I see adoption as essentially like that. It could cripple, but it doesn't have to. It can be dealt with and accepted. I suppose that at different stages of his life the child who has lost a parent will have to reflect again upon that loss, reexperiencing its meaning and reintegrating it. And I imagine that adopted children have to reflect at various stages of their lives what it means that they were adopted. I suppose that as they grow up, as they experience life, as they mature, they will have to repeatedly reflect on the meaning of the fact that they were adopted, that their parents couldn't keep them, that somebody else had to raise them, that their biological parents were not there for them. I think that's a very complicated and difficult fact to accept, but I think that's all it is, and that it need not be turned into some life-controlling fact, which sits forever like an undigested lump in one's gut. After all, if being a parent is pretty much the same, whether the relationship is biological or adoptive, the same holds for being a child.

Susan: Thank you very much.

Afterword

Your children are not your children.
They are the sons and daughters of Life's longing for itself.
They came through you, but not from you,
And though they are with you yet they belong not to you.
You can give them your love but not your thoughts.
For they have their own thoughts.
You can house their bodies but not their souls,
For their souls dwell in the house of tomorrow, which you cannot visit,
    not even in your dreams.
You can strive to be like them, but seek not to make them like you.
For life goes not backward nor tarries with yesterday.
You are the bows from which your children as living arrows are
    sent forth.
The archer sees the mark upon the path of the infinite, and He bends you
    with His might that His arrows may go swift and far.
Let your bending in the archer's hand be for gladness;
For even as he loves the arrow that flies, so He loves also
The bow that is stable.
—Kahlil Gibran, *The Prophet*

All parents are faced with the difficult task of embracing their children's differences from them, though the necessity of this embrace is often obscured by physical likenesses and fantasies of genetic sameness. The adoptive parent, unable to invoke either of these obscurations, is faced with negotiating diversity from the start. We commit to try to love and care for whoever is entrusted to us. Parents do not adopt in order to carry banners against social ills. We adopt to have the joy of loving a child. Yet in our quiet negotiation of differences we make an important contribution to our culture's

217

concepts of the family and its relation to the wider world. Through adoption, the family ceases to be a preserve insulated from the rest of the world, valuing similarity and derogating difference. Rather, the adoptive family integrates diversity and uses it to form a permanent bridge to and from the wider world. In this way, marriage and adoption are similar; both rest on the capacity to love another without the illusion of sameness.

Adoptive parents, through their love and care of their children, find themselves taking on, in miniature, a central dilemma of modern society, what David Kirk has called "the necessity of heterogenous constituents becoming parts of cohesive units" (1988, p. 7). Through our children our families become connected to the social problems that resulted in our children's relinquishment: alcoholism, drug addiction, teenage pregnancy, prejudice against unmarried women and their children, the inferior status of women, the living conditions of the poor, child abuse and neglect, mental illness, economic inequity between first and third world countries, and so on. We find white parents scurrying to the public library for books on prejudice; middle-class parents, socialized to remain segregated in the suburbs, ferreting out and building neighborhoods where diversity is respected and appreciated; parents who listen to news from Korea and India with a different, more personally invested, ear; parents lobbying for special-needs children, for programs for drug-dependent pregnant mothers; parents involved in open adoptions often crossing racial and class barriers to form ties to their children's first family.

Although many adoptive parents are not socially active around the factors that affected the arrival of their child, all of our families are enriched by the diversity our children bring us—be it racial, religious, ethnic, or new temperaments and abilities. For all adoptive families, our children are a daily reminder of the world apart from our often middle-class lives. This revisioning of the family from an insular preserve—"our clan, our class, our race, our nationality"—to an active member of a global community is part of the adoptive legacy to us and our culture.

Quietly, our families are creating and living new meanings for adoption. Whereas in most cultures adoption has existed for the parents as a means of strengthening existing kinship bonds or increasing one's status by allying oneself with the ruling powers, it now exists for the benefit of the child as well. In more complex adoptions—those that introduce differences in race, religion, and social class—kinship loses its conventional meaning and is founded instead on "reciprocal need, caring, and affinity" (Benet 1976). Interestingly, adoption teaches us the young child's concept of "family": adults and children who live together, who have love and respect for each other. In other words, "family" is not essentially a legal and genetic set of relationships (Pedersen and Gilby 1986, pp. 119–20).

Our own fantasies of having been orphaned and adopted, which most children experience at least fleetingly, point to people's nascent sense of both vulnerability and interconnectedness with others outside our nuclear families. The adoptee's so-called genealogical bewilderment is not just a negative "adoption stress" but a process of imaginal variation, of inhabiting imaginally first this family and then that, breaking down the boundaries of the family that so often isolate us from one another in their efforts to protect us. Adoption, actual and imagined, "is a metaphor for the human condition, sending us forth on that mythic quest that will prove that we are connected to each other and to all the creatures of this world—and in the process, reveal to us who we really are" (Lifton 1988, p. 296). Adoption takes both children and parents on this quest.

The stories of our history—in their difficulties and graces—strengthen and shape each of us. The struggles we have suffered can be both diffi-cult and generative. This is as true for our adoptive children as it is for us. Our children carry their adoption variously over time—as fact, as pain, as odyssey. We hope that these pages will be a help in both the struggle and the joys surrounding adoption, an aid to our joining as partners with our children in our combined efforts to understand the legacy of adoption in our lives. Adoption is not a fact to be held secretly, with shame, regret, or fear. It is a fact that gives rise to many meanings for both child and par-ent: meanings to be witnessed and shared, to be clarified or tangled with, meanings that not only move us but change us, and for which gratitude is finally due.

Two Families Who Decided Not to Talk with Their Young Children about Adoption

Eric: One-Time Telling

My husband and I were working full time. He was going to law school in the evenings; I was teaching elementary school. We put off having a child until my husband was finished with his degree and I stopped working. Once that happened, I didn't get pregnant for some time. When I did, I had a miscarriage in the second month. Nothing happened for quite some time. We went to doctors for all the tests. It was a very emotional and frustrating time. We wanted a baby badly. At long last, there came the opportunity to adopt a nine-day-old baby boy. I was twenty-eight, my husband thirty-two.

Eric was a gorgeous, perfect child. From the day he entered our home, he became our very own "first" child. Eighteen months later, our second son was born, and fourteen months after that, our third son. Two years later, our fourth son completed this wonderful team. The children were certainly very close in age. They were brought up always equally, and everyone got along beautifully together. We loved them all the same. When Eric was about three years of age, we told him that he was the "special" one, that he was adopted, and that he came to us when we didn't think we would ever give birth to a child. That was it! The subject never came up again. Each son has his own personality, his own looks. In fact, none of the boys looks like us. I'm dark with dark brown hair. My husband is fair and blond. Eric had red hair when he was born and it became strawberry blond. Eric's brothers may have mentioned to their friends that Eric was adopted. This fact was accepted, and there were never any more explanations needed.

Eric was a leader, into all activities, mainly sports. He played basketball, baseball, soccer, and football in Little Leagues, on school teams, and in backyards. His brothers always followed. His interests and enjoyments became theirs. They were sometimes on the same teams. We supported each one by going to every game. We are fortunate to have always lived in places where the schools were excellent and athletic leagues brought together a whole community. To this day, Eric keeps in touch with boys he knew from elementary school. All four boys were bar mitzvahed, and we were involved in the local temples. Being the first, Eric paved the way for his brothers. As Eric's parents, we learned from him.

I went back to teach when my youngest son started elementary school. Teaching was, I believe, very beneficial in helping me to raise four boys. I was always home for them after school, on school vacations, and in the summer, and I learned to have a lot of patience, compassion, and understanding of all children, not only my own. Eric always had his mother, his father, and his three brothers to love and support him, as well as many, many friends. We had our expectations and dreams for all of them.

Eric was and will always be our number one son. His brothers adore him and still confide in him. They all followed him by going to college and graduating. Eric is now twenty-seven. He's happy, well-liked, and has a million friends. He has a good job. He has never asked about the circumstances of his adoption. We believe it's because he never felt for a minute that he was an addition to our family. He was simply the "first" son. In fact, he believes he is the handsomest one!

Jeremy and Chloe: Deciding to Postpone Telling until Latency

Our two children, Jeremy and Chloe, were adopted a few days after their birth, nine and ten years ago. They came to us after years of anguish and longing, only too familiar to adoptive parents. Their arrival dispelled all the past pain, and they continue to be the greatest source of joy in our lives.

There are many aspects of this experience that I could write about, but one seems to be unusual these days. I will recount just this part of our story, as it may be of most interest to adoptive and prospective adoptive parents.

After much thought and debate, my husband and I decided not to tell our children about their adoption until they were in latency. We had read several studies on the disproportionate numbers of adopted children with school and emotional problems, studies that recommend telling children later, as was once common practice. We felt that learning of one's adoption before having enough cognitive development to understand it or enough language to formulate questions about what one didn't understand might affect the forming of a good self-image. As our daughter was only eleven months old when our son arrived, it was possible to avoid the subject of adoption. When she first saw her brother, Chloe's words were, "Oh! woof, woof!" We also decided that until we told the children, we would not discuss it with anyone else who did not already know, including schools but not including doctors.

This may sound like a difficult or complicated thing to do, but it was very easy. The daily task of caring for infants is so consuming; the subject just never came up. Other women in the playground near our house "remembered" seeing me pregnant; strangers thought the children resembled us. I did not worry that anyone else might tell them because only our oldest friends and family knew about the adoptions, and they also knew that we had not yet told the children. When Jeremy and Chloe asked the inevitable question, "Was I in your tummy?" I answered what I thought they were really asking, just as one tries to answer a child's questions about sex by answering the implied question rather than the specific question. Thus, I would say, "Of course, you were born just like all babies." I did not feel more uncomfortable about this than I did about keeping alive the myth of Santa Claus or the Tooth Fairy.

The difficult part, of course, was finally telling the children. Originally we had planned to tell them when they were six and seven years old. At that time, however, our daughter, who had just had a learning disability diagnosed, was having a very hard time. We had to wait until she was nine and our son was eight. Certainly, it was a very difficult task to undertake, one that, obviously, would have been avoided by telling them from the beginning. We had the feeling that we were delivering a terrible blow and feared that nothing would ever be the same again. My husband, in fact, found the idea of telling the children so upsetting that he could hardly bring himself to think of it at all. I spent many hours rehearsing the event with a friend. My husband and I finally agreed to tell the children on a particular weekend at our country house. Even then, at the agreed upon time, he suddenly decided to take the children fishing! Ultimately, we did all sit down together and have the talk.

I told them how I had tried for many years to get pregnant and had not succeeded; how, luckily, families can be made in many ways, one of which is through adoption; and that we had adopted both of them. I told them that their adoptions had been arranged before they were born, that we had first located a young woman who was pregnant but who was not in a position to raise a child, and that, through a lawyer, we had arranged to adopt her baby, who was our daughter, Chloe. One year later the same thing happened with the adoption of our son, Jeremy. We talked about how very difficult it is to find a baby available for adoption and how incredibly lucky we had been to have the opportunity to adopt them. Most important, of course, were the stories of how sad we had been for years before they came and what it was like going to the hospital to bring them home—truly the happiest days of our lives.

The children were, of course, clearly surprised to hear all this. "Do you mean I'm really adopted?" they both asked. But surprise seems to have been the extent of their reaction. Ever since the children were born, I have recorded their childhoods in albums containing photos, announcements, cards, curls of hair, and other memorabilia. I had made album sheets for the trips to the hospital, for our court hearings, and for the parties we had afterward to celebrate. But these sheets I had kept apart from the first-year books. After we discussed the adoptions with the children, we put the extra pages in the albums, and Jeremy and Chloe took the opportunity of looking through the books again, as they love to do in general. They reminded themselves, I think, that everything they knew about their lives was still true, only now there was a piece of information they hadn't known before. The children were soon in their usual hurry to get out to play.

Once they had left the room, my husband wept but could not say why. I felt as though something I had been waiting for and dreading for a long time had both happened and not happened. I didn't feel relieved because what I feared had not happened—yet. For a while I kept waiting for some sign of distress or confusion from the children. It has been two years now and there is still no sign; I have stopped giving it much thought. The children told their friends—in the spirit of "Hey, guess what?"—but since then the subject hardly ever comes up. Someday, no doubt, Chloe and Jeremy will have questions about their biological parents and may want to trace them. Perhaps someday adoption will emerge as a problem for one or both of them. But perhaps not.

Looking back on the decision, I can't know for certain if it was a good one or not. Perhaps, had we told the children from the beginning, their sense of identity would have been different than it is—we'll never know. Telling them when we did seems for now to have worked for our family.

The issue of adoption in relation to the general experience of child rearing continues to be a much less salient element than we ever expected. Before we adopted and before we told the children about the adoptions, it loomed very large in significance and power. But, except for these two occasions, it shrinks to being just one of the myriad daily concerns involved with loving our children, helping them to grow and find their way, and trying to be the best parents we can.

Adoptive Comments, Questions, and Play Sequences of Adopted Children in the Stories, Arranged by Age[1]

Age

Year–Month

1–9   Toddler dreams that day-care teacher took her baby bear away. She awakes weeping, "Why did she do that? Why did she take my baby away?" Subsequently, child reenacts someone trying to take a baby away from her mother.

2–0   Child reenacts story told to her of the day of her adoption.

2–0   Child pretends to be small bunny or other animal in the woods, which adoptive parent comes upon while walking. "The bunny would initially surprise me or her father, then would want to come home with us to live in our house and be our baby bunny."

2–5   Child asks adoptive mother, "Just where does a baby grow?" "Well, then, I grew in your uterus?"

---

1. We have listed here all the children's talk, play, and dreams that the adoptive parents reported as possibly having to do with adoption. Obviously, particularly with the dream and play sequences, it is not always possible to prove that the child was actually concerned with adoption at the time.

2–6 on	Child has daily talks, primarily at bedtime, with mother's index finger, whom she imagines as Aranea, the daughter of the dead spider, Charlotte, in *Charlotte's Web*. In the story, after her mother's death, Aranea is cared for by Wilbur, the pig. Aranea, adopted by Wilbur, becomes the most consistent character in this girl's play. Child has others take good care of the baby spider and in her third year does some of this caretaking herself. Sometimes the narrative includes missing her mother, but other times wholly different themes present themselves.
2–6	"Did your [adoptive mother's] belly get big and fat when I was inside?" (Parent explains no.) "But I want to be in *your* belly."
2–6	For several days in a row child entertains her day-care peers at naptime with her adoption story, saying, "When I was a baby I took a long, long, long plane ride all the way from El Salvador, and Mom and Jenny and Mimi [her aunt] came to get me at the airport." The children ask, "Did you eat things on the plane?" Child replies, "Chicken and rice, and I threw my bottle down the aisle" (all true).
2–9	Child enacts someone trying to take a baby kitten away from its mother, and the mother vehemently objecting.
2–9	Child claims her [adoptive] mother is also her father's mother. When mother says no, she is his wife, that he has a mother, child replies, "I know. His other mother went away."
2–9 on	Child enacts play where a mother animal dies, and a baby animal is found and becomes the child of the mother who finds it.
2–11	Child reenacts Moses' adoption. A magic pony spots the bad pharaoh's coming. The babies are hidden, and the [adoptive mothers] lie that they haven't seen any babies in order to protect the children from the bad pharaoh.
2–11	"When are we going to take her [new adopted sibling] back to the airport?"
3–0	At her third birthday party, girl asks, "Well, is she coming? Is my lady coming?" [Adoptive] mother asks, "Which lady?" "You know," child replies, "the lady I grew inside. It's my *birth*day, isn't it?"
3–0	On first day at a new preschool, child announces to the group, "When I was a baby I drank milk from my mother," and proceeds to describe nursing to the group, an experience she did not have.

3–1	Child sees a pregnant woman and asks, "Where is she starting?" Mother asks what he means, and he replies, "Well, is she starting at the hospital or the airport?"
3–1	When new stepfather moves into house, child announces that she will not be living with her family anymore, but moving "to my other mom's house." Same child has imaginary grandmothers, uncles, brothers, sisters, and cousins.
3–1	Mother explains that child's aunt is pregnant and that that is why her belly is so big. He replies, "Just like I grew inside you." When mother says no, he sticks his thumb in his mouth, grows pensive, and acknowledges sadness.
3–2	"Take off my skin, Daddy!" "Take off my hands, Mom. I want yours."
3–2	"I was in your tummy, Mommy?" (Mother explains no.) "What was her [the birthmother's] name, Mommy?" "What was [my sister's tummy-mommy] called?" "Let's call her [my birthmother] [For]Sythia." Child enacts with mother the story of their union in India. Child asks, "Were you sad in India, Mommy?" "Was I a little afraid of you at first, Mom?" (when they first met, child was eight months).
3–2	"That factory does not make baskets . . . because it makes babies. That was where I was made." Mother explains how babies are made. "So, Mom, I grew in your uterus?" Mother says no. That night he says again, "I was made in a factory," and his mother explains that was not the case. "I so sad, Mommy. . . . I so sad I didn't grow in your uterus."
3–4	Indian child is hesitant to enter church where a party of Indian adoptees and their parents is being held. After a forty-five-minute wait outside with her father, she asks him if a white woman in a sari is her mother. When he assures her she is not, the child confides that she is confused about the differences between her mother, her tummy-mother from India, her godmother, also from India and expected at the party, and her grandmother.
3–4	Child says to her adoptive mother, "If Grandma is your birthmother, who is your adoptive mother?"
3–4	"You are not my mother!" child announces to her adoptive mother when a stranger approaches the child and singles out physical characteristics having to do in the woman's mind with

people from the child's birthcountry (characteristics that are different from the adoptive mother's).

3–4   Child replays adoption-day story, but asks mother to pretend that when she is picking up the baby she is choosing the wrong child. Then child corrects her cheerily, proclaiming that she *is* the right baby.

3–4   Child pretends that she is a nursing baby piglet. She has her adoptive mother ask pig-mother if piglet can live at her house. Pig-mother says yes. When at adoptive mother's pretend house, child has adoptive mother "squish" her. Child runs back to pig-mother, who protects her. Then piglet asks pig-mother if she can live with adoptive mother. Same scene recurs, with piglet returning and again asking to live with adoptive mother. First mother seems to keep watch on second mother, whom piglet keeps wanting to live with.

3–5   While riding in a car (in the United States), an Indian child sees an Indian man on the street. She asks her father, "Is that my real daddy?"

3–5   Child says to her adoptive mother, "You're not really my mother." Adoptive mother says she is. "But, you're not really, really my mother." Adoptive mother explains that she is really her mother but not her birthmother. Child continues, "You know what I want when I grow up? I want to get so tiny that I can get in your tummy."

3–5   "Mommy, do you know who my favorite friends are?" Mother guesses. "Mom, do you know who my favorite mommy is?" Child announces the name of her adoptive mother.

3–6   Adoptive mother states that child started asking questions about adoption, and everything else in the world, at this age.

3–6   "Did I drink from your breasts when I was a baby like Jeremy [sibling of a friend] does?"

3–6   "Mama, was I in your tummy?" Mother says no. A day later: "So I was in your tummy?"

3–6   Child asks mother to treat her like a baby; mother complies. Child asks, "Was I in your tummy?"

3–6   "I was in your tummy. I was in your tummy," child announces, several months after a conversation where she had seemed to understand she had a birthmother.

3–7   Child asks Indian woman who directed her orphanage when she was a baby, "Are you my mother?" After this woman's function has been explained to child, child throws her arms around her neck and says, "Thank you for my sweetie mommy. Thank you for my sweetie daddy."

3–8   Child expresses regret that adoptive mother did not nurse her. She tries to get mother to say she drank milk from mom's nipples instead of from a bottle. A week later, child creates a game of sucking mom's nose.

3–9   When mom asks if child knows she was in another woman's belly, child says, "Yes, I know. She had brown skin like me." A week later she refers to her "Indian mom" as her birthmother. "My Indian mom took care of me until you could come and get me. . . . You know, the one whose belly I was in!" Child asks where adoptive mother was when child was at orphanage. "Sometimes I cried for you when I was a tiny baby, when I was at the baby clinic."

3–9   Child has play character tell her mother, "Maya is sad . . . because she wants a mommy with brown skin, not skin like yours." She suggests that her mother could paint her skin, and that if it rains God could help them keep the paint on. Later, "You can be my mommy forever and ever, anyway."

3–10   "[Adoption] means that he loves me very much and he found me!"

3–10   Child says to a peer, "I was born in India. . . . I was in my brother's tummy! Then I came out and my sister came to find me. She's my mother. My sister is my mother!"

3–9   Child pretends she is her younger sib in her adoptive mother's stomach. Then she pretends she is being born out of her adoptive mother's tummy. Child alternates between pretending she is birthbaby of her adoptive mother and mother's going to Brazil to adopt her. At one point she says, "I don't want you to have gone to Brazil to get me. God says I'm coming from your tummy very soon."

3–10   "Someday, Mom, you should have skin on your hands my color."
"Why [do we have different colors]?"
"Did my [younger sister's] nurse have brown skin too?"
"Did her waitress have brown skin?"
"Mom, did mine have my skin?"
"But why did God give me my skin and [my sister] her skin?

Why are they different?"

"But what color was my lady's?"

"I don't like [my skin color]. I want brown skin like [little sister]."

3–10   Child reenacts Moses story she has heard, but has princess be the mother "forever and ever." Magic ponies help the princess protect the mother and child.

3–?[2]   Blonde child in darker family explains to friends that her doll is "the only one in the family who looks like me." "I'm the only member of this family with blonde hair. My daddy loves blondes."

3–?   Through adoption of younger brother, child becomes curious about her foster care before placement and enjoys hearing her adoption worker tell her stories about herself as a baby. She seems to understand that she and her brother had different birthmothers but the same foster home, which she and her mother call "the waiting house."

3–?   Child expresses pain over looking different from her parents and dons a blonde wig, wanting to pretend to be her blonde friends. Her peers had commented, "How can that be your mom? She doesn't look like you." Or they said, with slant-eyed demonstration, "Chinese, Chinese! You're Chinese!"

3–?   Child suggests to mother that they get rid of newly adopted baby brother, who is crying a lot and taking up much of mother's attention. While mother is feeding new baby, child urinates in kitchen pot and shows her mother: "See what I did?" Mother thinks child is trying to see if adoption is re- versible. If she or her brother is "bad," will mother return the child?

3–?   Child says adamantly and in protest, "I don't want brown eyes; I want blue eyes!" (like the rest of the family).

3–?   Referring to her adoptive mother, child explains, "My mommy came to India. My mommy loves me."

3–?   "Adopting means you love a baby very much and go find them."

3–?   Child thinks that when friend's baby is born it will be taken to the orphanage in India where she was adopted so that someone can find it.

------

2. A question mark has been used to indicate that the parent specified how old the child was at the time in terms of years only.

3–?	When asked what she thinks it means that her new stepfather is adopting her, a child (adopted in India by her adoptive mother) says, "It means that he loves me very much."
3 or 4 yrs.	Child asks adoptive mother, "Why did you adopt us?" After listening to answer, child says, "It's okay, Mom, you have us now."
3 to 4 yrs.	Child recites litany of friends who are adopted and the countries they come from.
3 to 6 yrs.	Korean child who is teased by peers thinks it is "stupid" to have a Korean middle name and wants little to do with anything Asian. Once the family has two foster Vietnamese children, she develops positive feelings toward chopsticks and hanboks.
4–0	Child has a play character whose mother has died explain to her adoptive mother that the child wants a brown mother (not white like her adoptive mother).
4–0	Child asks her adoptive mother if she is a queen. Then she asks what her "real mother" looks like.
4–0	"Some kids have lots of mothers."
4–0	Child asks her adoptive mother, "Why would a woman who grew a baby give that baby away? . . . But why would a mother give up a baby? . . . But I want to know why." Mother suggests that maybe she wants to know why the lady who gave birth to her did not become her mother. "Yes, why would she give me up?" Child agrees with mother that it is "awfully hard" to understand why.
4–0	Twins who were adopted at birth and know their birthmother announce matter-of-factly to their adoptive mother that they were in her tummy. When adoptive mother tells them they were in their birthmother's womb, the son asks, "Why?"
4–3	Several months later girl twin snuggles into adoptive mother's lap and asks tentatively if she was in her womb. When told again that she was in her birthmother's womb, she nestles right onto mother's stomach, almost burrowing, and says, "I wish I had been in your womb."
4–3	As child announces how many children she plans to have, she says, "Mom, I was definitely in your tummy." When mother says no, child says, "Nope, yours. Your tummy." Mother again says no. "Well, then, I was in Daddy's tummy." Mother says no. Child replies, "I'm going downstairs to check on the weather."

4–3	Child says to her adoptive mother, "I was not in your tummy. That nice lady went to the doctor, and I came out of her tummy to be with you. I was so happy to see you!"
4–4	After visit with birthmother, child says, while sobbing, that she will never go alone to see Mommy Michele (birthmother) ever again. Her adoptive mother asks her why. Child says, "You can't go shopping without me! Max [her twin brother] can go visit while you and I shop!"
4–6	"Why didn't my real mom want me?" Adoptive mother asks what the child thinks. He replies, "I think she didn't like me." After mother explains, she asks if he has been worrying about this. He says, "No, I just wondered." He wets his pants at nursery school that morning, the first and only time.
4–6	Child asks his adoptive mother, "Was I in Mommy Michele's [birthmother's] womb?" "And Lani [his twin sister] was there too?" Mother says yes to both questions. Child replies, "Oh, like a camel!"
4–7	Child argues with her three-year-old sister, saying, "My place [birthcountry] is more beautiful than yours. It's my turn, so we get to visit my country next. We just visited India [sister's birthcountry]. I miss my people." Parents tell her she has never been to India and determine that she confuses India with an Indian party her family recently attended.
4–8	Child thinks Brazilian woman who facilitated her adoption is her birthmother. At several other times, when strangers whom she thinks look like herself are particularly kind, she declares that the woman is her tummy-mommy.
4–9	Adopted twins announce to people that they have a birth-mom, that they were in her womb, and that they have an adopted mom.
4–9	Boy announces he will marry a friend. His sister cries and wonders why he won't marry her. He tries to comfort her and says, "Okay, first I'll marry Rebecca; then I'll marry you, and one can be the birthmom and one can be the adopted mom."
4–9	Child sees two pregnant women and exclaims, "There's two birthmommies!"
4–9	Adoptive mother asks how it feels to be adopted, and child says, "Great!"
4–9	"I ate turtle eggs in Brazil when I was a baby. [I drank milk] from my mother who came to visit us." Mother explains this

was the woman who facilitated her adoption, not her birth-mother. "I want my tummy-mommy to come and visit us and see my school." Mother explains she can't come now. "But why? [The Brazilian adoption facilitator] came from Brazil. . . . I want to see her now."

4–9   Child while climbing on a jungle gym pretends she is on vacation with her adoptive mother in her birthcountry. Together they admire the sea, the mountains, and the lovely people on the beaches.

4–9   "Mom, if I didn't come out of your tummy, does that mean I can never have a baby come out of mine?" When reassured she will be able to, she says, "I want to have two babies: one girl and one boy. And they will love each other just like me and [my sister]."

4–10   "Mom, where does the mommy buy the seed [for the baby]? . . . Did Daddy give you my seed?" Mother explains about birth-mother and father. "I don't want to have one mommy and then another mommy. I want to have stayed in Brazil with [birth-mother]. . . . I miss her."

4–10   Child asks, "What is Salvador's name?" referring to her birth-mother by the ɩame of her birthcountry. Then she asks, "Does she have those lines [stretch marks] on her tummy like in the book [a book on reproduction recently given to her]?"

4–10   Child draws a picture at school and explains, "This is a picture of me and Max [her best friend] and my grandfather who lives in El Salvador." Child has no living adoptive grandfather and has been given no information about biological grandparents.

4–11   "You [adoptive mother] didn't have [to go to childbirth classes] for me 'cuz I was in someone else's belly."

4–11   "You know, it's funny. I don't remember anything about the plane ride from El Salvador" (when she was eleven months of age).

4 to 5   Child looks for people who look like her and wonders if they come from "my place," her birthcountry.

4–?   Child is upset that friend has teased that she could never "match" her mother.

4–?   Tan Brazilian child identifies herself with darkest babies, and compares and contrasts skin and hair color of her family members.

4–?	Child asks why he can't see his "birthday mother" since his foster brother could.
4–?	Child asks, "When did you come to the hospital to get me?" When mother explains that she didn't, he follows up with "Well, where did I go?" Mother explains that child had been at his birthlady's house for a while. He says, "Oh, I thought you got me at the hospital."
4–?	Child asks name of birthmother.
4–?	"Joey [a friend] is lucky because his mother is three things" (his mother, birthmother, and teacher). "Why can't you [adoptive mother] be three things?"
4–?	Child asks where his birthparents are from.
4–?	"But lots of brothers have different birthmothers. Right, Mom?" (Child had a foster brother.)
4–?	Child observes who has adoptive children and notes this.
4–?	Child wants to hear story of adoption again.
4–?	Child tells friend that her birthmother is "just gone away, not dead."
4–?	Child explains to a peer: "The way I see adoption is like this. Somebody has the baby but can't keep the baby and goes 'Wah, wah, wah. Good-bye, Baby,' and somebody who can't get a baby in their tummy says, 'Oh great, a baby. Goody, goody, goody. Hello, Baby.' You know, somebody wins and somebody loses!"
4–?	Child exhibits pain in her wish to have come out of her adoptive mother's tummy and insists that her adoptive mother breastfed her. This child shows absolute determination to be exactly the same as her adoptive mother.
4–?	"Mommy, sometimes children from China have parents who don't look like them." (Hispanic child in Caucasian family remarks this, while observing two Korean children with Anglo parents.) "I'm not Chinese and neither are you [Mom]."
4–?	Child asks his adoptive mother, "So, where is he, my real father?" "Why don't you know where he is now?" "I don't want him to find me." "He'd take me away. He'd change his mind. I'd get kidnapped by him." "Why didn't he want me?" Child wonders with adoptive mother whether he was relinquished because he was a bad baby or the father was a bad father.

4–?	"Mom, you know I'm adopted? . . . You know adoption is forever."
4 to 5	Child repeatedly rescues real and imaginal baby animals who have been left by their mothers, and mothers them herself. She also mates her actual pets, takes care of the babies, and then "adopts" them out.
4 to 5	Child becomes more aware of people's skin color and hair texture. "What do you call my skin?" "I have shiny black hair and you have orange hair." "Your skin is pink." These things are observed without value judgment, except when she says to the parent of a curly-haired, blonde child, "I don't like her kind of hair."
4 to 5	Child begins to show interest in her Salvadoran heritage, looking at books with pictures and showing souvenirs to guests. She assumes that other nonadopted Salvadoran children she knew have also been adopted.
5–0	Child plays out a scene in which a wicked woman takes a child away from her good mother. She has the girl say to the wicked lady, whom she has her mother play, "If it hadn't been for you, I would be with my real mother." Child then confides to her adoptive mother, "Yeah, if it hadn't been for you, I would still be with her. You came and took me away."
5–0	Child says to his adoptive mother, "Wrap me up the way you did when you got me. . . . Now hold me like you did when you got me. Tell me the [adoption] story again." He says sadly, "I wish I had been in your tummy." "Why didn't she [the birthmother] want me?" "How old was she?" "Oh, ho! She was a *teenager*." "If she was a teenager then, is she a teenager now?" "Well, I love her and I want to see her."
5–11	Peer whispers to adopted child something about "you're adopted" and "not in your mommy's tummy." Child replies matter-of-factly, "Of course, I'm adopted. Yeah, sure, I wasn't in my mommy's tummy. I was in this nice lady's tummy, and she was too young to be a mommy. So I came out of her tummy, and my mommy and daddy were waiting for me and my mom's been happy ever since!"
5–?	Child adopted from Korea is asking her adoptive mother questions about where babies come from, the birth process, and nursing, and then tells her version of how she was born—that her mother went to Korea, gave birth to her, came back here, and adopted her.

5–?	Child enters room where television is showing footage of the bombing of a Salvadoran village in her homeland. She says, "Mommy, look at all the volcanoes exploding. El Salvador has beautiful volcanoes!"
5–?	Child asks why soldiers have guns and shoot people in her birthcountry, El Salvador.
5–?	Adopted sibs talk about how "something doesn't work right" in their adoptive mother's body, so she can't have babies. They wonder if this means that she is sick and whether it is contagious. Daughter particularly wants to know if she will be able to have babies.
5–?	Son remarks to adoptive mother when they take the dog to be spayed, "Oh, I see, that's what happened to you. You were *fixed!* That's why you can't have babies!"
5–?	Child wonders looking at her photo album if her Korean foster mother was really her birthmother.
5–?	Friend of adopted child asks adoptive mother, "Why didn't her mother keep her?"
5–?	Child asks why she was given up for adoption.
5–?	Child asks his birthmother's name. He also asks (though the time is unspecified) what his birthparents looked like, what ethnic and religious backgrounds they were, what their interests were.
6–2[3]	Child explains that her birthcountry and that of her sister are "different planets"—Brazil and India.
6–4	Child wants to meet her birthmother and visit her birthcountry. She explains to her peers in kindergarten that she vacations each summer with her family in her birthcountry and visits with her "tummy-mommy." (This had never actually happened.)
6–6	Child asks her adoptive mother if her godmother is her tummy-mommy. She says, "I want to be with her [birthmother]" and asks "How long was I with her before you came [for me]?" On hearing "sixteen days," child says, "Good, sixteen days, that's a long time. I miss her."
6–6	Child says to her brother who was also adopted, "You are not

3. Many of the children in these stories were still not six years old, since we were especially curious about younger children and wanted parents' memories of this early time to still be fresh. The paucity of remarks after five years of age, therefore, does not mean that children talk about adoption less with their parents. Far from it!

my real brother. You are my fake brother. We are adopted. I was born from a lady in Georgia who really loved me a lot and she took care of me for a month and I was her Georgia peach. Then she gave me to Mom and Dad who adopted me and they are my fake parents. And we are a fake family."

6–9 Child asks adoptive mother, "Hey, Mom, what happens if a pregnant woman gets sick? I mean, what if she dies?" "What if you and Dad hadn't been there when I came out of the lady I was born from?" When asked what he thinks would have happened, he answers, "They would have killed me." (Mother remarks that the son was perfectly cheerful throughout this talk.)

6–10 "What did she [the birthmother] say when she saw me?" "Did she kiss me?" "Only you should have kissed me because you're my parents."

7–0 Child says to her family at supper, "You know it is not a nice thing for a man to give a woman a seed if she can't be a good mother yet. . . . I've been trying to think this out in my head."

7–1 Child says to her adoptive mother, "I love my Lizzie doll. You got her for me when I was four years old. You got her for me because she looks like me. She has my blue eyes and my yellow hair and my peach-colored skin. You are my best mom. You are my real grand mom. The lady I was born from, she loved me a lot but she only knew me for one day. You and Daddy have known me ever since I was a month old, and you cried every day for a month when you were waiting to get me out of Georgia. You are my real mom and my best mom."

7–2 "My [birth]dad is a jerk." "He left my [birth]mom by herself."

7–2 Friend of adopted child asks him, "Well, when are you going to look for your real mother?"

7–2 To friends: "See, being adopted is better because you're chosen. There was this lady, my biological mother. She was too young and too poor to be a mom, so when I came out of her vagina, my parents were waiting for me, and it was the happiest day of their lives." His friend then wonders when he will look for his real mother. "Richard, you don't understand. *This* is my real mother."

7–10 "But do you know what the very best thing in the world is? To be part of a family and to love them."

7–11 "Why didn't [my sister's birthmother] want her?" "Why didn't my mother want me?" "How old was she [the birthmother]?"

"Exactly how old was she? It matters. It matters." "What was her name?" "How can I find her if I don't know her name?" "[You are] sort of [my mother]" (said to adoptive mother). "Where is the blanket you took me home [from the hospital] in?" Parents get the blanket. Child says, "I love this blankie. I'm going to keep it my whole life. Tell me the story again, about how you got me. . . . Wait, let's go find Daddy and you tell the story when Daddy's there." (This is the first time child requests father's presence at telling of the adoption story.) Child wants to know how much the champagne cost that celebrated his arrival. "And you know if anyone had tried to take you [adoptive mother] from me, my father would have killed them." Child asks what he looked like when his adoptive parents first saw him, how they felt, how big his eyes were, how happy his adoptive mother was.

7–?   Child asks if foster sib's first foster parents who had the same last name as his birthparents were his birthparents.

7–?   Child asks if he could meet his birthparents.

7–?   Child goes to Korean culture camp and returns to school no longer trying to conceal her heritage, but proud of it. She takes Korean and adoption things to weekly "show and tell."

7–?   Child expresses desire to meet her birthmother and to know who she is.

7 and 8   Child talks with mother about teenage pregnancy and how she thinks a teenage mother should keep her baby, how she would like to have a baby as a teenager and keep it. Child does not think a teenager should necessarily get married if she is going to have a baby.

8–0   "Did you choose me?" Mother says no, that the birthmother chose them. Child remarks, "That's good 'cuz if you buy something in the store and choose it, you can return it. Was it the same with [my sister]?" Child then asks lots of questions about his biological mother. Then he says, "I'm so glad you adopted me. . . . You were spared the pain of childbirth."

8–1   "I love Dad so much. I love you so much. . . . Mom, is it better to have adopted me or given birth to me?" Mother asks what he thinks, and boy replies, "I think it is just different." Mother tells her son that she cannot imagine being any closer to him if she had given birth to him. He replies, "Me neither. Me neither. I want you for my mother."

8–3	Child wants to know how old the mother of his sister's friend was when she gave birth. Then he asks, "And how old was my birthmother?" He learns that his birthmother was two years younger. "Sixteen. Ah, that's younger, isn't it? Tell me some more about her." "I'm good at math and science too [like his birthmother]. I bet I got it from her. She doesn't know me since I was a day old, so you will have to tell me what I was like when I was a baby."
8–6	"Am I Indian? . . . Tell me about those Indians. . . . Those people were very smart . . . like me. . . . And my birthmother—where was she from?" When mother says Greece, child shouts, "That's what Daddy studies! . . . I'm going to tell my art teacher. She's been wanting to know. I'm Indian and I'm Greek."
8–?	"Mom, making German flags [adoptive mother's ethnic background] will look dumb," child explains while trying to complete a school project on parents' ethnic background. She decides to make four flags, one for each parent, birth and adoptive.
8–?	Korean-born child explains the citizenship process to her class. A boy asks, "Why didn't your real parents want you?" Child replies, "Well, actually, I think I was always wanted. My [adoptive] parents wanted me even before I was born."
8–?	Child wants to know if he will be bald and asks if his birthfather was bald.
8–?	"Who is right, Mom, my birthmom [for relinquishing me as a teenager] or Jane [a teenager who is going to keep her baby]?"
8–?	Child comments how lucky she is to have had more than two parents without having to endure a divorce.
9 on	Child says to his adoptive mother, "My real mother would let me—"
9–?	"Hey, Mom, what [ethnicities] am I again?"
9–?	Child says he no longer likes to tell his adoptive story because this year he "feels sad about it, not glad." He wants to present himself at school as "normal"—not adopted.
9–?	Child asks his adoptive mother if his learning disability is a result of his "[birth]parents being stupid people." He expresses some anger at birthmother for drinking while she was pregnant with him.

9–?	Child asks mother to get diapers for her baby doll. Then she asks mother why her birthmother and birthfather had planted the seed that was to become her if they were not able to parent. After answer, child says, "She didn't give me away. She had a baby. She gave birth to me. But she didn't give *me* up." Then she asks, "What happens if the lady doesn't want to grow a baby [and the man planted the seed]?" Mother explains about abortion, to which the child replies, "I guess it's really good that she chose to let me grow. She was my mother while I was growing in her uterus, and you are my mother since I was born. You know which is the harder job." Mother asks her which, and the child replies, "My birthmom's, of course, because having a baby is so painful."
9–?	Child differentiates between her birthmother's experience, who had not wanted to be a mother, and her brother's birthmother, who tried to be a mom and was unable to do a good enough job. Child feels some sadness for each birthmother.
10	Child consciously links his fondness for animals, math, and science to his birthparents' interests and incorporates them into his ambition to be "some kind of scientist who works with animals because I love animals and think they're very important."
10–3	When peer tells Korean adoptee of another Korean adoptee, the child asks, "Well, is she from South Korea or North Korea? She better be from South Korea, because that's where I'm from; that's all I can say." When it seems likely she is, child replies, "Well, good then, she's fine." Several days later when adoptive mother is reassuring child that she will never have to change families the way the other Korean adoptee had, the child volunteers, "That happened to Tyler [the family cat], too. When we got him, first, one family adopted him, but they couldn't take care of him, so they brought him back to the pet store, and then we adopted him."
10–6	"Tell me about my birthmother." Child is interested in factual information about history and lineage. Child says that he is happy his birthmother gave him to adoptive parents because he loves them very much. Then he says, "Okay, Mom, I know it's different for you. I really do. But this is how it is for me. You will never be fully mine. Because I did not come out of your body. Because I was not made from your egg and daddy's sperm. That is how it is for me."

10–6   In response to his adoptive mother's saying, "It's hard, isn't it, being adopted?" child says: "Last August, at sailing camp, that Tuesday night when I went to the social. The kids were all talking about how glad they were they weren't adopted. And I didn't tell them I was adopted because I was afraid they would tease me." Later that night child is very gay and kids his parents about being so glad they adopted him.

10–6   Boy's adoptive sister announces that he is a fake brother because they are both adopted. Boy says to his younger sister, "Lizzie, let me explain all this to you. Let me tell you about you. No, I'll tell you what happened to me. You see, there was this lady and she was my birthmother and she loved me a lot, but she was only sixteen and she was too young and too poor to take care of me so she found Mom and Dad."

Teenager   Child says she wants to find her birthmother.

References

Anastasi, A. 1976. *Psychological Testing*. 4th ed. New York: Macmillan.

Anthony, E. J. 1987. Risk, vulnerability and resilience: An overview. In E. J. Anthony and B. J. Cohler, eds., *The Invulnerable Child*. New York: Guilford.

Benet, M. K. 1976. *The Politics of Adoption*. New York: Free Press.

Berger, M., and Hodges, J. 1982. Some thoughts on the question of when to tell. *J. Child Psychotherapy*, 8:67–88.

Bernard, V. W. 1963. Application of psychoanalytic concepts to adoption agency practice. In E. Smith, ed., *Readings in Adoption I*. New York: Philosophical Library.

––––––. 1970. *Adoption*. New York: Child Welfare League.

––––––. 1974. Adoption. In S. Arieti, ed., *American Handbook of Psychiatry*. Vol. 1. 2nd ed. New York: Basic Books.

Bernstein, A. C., and Cowan, P. A. 1975. Children's concepts of how people get babies. *Child Development*, 46:77–91.

Block, N. J., and Dworkin, G. 1976. *The IQ Controversy*. New York: Pantheon.

Blum, H. P. 1983. Adoptive parents: Generative conflict and generational continuity. *Psychoanal. Study Child*, 23:141–163.

Blum, L. H. 1976. When adoptive families ask for help. *Primary Care*, 3(2):241–249.

Bohman, M. 1970. *Adopted Children and Their Families: A Follow-up Study of Adopted Children, Their Background, Environment, and Adjustment*. Stockholm: Proprius.

––––––. 1971. A comparative study of adopted children, foster children and children in their biological environment born after undesired pregnancies. *Acta Paediatrica Scandinavia*, Supp. 221:1–38.

––––––. 1972. A study of adopted children, their background, environment and adjustment. *Acta Paediatrica Scandinavia*, 61:90–97.

Bohman, M., and Sigvardsson, S. 1978. An 18-year prospective, longitudinal study of adopted boys. In J. Anthony, C. Koupernik, and C. Chiland, eds., *The Child in His Family: Vulnerable Children*. London: Wiley.

––––––. 1980. A prospective, longitudinal study of children registered for adoption: A 15-year follow-up. *Acta Paediatrica Scandinavia*, 61:339–355.

Boomsma, D. I. 1987. Absence or underestimation of shared environment? *Behavioral and Brain Sciences*, 10:1, 19–20.

243

Bouchard, T. J., Jr.; Lykken, D. T.; McGue, M.; Segal, N. L.; and Tellegen, A. 1990. Sources of human psychological differences: The Minnesota study of twins reared apart. *Science,* 250:223–228.

Braff, A. 1977. Telling children about adoption. *Amer. J. Maternal and Child Nursing,* 2:254–259.

Brinich, P. M. 1980. Some potential effects of adoption on self and object representations. *Psychoanal. Study Child,* 35:107–133.

———. 1990. Adoption from the inside out: A psychoanalytic perspective. In D. M. Brodzinsky and M. D. Schechter, eds., *The Psychology of Adoption.* New York: Oxford University Press.

Brodzinsky, A. 1986. *The Mulberry Bird: Story of an Adoption.* Fort Wayne, Ind.: Perspective Press.

Brodzinsky, D. M.; Pappas, C.; Singer, L. M.; and Braff, A. M. 1981. Children's conception of adoption: A preliminary investigation. *J. Pediatric Psych.,* 6(2):177–189.

Brodzinsky, D. M., and Schechter, M. D. 1990. *The Psychology of Adoption.* New York: Oxford University Press.

Brodzinsky, D. M., Schechter, D. E., and Brodzinsky, A. B. 1986. Children's knowledge of adoption: Developmental changes and implications for adjustment. In R. D. Ashmore and D. M. Brodzinsky, eds., *Thinking about the Family: Views of Parents and Children.* Hillsdale, N.J.: Lawrence Erlbaum, 2:177–189.

Brodzinsky, D. M., Singer, L. M., and Braff, A. M. 1984. Children's understanding of adoption. *Child Development,* 55:869–878

Canape, C. 1986. *Adoption: Parenthood without Pregnancy.* New York: Crown.

Caplan, L. 1990. *Open Adoption.* New York: Farrar, Straus and Giroux.

Capron, C., and Duyme, M. 1989. Assessment of effects of socio-economic status on IQ in a full cross-fostering study. *Nature,* 340:552–554.

Cattell, R. B., Eber, H., and Tatsuoka, M. M. 1970. *Handbook for the Sixteen Personality Factor Questionnaire.* Champaign, Ill.: Institute for Personality and Ability Testing.

Clarke, A. M., and Clarke, A. D. B. 1976. *Early Experience: Myth and Evidence.* New York: Free Press.

Cohler, B. J. 1987. Adversity, resilience, and the study of lives. In E. J. Anthony and B. J. Cohler, eds., *The Invulnerable Child.* New York: Guilford.

———. 1992. Culture, vulnerability, and resilience in the study of risk for major psychopathology. In D. Cicchetti and D. J. Cohen, eds., *Manual of Developmental Psychopathology.* New York: Wiley.

Cole, E. S., and Donley, K. S. 1990. History, values, and placement policy issues in adoption. In D. Brodzinsky and M. D. Schechter, eds., *The Psychology of Adoption.* New York: Oxford University Press.

Damon, W. 1977. *The Social World of the Child.* San Francisco: Jossey-Bass.

Daniels, D. 1985. Differential experiences of siblings in the same families as predictors of adolescent sibling personality differences. *J. Personality and Social Psych.*, 51(2):339–346.

Demick, J., and Wapner, S. 1988. Open and closed adoption: A developmental conceptualization. *Family Proc.*, 27:229–249.

Deutsch, H. 1945. Adoptive mothers. In *The Psychology of Women*. Vol. 2. New York: Grune and Stratton.

Deykin, E. Y., Patti, P., and Ryan, S. 1988. Fathers of adopted children: A study of the impact of child surrender on birth fathers. *Amer. J. Orthopsychiatry*, 58:271–280.

Eldred, C. A.; Rosenthal, D.; Wender, P.; Kety, S.; Schulsinger, F.; Welner, J.; and Jacobsen, B. 1976. Some aspects of adoption in selected samples of adult adoptees. *Amer. J. Orthopsychiatry*, 46:279–290.

Elonen, A. S., and Schwartz, E. M. 1969. A longitudinal study of emotional, social and academic functioning of adopted children. *Child Welfare*, 48:2, 72–78.

Emde, R. N. 1988a. Development terminable and interminable. I. Innate and motivational factors from infancy. *Int. J. Psychoanal.*, 69:23–42.

———. 1988b. Development terminable and interminable. II. Recent psychoanalytic theory and therapeutic considerations. *Int. J. Psychoanal.*, 69:283–295.

Erikson, E. H. 1959. *Identity and the Life Cycle—Selected Papers*. Psychological Issues, 1:1. New York: International Universities Press.

Eyer, D. 1992. *Mother-Infant Bonding: A Scientific Fiction*. New Haven: Yale University Press.

Fanshel, D. 1972. *Far from the Reservation: The Transracial Adoption of American Indian Children*. Metuchen, N.J.: Scarecrow Press.

Farber, S. 1977. Sex differences in the expression of adoption ideas: Observations of adoptees from birth to latency. *Amer. J. Orthopsychiatry*, 47(4):639–650.

Fast, I. 1978. Development in gender identity: The original matrix. *Int. Rev. Psychoanal.*, 5:265–273.

Feigelman, W., and Silverman, A. 1983. *Chosen Children: New Patterns of Adoptive Relationship*. New York: Praeger.

———. 1984. The long-term effects of transracial adoption. *Social Service Rev.*, December, 588–602.

Fisher, S. M. 1984. The psychodynamics of teenage pregnancy and motherhood. In M. Sugar, ed., *Adolescent Parenthood*. New York: Spectrum.

Fisher, S. M., and Scharf, K. R. 1980. Teenage pregnancy: An anthropological, sociological and psychological overview. *Adolescent Psychiatry*, 8:393–403.

Forrai, M. S., and Anders, R. 1976. *A Look at Prejudice and Understanding*. Minneapolis: Lerner.

Fraiberg, S. H. 1959. *The Magic Years*. New York: Charles Scribner.

Freud, S. 1909. Family romances. In J. Strachey, ed., *The Standard Edition of the Complete Psychological Works of Sigmund Freud*. Vol. 9. London: Hogarth Press.

Freudberg, J., and Geiss, T. 1986. *Susan and Gordon Adopt a Baby.* New York: Random House.

Frisk, J. 1964. Identity problems and confused conceptions of the genetic ego in adopted children during adolescence. *Acta Paediatrica Psychiatrica,* 31:6–12.

Gibran, K. 1971. *The Prophet.* New York: Knopf.

Gill, O., and Jackson, B. 1983. *Adoption and Race: Black, Asian and Mixed Race Children in White Families.* New York: St. Martin's.

Gilman, L. 1984. *The Adoption Resource Book.* New York: Harper and Row.

Giorgi, A. 1975. An application of phenomenological method in psychology. In A. Giorgi, W. Fischer, and R. von Eckhartsberg, eds., *Duquesne Studies in Phenomenological Psychology.* Vol. 2. Pittsburgh: Duquesne University Press.

Goodman, J. D., Silberstein, R. M., and Mandell, W. 1963. Adopted children brought to child psychiatric clinics. *Arch. Gen. Psychiatry,* 9:451–456.

Gould, S. J. 1981. *The Mismeasure of Man.* New York: Norton.

Grotevant, H. D., McRoy, R. G., and Jenkins, V. Y. 1988. Emotionally disturbed adopted adolescents: Early patterns of family adaptation. *Family Proc.,* 27:439–457.

Holt, D. 1973. *Good Friends Come in Many Shapes.* New York: Children's Press.

Hoopes, J. L. 1982. *Prediction in Child Development: A Longitudinal Study of Adoptive and Nonadoptive Families—The Delaware Family Study.* New York: Child Welfare League of America.

———. 1990. Adoption and identity formation. In D. M. Brodzinsky and M. D. Schechter, eds., *The Psychology of Adoption.* New York: Oxford University Press.

Hoopes, J. L.; Sherman, E.; Lawder, E.; Andrews, R.; and Lower, K. 1970. *A Follow-up Study of Adoptions: Post-Placement Functioning of Adopted Children.* Vol. 2. New York: Child Welfare League of America.

Horn, J. M. 1983. The Texas adoption project: Adopted children and their intellectual resemblance to biological and adoptive parents. *Child Development,* 54:268–275.

Horn, J. M., Loehlin, J. L., and Willerman, L. 1979. Intellectual resemblance among adoptive and biological relatives: The Texas adoption project. *Behavior Genetics,* 9:177–207.

Jaffee, B. 1974. Adoption outcome: A two-generation view. *Child Welfare,* 53:4.

Jaffee, B., and Fanshel, D. 1970. *How They Fared in Adoption: A Follow-up Study.* New York: Columbia University Press.

Jensen, A. R. 1969. How much can we boost IQ and scholastic achievement? *Harvard Educ. Rev.,* 33:1–123.

Jewett, C. 1982. *Helping Children Cope with Separation and Loss.* Harvard, Mass.: Harvard Common Press.

Johnston, P. 1991. Degrees of openness: A matter of choice. *Adopt Net.,* May–June.

Kadushin, A. 1970. *Adopting Older Children*. New York: Columbia University Press.

Kagan, J. 1980. Perspectives on continuity. In O. G. Brim, Jr., and J. Kagan, eds., *Continuity and Change in Human Development*. Cambridge, Mass.: Harvard University Press, pp. 26–74.

Kamin, L. J. 1989. Researchers continue to try to isolate genetic, environmental effects. *Adopted Child* (ed. L. Melina), 8(9):3.

Kaye, K. 1988. Turning two identities into one. *Psychology Today*, November, 46–50.

———. 1990. Acknowledgment or rejection of differences? In D. M. Brodzinsky and M. D. Schechter, eds., *The Psychology of Adoption*. New York: Oxford University Press.

Kaye, K., and Warren, S. 1988. Discourse about adoption in adoptive families. *J. Family Psych.*, 1(4):406–433.

Kellam, S. G., Ensminger, M. E., and Turner, R. J. 1977. Family structure and the mental health of children. *Arch. Gen. Psychiatry*, 34:1012–1022.

Kim, D. S. 1976. *Intercountry Adoptions: A Study of Self-concept of Adolescent Korean Children Who Were Adopted by American Families*. Ph.D. diss., University of Chicago.

———. 1977. How they fare in American homes: A follow-up study of adopted Korean children in U.S. homes. *Children Today*, 6:2–6, 36.

Kirk, H. D. 1964. *Shared Fate: A Theory of Adoption and Mental Health*. New York: Free Press.

———. 1981. *Adoptive Kinship: A Modern Institution in Need of Reform*. Toronto: Butterworth.

———. 1984. *Shared Fate: A Theory and Method of Adoptive Relationships*. 2nd ed. Port Angeles, Wash.: Ben-Simon Publications.

———. 1988. *Exploring Adoptive Family Life: The Collected Adoption Papers of H. David Kirk*. Port Angeles, Wash.: Ben-Simon Publications.

Kornitzer, M. 1968. *Adoption and Family Life*. London: Putnam.

Kowal, K. A., and Schilling, K. M. 1985. Adoption through the eyes of adult adoptees. *Amer. J. Orthopsychiatry*, 53(3):354–362.

Krementz, J. 1982. *How It Feels to Be Adopted*. New York: Knopf.

Krugman, D. C. 1964. Reality in adoption. *Child Welfare*, 43:349–358.

———. 1968. A new home for Liz: Behavioral changes in a deviant child. *J. Amer. Acad. Child Psychiatry*, 7:398–420.

Lawder, E. A.; Lower, K.; Andrew, S. R.; Sherman, E.; and Hill, J. 1969. *A Follow-up Study of Adoptions: Post Placement Functioning of Adoptive Families*. Vol. 1. New York: Child Welfare League of America.

Lewontin, R. C., Rose, S., and Kamin, L. J. 1984. *Not in Our Genes: Biology, Ideology, and Human Nature*. New York: Pantheon.

Lifton, B. J. 1988. *Lost and Found: The Adoption Experience*. New York: Harper and Row.

Livingstone, C. 1978. *Why Was I Adopted?* Secaucus, N.J.: Lyle Stuart.

Loehlin, J. C., Horn, J. M., and Willerman, L. 1989. Modeling IQ change: Evidence from the Texas adoption project. *Child Development*, 60:993–1004.

Loehlin, J. C., and Nichols, R. C. 1976. *Heredity, Environment and Personality*. Austin: University of Texas Press.

Loehlin, J. C., Willerman, L., and Horn, J. M. 1987. Personality resemblance in adoptive families: A 10-year follow-up. *J. Personality and Social Psych.*, 53(5): 961–969.

Lowe, M. 1975. Trends in the development of representational play in infants from one to three years: An observational study. *J. Child Psych. and Psychiatry*, 16:33–47.

Margolis, M. L. 1985. *Mothers and Such: Views of American Women and Why They Changed*. Berkeley: University of California Press.

Marquis, K. S., and Detweiler, R. A. 1985. Does adopted mean different? An attributional analysis. *J. Personality and Social Psych.*, 48(4):1054–1066.

Martin, N., and Jardine, R. 1986. Eysenck's contributions to behavior genetics. In S. Modgil and C. Modgil, eds., *Hans Eysenck: Consensus and Controversy*. Philadelphia: Falmer Press.

McRoy, R. G., and Grotevant, H. D. 1988. Open adoptions: Practice and policy considerations. *J. Social Work and Human Sexuality*, 6:119–132.

McRoy, R. G., Grotevant, H. D., and Zurcher, L. A. 1988. *Emotional Disturbance in Adopted Adolescents: Origins and Development*. New York: Praeger.

McRoy, R.; Zurcher, L.; Lauderdale, M.; and Anderson, R. 1982. Self-esteem and racial identity in transracial and inracial adoptees. *Social Work*, 27:522–526.

McWhinnie, A. M. 1967. *Adopted Children and How They Grow Up*. London: Routledge.

———. 1969. The adopted child in adolescence. In G. Caplan and S. Lebovici, eds., *Adolescence*. New York: Basic Books.

Mech, E. V. 1973. Adoption: A policy perspective. In B. Caldwell and H. Ricciuti, eds., *Review of Child Development Research*. Vol. 3. Chicago: University of Chicago Press.

Melina, L. R. 1984. Children under five confused about adoption. *Adopted Child*, 3(2):1–4.

———. 1986. *Raising Adopted Children: A Manual for Adoptive Parents*. New York: Harper and Row.

———. 1987. *Adoption: An Annotated Bibliography and Guide*. New York: Garland.

———. 1989a. Researchers continue to try to isolate genetic, environmental effects. *Adopted Child*, 8(9):3.

―――. 1989b. *Making Sense of Adoption: A Parent's Guide.* New York: Harper and Row.

Menlove, F. L. 1965. Aggressive symptoms in emotionally disturbed adopted children. *Child Development,* 36:519–532.

Millen, L., and Roll, S. 1985. Solomon's mothers: A special case of pathological bereavement. *Amer. J. Orthopsychiatry,* 55:411–418.

Nickman, S. L. 1985. Losses in adoption: The need for dialogue. *Psychoanal. Study Child,* 40:365–398.

Panel. 1967. Psychoanalytic theory as it relates to adoption. (M. D. Schechter, reporter.) *J. Amer. Psychoanal. Assoc.,* 15:695–708.

Parsons, M. 1988. Psychoanalytic insights into problems of adoption: Report of Association of Child Psychoanalysis meeting at University College, London. *Newsletter,* Winter.

Pederson, D. R., and Gilby, R. L. 1986. Children's concepts of the family. In R. D. Ashmore and D. M. Brodzinsky, eds., *Thinking about the Family: Views of Parents and Children.* Hillsdale, N.J.: Lawrence Erlbaum.

Peller, L. 1961. About "telling the child" of his adoption. *Bull. Philadelphia Assoc. Psychoanal.,* 11:145–154.

―――. 1963. Further comments on adoption. *Bull. Philadelphia Assoc. Psychoanal.,* 13:1–14.

Person, E. 1980. Sexuality as the mainstay of identity, psychological perspectives. *Signs: J. of Women, Culture and Society,* 5(4):605–630.

Plomin, R. 1989. Environment and genes: Determinants of behavior. *American Psych.,* 44(2):105–111.

―――. 1990. The role of inheritance in behavior. *Science,* 248:183–188.

Plomin, R., and Daniels, D. 1987. Why are children in the same family so different from one another? *Behavioral Brain Sciences,* 10(1):1–59.

Plomin, R., DeFries, J. C., and Fulker, D. W. 1988. *Nature and Nurture during Infancy and Early Childhood.* New York: Cambridge University Press.

Raleigh, B. 1954. Adoption as a factor in child guidance. *Smith College Studies in Social Work,* 25:53–71.

Raymond, L. 1955. *Adoption . . . and After.* New York: Harper and Row.

Raynor, L. 1980. *The Adopted Child Comes of Age.* London: George Allen and Unwin.

Reid, J. 1957. Principles, values and assumptions underlying adoption practice. In E. Smith, ed., *Readings in Adoption.* New York: Child Welfare League of America.

Reiss, D., Plomin, R., and Hetherington, E. M. 1991. Genetics and psychiatry: An unheralded window on the environment. *Amer. J. Psychiatry,* 48(3):283–291.

Rondell, F., and Michaels, R. 1975a. *The Adopted Family. Book I. You and Your Child: A Guide for Adoptive Parents.* New York: Crown.

————. 1975b. *The Family That Grew*. New York: Crown.

Rose, R. J., and Kaprio, J. 1987. Shared experience and similarity of personality: Positive data from Finnish and American twins. *Behavioral and Brain Sciences*, 10(1):35–36.

Rutter, M. 1981. *Maternal Deprivation Reassessed*. 2nd ed. London: Penguin.

Rynearson, E. K. 1981. Relinquishment and its maternal complications. *Amer. J. Psychiatry*, 139:338–340.

Sander, L. 1983. Polarity, paradox, and the organizing process in development. In J. D. Call et al., eds., *Frontiers of Infant Psychiatry*. New York: Basic Books.

————. 1985. Toward a logic of organization in psychobiological development. In H. Klar and L. Siever, eds., *Biologic Response Styles: Clinical Implications*. Washington, D.C.: American Psychiatric Press.

Sants, J. H. 1964. Genealogical bewilderment in children with substitute parents. *Brit. J. Med. Psych.*, 37:133–141.

Scarr, S., and Weinberg, R. A. 1976. IQ test performance of black children adopted by white families. *Amer. Psych.*, 31:726–739.

————. 1978a. The influence of "family background" on intellectual attainment. *Amer. Sociological Rev.*, 43:674–692.

————. 1978b. Attitudes, interests, and IQ. *Human Nature*, 1:99–136.

————. 1983. The Minnesota adoption studies: Genetic differences and malleability. *Child Development*, 54:260–267.

Schafer, R. 1974. Problems in Freud's psychology of women. *J. Amer. Psychoanal. Assoc.*, 22:459–483.

Schaffer, J., and Lindstrom, C. 1989. *How to Raise an Adopted Child*. New York: Crown.

Schechter, M. D. 1960. Observations on adopted children. *Arch. Gen. Psychiatry*, 3:21–32.

Schechter, M. D.; Carlson, P. V.; Simmons, J. Q.; and Work, H. H. 1964. Emotional problems in the adoptee. *Arch. Gen. Psychiatry*, 10:109–118.

Schiff, M.; Duyme, M.; Dumaret, A.; Stewart, J.; Tomkiewicz, S.; and Feingold, J. 1978. Intellectual status of working-class children adopted early into upper-middle-class families. *Science*, 200:1503–1504.

Schiff, M.; Duyme, M.; Dumaret, A.; and Tomkiewicz, T. 1982. How much *could* we boost scholastic achievement and IQ scores? A direct answer from a French adoption study. *Cognition*, 12:165–195.

Schoenberg, C. 1974. On adoption and identity. *Child Welfare*, 53:549.

Schwartz, E. M. 1970. The family romance fantasy in children adopted in infancy. *Child Welfare*, 49(7):386–391.

Siegel, S. E. 1989. *Parenting Your Adopted Child*. New York: Prentice-Hall.

Silverman, M. 1981. Cognitive development and female psychology. *J. Amer. Psychoanal. Assoc.*, 29:581–605.

Simon, N. 1975. *All Kinds of Families*. Niles, Ill.: Albert Whitman.

———. 1976. *Why Am I Different?* Niles, Ill.: Albert Whitman.

Simon, N. M., and Senturia, A. G. 1966. Adoption and psychiatric illness. *Amer. J. Psychiatry*, 122:858–868.

Singer, L. M.; Brodzinsky, D. M.; Steir, M.; and Waters, E. 1985. Mother-infant attachment in adoptive families. *Child Development*, 56:1543–1551.

Smith, C. R. 1984. *Adoption and Fostering: Why and How*. London and Basingstoke: Macmillan.

Smith, E., ed. 1963. *Readings in Adoption*. New York: Philosophical Library.

Sorosky, A. D., Baran, A., and Pannor, R. 1975. Identity conflicts in adoptees. *Amer. J. Orthopsychiatry*, 45(1):18–27.

———. 1977. Adoption and the adolescent: An overview. In S. C. Feinstein and P. Giovacchini, eds., *Adolescent Psychiatry*. Vol. 5. New York: Jason Aronson.

———. 1978. *The Adoption Triangle*. Garden City, N.Y.: Doubleday.

Speir, P. 1980. *People*. Garden City, N.Y.: Doubleday.

Stein, L. M., and Hoopes, J. L. 1985. *Identity Formation in the Adopted Adolescent: The Delaware Family Study*. New York: Child Welfare League of America.

Stern, D. 1985. *The Interpersonal World of the Infant*. New York: Basic Books.

Sweeney, D. M., Gasbarro, D. T., and Gluck, M. R. 1963. A descriptive study of adopted children seen in a child guidance center. *Child Welfare*, 42:345–349.

Tienari, P.; Lahti, I.; Sorri, A.; Naarala, M.; Moring, J.; Wahlberg, K.; and Wynne, L. 1987a. The Finnish adoptive family study of schizophrenia. *J. Psychiatric Res.*, 21(4):437–445.

Tienari, P.; Sorri, A.; Lahti, I.; Naarala, M.; Wahlberg, K.; Moring, J.; Pahjola, J.; and Wynne, L. 1987b. Genetic and psychosocial factors in schizophrenia: The Finnish adoptive family study. *Schizophrenia Bull.*, 13(3):477–484.

Triseliotis, J. 1973. *In Search of Origins: The Experience of Adopted People*. London: Routledge.

Watkins, M. 1977. A phenomenological approach to organismic-development research. Manuscript, Clark University.

———. 1986. *Invisible Guests: The Development of Imaginal Dialogues*. Hillsdale, N.J.: Analytic Press.

Watson, J. B. 1928. *Psychological Care of Infant and Child*. New York: Norton.

Waybill, M. A. 1974. *Chinese Eyes*. Scottsdale, Pa.: Harold Press.

Wieder, H. 1977a. The family romance fantasies of adopted children. *Psychoanal. Q.*, 46:185–200.

———. 1977b. On being told of adoption. *Psychoanal. Q.*, 46:1–22.

———. 1978. On when and whether to disclose about adoption. *J. Amer. Psychoanal. Assoc.*, 26:793–811.

Wilkinson, H. S. P. 1985. *Birth Is More Than Once: The Inner World of Adopted Korean Children*. Bloomfield Hills, Mich.: Sunrise Ventures.

Willerman, L. 1979. Effects of families on intellectual development. *Amer. Psych.*, 34:923–929.

Witmer, H. L.; Hertzog, E.; Weinstein, E. A.; and Sullivan, M. E. 1963. *Independent Adoptions: A Follow-up Study.* New York: Russell Sage Foundation.

Index

abandonment fears, 82–84. *See also* kidnapping fears

abortion, 92

adjustment, 43

adolescent adoptees, 5, 32, 44–45, 88, 89; transracial, 76–77; perceptions of adoption, 91–93

Adopted Child, The (newsletter), 86*n*8

adoption agencies, 82

Adoption and Fostering (Smith), 39

adoption as "no big deal," 203–207

adoption groups, 86*n*8

adoption practice, 1–10. *See also* child's perceptions of adoption; parents' perceptions of adoption

adoption research, 25; psychiatric-psychoanalytic tradition, 26–36; infants and bonding, 36–38; clinical and nonclinical populations, 38–45; open adoption, 46; genetic research, 46–55

adoption story, 68–70; importance of telling, 99–100; acting out, 101, 118, 148–149; child's love of, 133–134

Adoptive Families of America, 86*n*8

adoptive father: perspective of, 207–216

adoptive parents: advice to, 1–2; anxieties of, 5, 88, 89–90. *See also* parents' perceptions of adoption

adult adoptees, 3, 203–204

age factor, 38

alcohol abuse. *See* substance abuse

ambivalence, 15, 20

anger, 15, 34, 90, 95, 100, 161, 162, 168, 171

animal imagery, 64, 70, 167; in child's play, 101–102, 104, 116–118

attachment to child, 14–15

attitudes toward adoption, 1–2, 8, 13–14

baby as symbol of purity, 22, 23

"bad baby" theme, 98

"bad seed" notion, 19

Baran, A., 79*n*6, 81

Benet, M. K., 71*n*4

Bernard, Viola, 21, 26*n*1

biological continuity, 14, 31. *See also* genetic research

birthfather, 77, 78, 141, 154, 156; "my real father," 97–99

birthmother: child's interest in, 77, 107–108; fears of, 81

birthparents: attitudes toward attachment, 14, 15; child's interest in, 30, 32, 80, 87, 125–127; adoptive parents' view of, 90. *See also* parents' perceptions of adoption; relinquishment of child; search for birthparents

birth stories, 69*n*3, 70–72

blood ties, 14, 15, 92, 93

Blum, L. H., 44

Bohman, M., 41

bonding of mother and infant, 36–38

Boomsa, D. I., 54

Braff, A. M., 59, 61

breast-feeding issue, 101, 132, 150, 174

Brinich, P. M., 81

Brodzinsky, D. M., 59, 61, 62, 80, 85*n*7

Capron, C., 51

caretaking: child's play of, 64

Charlotte's Web (White), 119

child's perceptions of adoption, 2–3, 7, 57–58; losses and issues, 7–9; stages